AND IT ONLY TOOK 100 YEARS...

ALAN SHAYNE

Library of Congress Control Number: 2026932790
First Printing, 2025

Rand-Smith Publishing
www.RandSmithBooks.com

CONTENTS

Preface

I seldom write a preface—most readers don't want to waste their time reading one. They just want to get right to the story. However, something happened that changed my mind. I was in my doctor's office, submitting to the indignity of letting his nurse take my vitals, when a woman in a chair nearby spoke to me.

"Excuse me," she said. "I couldn't help overhearing you."

"I'm sorry," I replied. "I must have gotten excited about my blood pressure numbers."

"No, not that," she said. "You gave your birth date. November 21, 1925."

"Oh," I said, "forgive me, but you know we all have to give our date of birth for the blood samples."

"I couldn't believe my ears. You're about to be 100. You look so young."

"Thank you," I replied. "You've made my day."

She beamed. "Congratulations! I've never met anyone who was 100. Are you having a big party to celebrate?"

"I'm afraid most of my friends are gone."

"I'm sorry—"

"Don't say that. Even longevity has its price."

She laughed. "You must have seen so much—the start of talkies, television, World War II. You must have so many stories."

Before I could answer, the nurse called her in. She started to walk away and then turned back to me. "You must tell me everything you've learned about the meaning of life when we see each other again." She blew me a kiss and disappeared.

I looked around. No one else had paid the slightest attention to the woman or to the 100-year-old man.

Later, in the backseat of the car (I gave up driving when I realized an accident was only a matter of time), I thought about the woman's excitement. A party? Celebrate what, simply persisting? The fuss over my endurance seemed odd, as if I'd achieved something worthy of the Nobel Prize. So what if I am 100? People act as if I've scaled Mount Everest, when all I've done is wake up each morning. I didn't plan it or earn it.

Out of the blue, I remembered that when I was a kid, one night in Brookline, I decided I would walk around the kitchen table, and the number of times I completed circles would be the number of years I would live. I was afraid that if I stopped at any number, God would be watching and He would pick that one as the year I would die. Exhausted, as I was, I finally got to 100 and stopped, so I guess God was watching me after all.

Truthfully, reaching this age feels more like a curiosity than a triumph, mostly for others. They expect revelations, as if living this long grants secret knowledge. Of course, not everyone gets here, and therein lies the mystery.

I've buried more friends than I care to count—lovers, rivals, dazzling personalities. And yet, here I am, a centenarian. What a peculiar word. It makes me sound like a relic in a museum, a curiosity behind glass. Sometimes I feel as if I'm expected to stand at a lectern and give out wisdom.

But I do have stories—loving stories, hidden stories, and funny stories, all ready to be told. For instance, I was born just 25 years after Oscar Wilde was imprisoned for being homosexual, and I've lived to see men marry men and women marry women, with some of those weddings even featured in *The New York Times*.

That's just the freedom of loving who you choose, and that's only part of my life. There's also the story of a young, barely educated boy from a poor family who worked his way to unimaginable success. Are those the stories about the meaning of life that the woman wants to hear?

The only way to find out is for me to start from the beginning. What follows is the truth as I have lived it.

Introduction

Norman and I were settling into our new West Palm Beach condo, arranging furniture and feeling excited about this fresh chapter in our lives. Suddenly, the telephone rang. I almost let it go. After all, no one had the number yet, but curiosity got the better of me.

I picked up the phone and, before I could say much, a warm voice asked, "Is this Mr. Shayne or Mr. Sunshine? The desk gave me your number. I've been looking for you everywhere."

"Who is this?" I asked, surprised.

"I'm with the local women's group, and I'd love for both of you to speak at my Lunch and Learn series at the Kravis Center." My irritation melted away, being replaced by curiosity.

"Forgive me," I said, "we're just moving in. I hope I wasn't too abrupt."

She laughed, "It's not for several months, so the only rush is for you to say yes! I promise it's enjoyable and will bring wonderful attention to your book."

Norman and I co-authored a book called *Double Life*, which garnered some attention. We had held several promotional events mostly around New York, but the attention had subsided, so I was surprised that people in our new location were familiar with us.

"Have you read our book?" I asked.

"Not yet, but it comes highly recommended!"

"And your audience?"

"Oh, women of a certain age."

"You know it was written by two gay men?"

"Of course!" she said warmly. "That's why I'm calling. The ladies will be fascinated." Her enthusiasm was infectious, and we eagerly set a date to discuss everything over lunch.

We met at a rather ordinary restaurant, where she was joined by a friend who had recommended the book, a young man who would introduce us at the event, and our hostess, who would conduct the interview.

The woman was brilliant and persuasive, making the opportunity sound so appealing that by the end of the meal, we were nearly begging to be her speakers. Still, I wondered why the wealthy women of Palm Beach would be interested in a love story about two men so different from themselves. She insisted that they would, and we agreed to the date.

The day of the event dawned brisk and sunny, setting the perfect mood. Norman and I, excited and dressed in our best blazers, arrived early. The Kravis Center was buzzing with energy, the parking garage already full.

Upon entering, we were awestruck by the crowd. The room overflowed with elegantly dressed women, each one radiating style and confidence. The air sparkled with the scent of fine perfume and lively conversation. Norman and I found a spot near the edge, soaking in the anticipation and feeling grateful to be part of something so special.

When the doors finally opened, we entered a breathtaking auditorium filled with flower-laden tables and elegant china. On either side of the stage hung massive posters of our book's cover, our faces strikingly oversized. It was all quite overwhelming. We were ushered to our assigned table, where we enjoyed a delicious lunch, nerves and excitement mingling.

After dessert, the lights dimmed, and a surprise awaited us: huge screens illuminated the room with a documentary about our lives and careers. We had sent a few photos over the past few weeks, but we never imagined something so beautiful would come of it. Music played throughout, and interviews with friends were seamlessly woven into the film's narrative. It ended with us, arms around each other, strolling by our Connecticut lake as Frank Sinatra's "Our Love Is Here To Stay" played. When the lights came back on, many in the audience wiped away tears. I lightened the mood by quipping, "I haven't cried so much since *Gone With The Wind*!"

What followed was a joyful afternoon filled with laughter and genuine curiosity. Norman, who'd been nervous about public speaking, shone brightly as he shared stories of his advertising triumphs, like creating the slogan "What Becomes A Legend Most." I shared tales from my Hollywood days, regaling the audience with stories about stars like Bette Davis, Katharine Hepburn, and Marlon Brando. We spoke openly about our life together, answering every thoughtful question with honesty and warmth.

When the event ended, Norman and I stepped into the lobby to a long line of women waiting for us to sign their books. Nearly everyone shared that they had a loved one who was gay and expressed how proud they were that their family member was living authentically and happily.

One grandmother, hoping to support her granddaughter, asked if she should say anything about her suspicion that the girl was a lesbian. I encouraged her to wait and let her granddaughter come to her. Years later, we ran into her and she told us that waiting brought them closer than ever.

The event and those interactions were a powerful reminder of the immense love and acceptance that exists in the world and how important it is for this story to be told.

One

Packing up the tiny 1937 Willys took nearly an hour. It was June of 1941, already warm enough that the sun turned the metal door handles hot to the touch. My bicycle was tied to the back bumper, padded with blankets to protect Dad's prized car. Inside, suitcases, food bags, and a kerosene stove for Dad's vegetarian meals were wedged together. Dad refused sandwiches, so Mother had to cook him soybean "meat" on the road. He claimed it tasted like hamburger, but I could barely choke it down once.

After shuffling bags in the backseat, I had just enough space to squeeze in. By then, it was late, and Mother's face was tight with frustration.

"I was ready at 8:30," she said as we finally pulled away.

"Well, I was ready," Dad answered. "Why didn't you say something?"

"You were reading your health magazines. The least you could have done—"

"Let's not discuss it," Dad cut her off. "Let's try to enjoy the day."

The drive from Brookline to Falmouth, just 80 miles, took three hours. Dad drove slowly, and lunch dragged on as Mother cooked soy patties on the stove. Another argument erupted when Dad turned on classical music.

"Must you play that dreary music? It gives me a headache."

"Can't you ever try to improve your mind?" he snapped. After that, they didn't speak at all.

I never understood why they couldn't get along. Once, I discovered a book of postcards from their engagement—Mother in Kansas, Dad in Boston—full of sweetness. I also found a women's health book, hidden on a shelf, with dates scribbled inside, tracking their intimacy. But mostly, I felt the tension: heat lightning on a summer night, always threatening a storm that never broke.

As we neared the Cape, bags and boxes slid onto my lap, but I didn't mind. Not even the gray sky could dampen my excitement. I watched for every familiar landmark: the stone pillars, Dutchland Farms with its wooden-spoon ice cream, the "Herring Run" sign, and finally the Blue Moon dance hall in Buzzards Bay.

When the stone pillars appeared, my heart leapt. We were close. Even the thought of having to work for my difficult grandmother couldn't dim my joy. Passing the dance hall, I dreamed of one day going inside. The paint peeled from the Blue Moon sign, but I imagined it glowing by the start of summer.

We crossed the Cape Cod Canal, the railroad bridge towering overhead for a passing ship. Beyond stretched scrub pines and the salty tang of the sea. Each arrival brought a feeling I couldn't explain, a freedom I found nowhere else.

Mother's voice broke my reverie. "I have the worst heartburn."

"That's because you upset yourself," Dad said.

"You know your mother's been waiting all day," she countered.

"We'll get there," he replied calmly. Then he added, "I wish you'd stop drinking coffee."

"Dearie, please. Coffee doesn't give me heartburn."

"Why don't you just try my coffee substitute? You'll feel 100% better."

I tuned them out and looked out the window, breathing the Cape air.

At last, the Falmouth sign appeared. Shabby houses gave way to larger ones. We passed the house where Uncle Louis and Aunt Rae used to live. Aunt Rae had an affliction that made her speak her thoughts aloud. At dinner, she'd offer food, then mutter, "Why should I wait on these people? They eat all our food and don't do a damn thing." She never realized she was speaking, so no one responded. I struggled not to laugh, though I pitied her.

We finally reached Queen's Byway, where my grandmother's shop stood among three others: a dress shop, a candy store, and one empty storefront. Nana's had two wide windows styled to look eighteenth-century and a bright red door with a sign: Opening July 1. Through the glass, tables were piled with merchandise and boxes—my work was clearly cut out for me.

Dad parked, and we piled out. He called, "Mother, Mother!"

Nana appeared through a curtain, chewing rye bread with cottage cheese. She wore a stained blouse under a sagging sweater; her skirt was dusted with powder. With her wild clothes and bulging bags of stockings for rug-making, people sometimes mistook her for a Seminole Indian.

Dad made a kissing sound, lips never touching her cheek. Mother kept her distance with a brief hello. I leaned in dutifully: "Hi, Nana."

"You said you'd be here early," she glowered.

"We got a late start," Dad said. "It's all right, we'll help you tomorrow."

"The clothes have to go to the house," she insisted. "It's too late now. Mrs. Hotchkiss stops serving at 7:00." So, we went to dinner.

The Elm Tree Inn was only a corner away, though we drove. Its weather-beaten sign swung in the rain. Inside, the fat Irish proprietress, Mrs. Hotchkiss, scolded us for being late, then beamed, shaking hands one by one. Dad clearly loathed the contact but couldn't escape.

Menus came. "Nothing but meat and chicken," Dad complained.

"A little piece of chicken won't hurt you," Mother said.

We ate in silence. Nana hunched over her plate, slurping, her false teeth clicking. Mother didn't even look at her. I remembered when we lived in Nana's house. Mother did all the work while my grandmother complained. Night after night, I'd fall asleep with Mother begging my father to get her a place of her own. Only after my grandfather died did we move to Brookline. Now Nana spent winters in Florida and summers on the Cape. Mother never forgave her.

After dinner, we drove through the rain to where Nana lived, a shabby frame rooming house with a crooked "Guests" sign on the patchy lawn. The landlady, thin and severe, opened the door. Inside, we hauled Nana's things through the dark. My parents would take my room for the night; I was given a cot in a windowless alcove a few feet from Nana's bed

As I undressed, I stared at the glass of water by her bed, her false teeth floating inside. I lay down, trying to ignore her snores and wheezes. At least when my parents left, I thought, I'd finally have a room of my own.

***

When I woke, sunlight filled the room, and we all went to clean the shop. I washed the small windowpanes. Dad unwrapped Mexican dishes, holding each one carefully away from his body as if he feared foreign germs. Mother swept the worn carpet that covered most of the floor.

We worked silently until Nana broke the quiet. "Do you have to make so much dust?" she snapped at my mother. "It's getting all over the jewelry I'm trying to put away."

Mother had had enough. "How else can I get rid of this filth?"

"Couldn't you sweep a little easier? It's going over everything."

Nana grabbed the handle. "I don't need your help. I'll do it myself."

They tugged the broom back and forth until Mother yanked it free and threw it to the floor with a sharp crack. "Take it," she shouted, stomping out the side door.

Nana turned on my father.

"What's the matter with her? I don't need help from any of you!"

"Mother, don't aggravate yourself," Dad pleaded.

I kept washing the windows. I'd seen too many of these arguments. Eventually, they retreated to opposite corners, and the situation quieted down.

After another tense meal, my parents prepared to drive back to Brookline. They dropped Nana at the rooming house while I pedaled behind on my bicycle, finally freed from the back bumper.

When I arrived, Mother and Dad were waiting to say goodbye.

"Be careful with your bike," Dad said. "Tonight, you can ride it, but from now on, when it gets dark, walk it home." I pictured myself dragging the bike a mile every night. It had a perfectly good headlight, but I didn't argue.

He wasn't finished. "Don't go swimming where the water's over your head. Currents could take you out to sea. Don't show off just because the other kids do."

Mother covered me with kisses I hated but endured. "I love you so much," she kept repeating.

Dad broke in again. "Don't exercise too much. And don't eat too much meat."

Nana grew impatient. "For God's sake, go if you're going. It's getting cold."

I kissed Dad perfunctorily, waved as the car pulled away, and followed Nana inside.

For the first time, I had a room with a lock. Turning the key gave me a thrill of independence. I unpacked neatly, arranging my things in the dresser drawers. For now, I hid my collection of nude photographs under my clothes, planning to find a better spot before the landlady cleaned.

The room was plain, with four windows, white beaverboard walls, green paper shades, dingy spreads on the twin beds, and homemade braided rugs. At night, headlights from passing cars danced across the walls.

Later, in pajamas, I climbed into bed with my diary. I dated the page June 23 and drew a capital T with a circle beneath it, my private symbol to keep track of how often I masturbated to be sure I didn't do it too much.

Then I pulled out the photographs. The first set showed a nude girl posing against a maple tree. She wasn't pretty, but she looked sexy. The newest picture was a close-up of a naked boy held by two older boys who laughed as they forced him to show himself to the camera. It felt strangely exciting, like the Strength and Health magazines I peeked at in the bookstore. With the locked door and no interruptions, I could finally explore those feelings freely.

The next day, I started a ritual that only changed on Sundays. After I got up, I took a shower and dressed, then bicycled a mile to the store, had some juice and coffee, and began work. I wanted to make the store look as good as the other stores on the Byway. It was a hopeless task, but I felt I had to do it.

My grandmother always ordered too many things from the salesmen who flattered her. As a result, there wasn't enough room on top of the tables in the shop to put all the merchandise that arrived, so she shoved a lot of it underneath them. Cloths with India prints covered the tables and went all the way to the floor, so nobody could see the mess. The trouble was that when Nana wanted something from under one of the tables, she pulled out all the boxes, like an animal digging for food, and everything was thrown around until she found what she was looking for. Then she'd grab onto the table, hoist herself up, and walk away from the mess.

I always had to clean it up and put everything back in place. When I finished, I swept the sidewalk in front of the store and arranged the Mexican baskets and colorful chairs under the windows. My favorite moment was standing back to admire my handiwork and breathing in the fresh air before heading back inside to the dust and disorder.

Instead of thanking me, my grandmother put everything back the way it was, restoring the jumble she preferred.

"Nana," I said, "please don't make a mess again. I just straightened that table."

"It's better the way it was," she replied.

"But nobody can see anything the way it was," I said.

"I can see it," she said.

I waited on customers most of the day, usually older women with blue hair who called me "cute." I had to ask Nana for prices on anything they wanted. Instead of telling me, she would rush over to take over the sale herself, eyes narrowing as she tried to control her excitement.

Finally, there was some activity in the store next door. I looked out the window and saw a van drawn up in front of it. A good-looking Irishman, around forty, got out and started to lug dresses into the shop. It wasn't that hot, but this guy was sweating like a pig. His face was red and blotchy. Then Mrs. Goodell, whom I'd known slightly for many summers, opened the door by the driver's seat.

She looked older and tired, her features severe. Clearly, she wasn't happy with how the man worked. She grabbed an evening dress before it hit the sidewalk and quickly scooped up a belt from a garment bag. I could hear her giving instructions that he ignored.

I went outside thinking I'd say hello and offer to help. But they had disappeared, so I went back into the store. The next day, I ran into Mrs. Goodell, who greeted me with, "How handsome you've gotten, Alan." I was surprised she even remembered my name.

"How's your mother?" she asked.

"Fine," I said.

"We have to have a good visit, but I'm so busy now getting the store ready. As soon as we're squared away, I want to know everything you're up to." She grabbed my chin and pinched it. "See you soon."

A few days later, I had the opportunity to speak with Mrs. Goodell, but we exchanged only a few words. Everybody called her Mrs. G. She barely spoke to the girls or anyone else. She was haughty, and she lumbered around when she moved. Liz, a good-looking brunette in her thirties, had arrived to help Mrs. G. sell the dresses.

During one of her cigarette breaks behind the store, Liz told me that a man named Jim was Mrs. G.'s lover, and he was a drunk. Liz said all Mrs. G. did was order Jim around, and he drank to get the courage to stand up to her.

At last, I thought Liz would be somebody I could spend time with. But when I asked her about going to the beach on Sunday, she said she was busy getting the lay of the land. She said she'd be free the following week.

One night at the Inn, I sat with my grandmother for dinner and found myself watching the other tables filled with older people. The scene left me feeling down. Mrs. Hotchkiss made it worse with her loud laugh and constant put-down of her middle-aged son, Eddie. She would yell at him to get people to order so she could close the kitchen and then scream, "Get your little farts out of here." I wondered why any adult would tolerate that. As for me, I had no choice but to put up with my grandmother.

After dinner, I would go back to the house and my dreary room. I tried to read, but the landlady's lamp had a weak bulb. My only escape was my diary and my photographs. Sometimes I would take off all my clothes and stand where the headlights of the oncoming cars would pummel my pale body. I wanted to cry out, "Look at me! I'm somebody you would like to know!" They couldn't see me, but for a fleeting moment, it made me feel alive.

Then in the morning, everything changed. Once I had a shower, put on a newly washed shirt, some pressed slacks, and combed my hair carefully, I was a different person. Maybe this would be the day something wonderful would happen. I raced my bike to the shop and began setting up the baskets in neat rows on the sidewalk like a Mexican market. The sun was on the other side of the Byway, so it was cool and dark. The baskets gave off the sweet scent of newly mowed grass, perfuming the fresh, clean air.

I saw a young blond guy sweeping in front of the newly opened men's store across the street. He was probably only a couple of years older than me, but he looked grown-up. He was wearing a yellow pullover shirt and white and brown saddle shoes that my parents wouldn't buy for me. He even had a crew cut. He reminded me of a cheerleader at a football game.

He looked up and saw me. "Morning," he yelled.

"Morning," I replied.

He leaned the broom against the front of his store and walked across the street. He had a cocky, sure-of-himself stride. "You work here?" he asked.

"Yuh," I said, trying not to seem too excited about this older boy stopping to talk to me.

"I'm Dudley," he said.

"I'm Alan."

Dudley extended his hand, and I shook it. His grip was strong, as if he was making an extra effort not to have a wishy-washy handshake. "Do you know any girls?" he asked.

Actually, several from my class at school were going to a girls' camp a few miles away. "I do," I said, "but they're in Silver Beach—"

He cut me off. "That's okay. I've got a car, so why don't you set up a double date for Saturday?"

"I'm not sure they can leave the camp at night."

Dudley was persistent, "Why don't you find out and let me know?"

"I'll call them tonight," I said.

"Good," Dudley said. He went back across the street and opened the door of his shop. He turned back and yelled, "Let me know."

I was puzzled. Dudley didn't seem friendly at all, but he did want to double date with me. Maybe he'd change after he got to know me better. I sure needed a friend, so I thought I'd better make allowances for him and see what happened.

I called Nancy Williams that night. She wasn't my girlfriend, but we used to hang out a lot at school. Her family was rich, and she'd take me to her parents' mansion for lunch once in a while. She was a jock and consistently won silver and gold cups for tennis. We had an understanding that there was nothing romantic between us. That seemed to suit us fine. When she finally came to the telephone, she seemed excited to hear from me, but she said the girls weren't allowed to leave the camp.

"There is a dance here on Saturday night," Nancy said. "Why don't you come and bring your friend if you can find a way to get here?"

"Oh, okay," I told her, "my friend has a car. Just give me directions."

When I saw Dudley the next day and told him about it, he seemed excited. "This place is a morgue," he said. "We'll liven it up!"

It was a beautiful night. The moon was almost full, and it was cool enough to wear a jacket and tie without sweating excessively. I was nervous about Dudley picking me up. I was embarrassed to be living in such a seedy rooming house, but Dudley didn't mention it, so I felt relieved. I slid in beside him and gave him the directions to the camp. There was something exciting in the air, and the smoke from Dudley's cigarette made me feel almost lightheaded. After about twenty minutes, we turned off the main road and followed a driveway through piney woods to a huge, shingled house.

We knocked on the front door, but when no one came, we figured they couldn't hear over the music. The door was open, so we walked into this huge living room, almost like a barn, with a beamed ceiling and an enormous stone fireplace. The wicker furniture was stacked up and pushed close to the wall, along with the rugs that had been rolled up. There must have been about 30 kids dancing to a record player, most of them girls and a half dozen boys.

Nancy approached us, and I introduced her to my new friend. "I have just the girl for you, Dudley."

She ran over to where some girls were sitting and returned with a plain-looking one who had pimples covered with white cream. We split up and began to dance. Nancy wasn't a good dancer, so she talked through the music as if to cover up her bad moves. The top of her head only came to my chest, so I had to bend over to hear her.

"I had this terrible sumac poisoning," she said, "but since I was entered in the Cape Cod Championship, I couldn't back out of it."

The record player changed automatically, and romantic numbers like "Between a Kiss and a Sigh," "I'm Waiting for Ships That Never Come In," and "Be Careful It's My Heart" played, so I couldn't jitterbug to them. I had to hold Nancy close, but I was careful not to touch my body to hers below the waist. Not that I was attracted to her, but when I danced with Ronnie Markson, whom I took to the junior prom, she pressed her body right against me, and I had to try like crazy not to get a hard-on. I wasn't going to take any chances with Nancy.

The dances seemed interminable, and my shoulders ached from trying to move Nancy around. I looked for Dudley and saw him dancing close to a pretty girl who was laughing a lot. Then he rushed over to me. "I've got to go," he said.

Nancy protested, "We haven't had refreshments yet."

"I gotta work tomorrow," he said.

"But it's Sunday," she replied, "nobody works on Sunday. Besides, there are more girls I want you to meet."

"Sorry," Dudley said, "I have to do an inventory. Some other time."

We said goodnight and walked outside to the car. We got in, and Dudley took hold of the steering wheel without starting the car. I figured he'd had a lousy time, so I didn't say anything. I just waited for him to speak, but he just stared straight ahead. I felt these waves from him that made me tingle. Finally, he started up the car, and when we'd driven well away from the house, he pulled over. "I gotta pee," he said.

I got out with him, and we both walked across the road over to the edge of the woods. Dudley peed, making a loud sound as his stream hit the ground. I suddenly felt hot in the muggy air, and my pee wouldn't come. I'd always had trouble peeing next to another guy, and I avoided it in school if I could. I'd wait until I was alone or try to find an empty stall. I figured Dudley would think I was peculiar if I didn't join in, so I tried desperately to think of warm water. I could feel Dudley looking at me, and I began to get excited.

We got back into the car, and Dudley drove me back to my room. Neither of us spoke until I got out of the car. "Night," I said.

"Night," he replied, and he zoomed down the highway.

I went up to my room, undressed quickly, went out to the hall bathroom, brushed my teeth, returned to my room, locked the door, and got into bed. I was glad to be by myself. I had to figure out what had happened. It wasn't just my imagination, but I had the feeling Dudley was waiting for something, something I was supposed to do. And then I started to remember what had happened that spring.

Two

March was cold and damp. With the weekend approaching and no plans, I was surprised when the phone rang for me. Lenny Myers, an athlete from school whom I barely knew, was on the line.

"Any plans this weekend?" Lenny asked.

"Nothing," I said.

"My dad and I are opening the camp in Maine. Want to come?"

I'd never been to Mr. Myers's camp. "I'd like to, if my parents agree."

"Ask and let me know. We'll be painting, but it's not hard."

"Sounds good," I said.

"Well, let me know." Lenny hung up.

They probably hoped I'd want to go to camp that summer, but it sounded better than nothing. I knew my parents would say yes.

Friday after school, I packed old clothes and a bathing suit, though I doubted I'd swim in a cold lake. Lenny and his father arrived in a beat-up station wagon packed with boxes, and I squeezed into the back.

Mr. Myers, with his rimless glasses and gray hair, asked about school as we left, but the noisy car soon ended the conversation.

It was already dark when we reached "Camp Emoh for Boys." Lenny told me Emoh was "home" spelled backwards. Mr. Myers announced Lenny's first task would be to repaint the sign.

We turned down a long dirt road, headlights glinting off puddles. Beyond the trees, a clearing revealed cabins and a larger building—the dining hall.

Mr. Myers unlocked a cabin, then stormed out, frustrated. "I told them to turn on the electricity, and it's not working."

By morning, the electricity and water were working. After breakfast and showers, Mr. Myers assigned us to paint the dining room chairs. We considered walking in the woods, but the rain sent us back to work.

By day's end, many chairs remained, but Mr. Myers praised our work. Dinner was bland, but I ate it to show I wasn't picky. The rain on the roof helped me sleep, though I woke up to damp sheets.

The next morning, Mr. Myers had errands in town. "You're on your own—take out a rowboat and enjoy the lake," he suggested.

After breakfast, Lenny and I cleaned up, then showered. The cabin was still messy. I dug through a box of athletic gear and found a jock strap and a hard, curved shield. Lenny walked in, a towel around his waist, his athletic build immediately apparent.

"What are you doing?" Lenny asked.

I charged him and we wrestled, Lenny holding back his strength. He pinned me while I panted, still holding the shield. "What's this?" I asked.

Lenny's eyes narrowed. "You know what it is."

"No, I don't," I said.

"It's a cup," Lenny said, "it goes over your cock to protect you."

I placed the shield over Lenny's crotch; he pushed it away, but I put it back. He called me a horny bastard and grabbed me for another round of wrestling. Each time I touched him, he grew more aroused. Suddenly, Lenny grabbed his towel and covered himself. "Let's get out of here," he said.

Breathless, I followed Lenny to the lake. The sun broke through as we launched a rowboat. Facing him as he rowed, I noticed his arousal. He looked around nervously, though no one was nearby. I was excited, too.

Lenny rowed us into a secluded river. The sun warmed us, but I still shivered. He pulled the boat onto the sand, and we got out, silent.

Lenny stripped off his pants, and I followed suit. "Lie down on your belly," he said.

I lay down on the sand, ignoring the discomfort. Lenny lay on top of me but quickly stopped. I sat up and touched him.

"Stop," he said, pulling me up. We scanned the empty riverbank, then waded into the water. Lost in each other, we forgot to be cautious. I took hold of Lenny, and he reached out to me. Lenny's breathing quickened with desire. "Oh, oh, oh" came from his throat as if his heart was beating out the sounds. I began to come into the river. I kept coming and coming, and I worried I had broken something. But finally, it stopped.

Afterward, we avoided eye contact, washed in the river, and dressed. I felt ashamed as Lenny rowed us back. We barely spoke, and I longed to go home. We pretended to be friendly in front of Mr. Myers, but I knew we wouldn't see each other again.

That night, I mulled over what had happened. Was this what Dudley wanted from me?

On Monday, when I got to work, I saw Dudley across the street sweeping the sidewalk. When he saw me, he nodded and went inside his store. The next few days, I saw him occasionally through the shop's plate glass windows, but he never came out. Finally, by the end of the week, I made up my mind to go over and have it out with him. Why couldn't we be friends?

I opened the screen door of the men's shop and went in. There was a delicious smell of aftershave lotion and tables of cashmere sweaters in many colors. The whole place looked expensive. I felt grubby, like I didn't belong there. A man with a big chest, who looked like a football player, came from the back when he heard the door close. He was wearing white saddle shoes just like Dudley's.

"Is Dudley here?" I asked.

The man looked at me for a moment before he answered. "Dudley doesn't work here any longer. He's gone back to Boston."

"Thanks," I said. I went back across the street. I decided to try to forget the whole incident, but there was something mysterious about it. I wished I had a friend to talk to, someone older who could explain it, but I didn't.

I was beginning to feel more and more insecure. I tried to talk to my grandmother about it, since there was nobody else that I was even close to, but she was always preoccupied with selling in the store or reading her romance novels. When we had dinner at Mrs. Hotchkiss', she was so busy slurping her food and running her tongue over her false teeth that I couldn't even look at her, let alone talk to her. One night, I rode my bike until I caught up with her as she walked to the rooming house. I got off the bike and pushed it alongside her.

"I want to ask you something," I said as we walked.

"Vot?" she said suspiciously. (Her accent was especially noticeable in "w" words.)

"Well, it's a difficult thing to say."

"You vant to go home?" She stopped and looked at me.

I stopped too. "No, I'll stay 'til Labor Day, the way we arranged it."

"Vell, vat is it?"

"Am I good-looking?" I asked sheepishly.

"Vat do you vant to know that for?"

"I just do," I said. "Am I?"

"Och," she made a funny sound. "You're all right."

"That's not an answer," I said. "Am I?"

"Your nose is too big," she replied and walked on.

I got back on my bike and arrived at the rooming house before she did. I rushed to the bathroom and looked in the mirror. I turned my face in different ways, but I couldn't see my nose at an angle. I went to my room and locked the door. I couldn't bring myself to put what she said in my diary. I just went to bed and tried to forget it, but I couldn't.

The summer was going fast, and I still didn't have any friends. I never got to know any of the kids in town because I was always working in the shop. I didn't know how to approach them. The rich kids who lived in the Heights had their own cliques, and even at the beach, they didn't mix with anybody else. Mrs. Goodell always said "Hello," and "We've got to have that talk one of these days," but we never did, and Jim was always hungover.

The two girls at the candy store were locals, and I would occasionally go in to talk with them, but they were in their twenties. They teased me and fed me chocolates, and once dared me to eat one of each of the 21 different candies the store sold. I did it, but it turned me off chocolates for weeks. I thought Liz and I would be friends, but she was always rushing out of the store to go somewhere or arriving too late for work to stop and talk.

"Liz," I yelled one day, "What about the beach this Sunday?"

Liz walked over to me. "I've been meaning to tell you; I've been seeing this guy. I'm sorry for not spending time with you. You're a nice kid, but right now, I can barely make it to work."

She reached out to pat me on the shoulder, and something fell out of her purse. I picked it up for her. It was a thin, tin box with "R" and "L" in large letters on the front.

"What is this?" I asked. "Is it medicine? Are you sick?"

She looked at me for a minute. "Don't you know?" I shook my head. "R and L stand for rubber and lubricant."

"Oh sure," I said, pretending I knew, but I'd never heard about it before.

"Well, I gotta run." She zoomed off.

One day, Mrs. Goodell came by and told me she was going to church on Sunday and asked if I would like to go along.

"Oh, I don't want to go to church," I said nervously. "Maybe some other time."

"You don't have to go inside the church if you don't want to, but it's a lovely ride, and we'll have a picnic. I'll make some sandwiches. It'll do you good to get away from here."

I never had anything to do on Sunday, so I finally said yes. I just had to be with some people for a change. It would be a treat even though they were so much older. They might end up being friends.

It was a July day at its best, feeling more like a perfect day in June. Soft miniature clouds hid the sun, but only for a second now and then. A fresh breeze rustled the heavy leaves drooping from the trees, and the summer seemed to be standing still, holding its breath.

I was in the backseat of Mrs. Goodell's car. I tried to ignore her and Jim's bickering as we drove out of Falmouth. I wondered why they were always fighting. They weren't married, so if they didn't like each other, why didn't they just separate? Jim was driving, and Mrs. Goodell had to turn around as far as she could to say something to me.

"You don't have to come into the church if you don't want to," she said," but I think it would do you a world of good."

"No, thank you," I replied, "I just don't feel right about it."

"Alan," she coaxed, "don't be absurd. I know what's bothering you. Lots of Jewish people are Christian Scientists. You won't feel uncomfortable."

"I just think I'd better not." In school, when we sang Christmas carols, I could never sing "Jesus" or "Christ" out loud because I was afraid it was a sin, so how could I go into a Christian church?

"Leave him alone," Jim interjected irritably. "He can wait in the car with me." Once again, Jim was hungover, and the prospect of sitting with him alone wasn't so great.

We pulled up in front of a long, white shed with a small cupola over the double doors that marked its entrance. Mrs. Goodell put on a hat and attached it to her hair with a long bobby pin. "I'll be about an hour," she said. "You two, behave."

I hadn't realized she'd be gone that long, and I knew it would be agony talking to Jim, so I said, "No, I'll come with you."

The two of us sat beneath an open window with the sun pouring in and spotlighting the flowers. I felt peaceful and listened to the simple sermon, which was quite different from the ones I'd heard when I went to temple with my parents. There was nothing formal or uncomfortable about it. It just seemed like ordinary life. It certainly wasn't mysterious. I put aside my fears and thought, "It's all right. God will understand."

As we were driving back to Falmouth after we'd had our sandwiches on the side of the road, Mrs. Goodell suddenly put her hand on Jim's arm. "This is Truro," she said, "isn't it?"

"Yuh, I think so," Jim answered.

"It's where Juddie lives," she said. "Let's go see him."

"You can't go barging in on someone without any notice," he said.

"I'm dying to see his house," she replied with relish, "and he told me to come by whenever I was in the neighborhood."

Jim lowered his voice. "What about him?" he whispered, turning his head slightly toward me as I listened more intently.

"You make me sick," Mrs. Goodell snorted. "What do you think he's going to do with us right there? I want to see that house!"

As we got out of the car, a plump man in his fifties, talking with a boy and a girl, spotted us. "Edith," he yelled, "what a delight." He came running up from a section of garden that curved around the side of the house and embraced her.

When we were in the house, I had to keep my mouth from dropping open. He told us that he'd added several wings onto the original building as he took us from one beautiful room to another. The floors and all the antique furniture were highly polished, and although the ceilings were low, as I knew they often were in early cottages, they still featured the original beams, gnarled with age. Hooked rugs with patterns of either flowers or animals were scattered over the floors. Oversized fireplaces filled with dried flowers dominated the tiny rooms. We climbed a staircase barely wide enough for us to get by, which took us to bedrooms with four-poster beds covered with comforters that matched the curtains.

"It's absolutely perfect," Mrs. Goodell said. "You've done it exquisitely. I've never seen anything like it."

Juddie's round face was flushed with pleasure. "Thank you, Edith," he said. "You can imagine what it's been like with these locals. They suggested taking up the random-width floors and putting in new ones."

Mrs. Goodell joined Juddie's laughter. "No," she screamed.

When we were downstairs again, he was particularly nice to me, encouraging me to ask questions about the implements in front of the fireplace that the colonials had used for cooking. He seemed to be having a good time showing us the house. There were little beads of perspiration on his forehead at the edge of his carefully combed silver hair, and his blue eyes sparkled with pleasure as he showed off his treasures.

The screen door suddenly burst open, and the young man and the girl I'd seen in the garden walked in. He was only wearing a tiny bathing suit, and his muscular body was dark as a chestnut.

"Oh, good, you're here," Juddie said, introducing them. "This is my niece Ann, and this is Johnny Parks, who's staying with me." We all shook hands. "I was just telling young Alan here how our ancestors cooked," he said, giving Johnny a look, "and now we must all have some coffee."

Johnny looked straight at him, ignoring us completely, and then ran out the door, pulling the girl behind him. We could hear their laughter as they romped in the garden.

Mrs. Goodell said, "We must be getting back."

"It's just as well," Juddie replied. "We're late for lunch, so you'll come another time. And do bring Alan again."

As we got into the car, I looked back at the house and saw the young man staring at me from the garden. I must have done something to annoy him, but I couldn't think what. I should think he'd be happy just staying in such a wonderful place, surrounded by beautiful things and all those flowers. He seemed to have everything. That's the way I'm going to live someday, I thought to myself.

When we were some distance from the house, Mrs. Goodell said, "Well, that was certainly interesting."

Jim, who hadn't said a word the whole time we were there, replied, "Is that the one he calls his nephew?"

"You notice he didn't call him that in front of his niece," Mrs. Goodell said.

They dropped me off at the shop to get my bike. I thanked them, and they drove off. Something was funny. All that about the nephew, and why did he give me such a look as we were leaving? I had a feeling there was some mystery they wouldn't talk to me about.

***

All summer, I passed a country store being transformed into an antique shop. It looked unusual, almost otherworldly, its brown wood weathered and old. A pulley hung above the double doors, with large shop windows below. The sign read "Antiquarium."

"Hi there." The voice startled me. "I'm Dave Garland."

I felt caught. "I was just admiring your store," I said, embarrassed.

"Wouldn't you like to see the inside?" he asked.

"Oh yes," I replied.

It was a relief to step out of the heat into the cool, dim room. Inside, the shop looked like a museum, filled with treasures: chandeliers, decanters, ivory boxes, chess sets, and needlepoint-covered chairs.

Dave turned on the lamps, and the chandeliers sparkled in the gentle light.

"How beautiful," I said. "I've been riding by every day on my way to work, but I had no idea it was anything like this."

"Come and see the garden," Dave said.

Dave led me through his bedroom and out the French doors to a terrace. The lawn was perfectly kept, bordered by flower beds and woods. A gardener worked nearby, making it all look like a magazine cover.

"I spend all my free time out here," he said. "Sit down for a minute."

I leaned on a wrought-iron chaise, breathing in the scent of grass and flowers. I wished I could live this way, peaceful and beautiful, like here or Juddie's cottage.

"Are you helping your grandmother in her shop for the summer?" Dave asked.

"Yes. She's getting older, so my parents wanted someone to watch her."

"I hope you're not working too hard," Dave went on. "Are you getting any time to swim?"

"Yes, I go to a small beach near Woods Hole at lunch," I said.

"I know a beach near Woods Hole where you can swim at night without a suit. Maybe it's the same place. Would you like to come with me sometime?"

"Thank you, but I'd be too embarrassed," I said.

"Why?" Dave asked. "We're just two men."

"I'm not comfortable with my body yet," I admitted.

Dave laughed. "You look fine. Maybe work on your biceps." He poked my arm and stood up. "Let's go back inside."

We walked back through the bedroom. Dave grabbed a book. "Have you read this?" he asked.

I looked at the title: Wind, Sand and Stars. "Not yet," I said as if I had read all the current best sellers.

"I think you'd enjoy it," he said. "An aviator wrote it."

"I'll get it at the lending library," I replied.

"No, I'm finished with it. You can borrow it."

"Thank you," I said, taking it from him. I was getting used to Dave's way of speaking, thinking he must be from an upper-class Boston family. I was about to ask him when he surprised me.

"I'll bet you masturbate a lot," he said.

No one had ever said that word out loud to me. I tried to hide my astonishment. I guessed it must be a subject that men of the world discussed openly, so I said, "Yeah, I suppose I do."

Dave pressed me further. "How often do you do it?"

"I try to keep it to once a day. Sometimes I cheat and don't write it in my diary so I can do it twice."

Dave walked over to the window and looked out. "There's nothing wrong with it," he said.

"Oh, I know everybody masturbates," I said the word forcefully to show how grown-up I was.

"Lower your voice," Dave said.

"Why?" I asked, surprised by his furtive tone.

"The gardener might hear us," Dave said. "You know the funny ideas these people can get."

My heart pounded. I sensed something unspoken, like the secrets Jim whispered to Mrs. Goodell or the odd moment with Dudley. Maybe Dave would explain it.

I was trying to summon up the courage to ask him when he suddenly said, "Your grandmother must be wondering what happened to you, and I've got to get back to work."

I felt I'd done something wrong, sensing a shift in Dave's attitude. He walked me to the door. I thanked him for the book, promising to return it. "No, you keep it," he said. "I have too many books, and I'm too busy to see people."

I went over to my bicycle. I suddenly thought, I'll go back and tell him I'll go swimming with him. Maybe then he'll tell me what all these secrets are about. But the door was closed. I put the book in the basket of my bike. I had a feeling that whatever had happened, Dave didn't want to see me again.

***

My grandmother and I arrived early to re-label merchandise. We covered "Japan" with "Cape Cod, Mass." since few people wanted to buy Japanese goods then.

By late August, I was preparing to return to Brookline after Labor Day. I felt I had little to show for the summer—no new friends, not much fun beyond a few movies.

While we worked, I asked my grandmother for a gift. "I've worked hard and haven't been paid."

"Vhat d'ya mean?" she replied. "You got your room and board, don't you?"

"But I want something to remember this summer by."

"You're crazy. I don't know vhat you're talking about."

"I want you to give me something. Something I'll always remember."

"Vhat?" Nana asked me suspiciously.

I picked up a cut glass decanter from a table. "This," I said.

"Vhat do you vant that for?"

"I'll put it in my New York penthouse one day," I said.

"That costs a lot of money. You don't need it."

"If you sell it, fine. If not, it could be my present. Either way, you win."

She finally sighed, "All right. Now leave me alone."

I was elated. Since the decanter hadn't sold all summer, I was sure it would be mine. If anyone showed interest, I'd mention the scratch on the stopper. It felt like a sign that my New York dream was about to come true.

On Sunday, I decided to go to the town beach for a change. I wanted to see people, but they were never on the small beach I visited near Woods Hole. I took a new book I'd gotten with the plays of Eugene O'Neill to read, so everyone would think I wanted to be by myself. The last week of August was stiflingly hot with clear skies.

I must have dozed off. When I woke up, the beach had filled. Near me, two women chatted with a handsome, older man whose tousled hair and protruding ears lent him a friendly look.

He and I exchanged glances. He smiled, an amazing smile. I tried to focus on my book but kept meeting his gaze. I felt uncomfortable, so I closed my eyes again and pretended to sleep.

"How's the book?"

I opened my eyes. It was the man. The women were gone. "I've just started," I replied, a little breathless and nervous.

"Can I sit down?" the man asked.

"Of course," I said, making room for him on my towel.

The man settled near me and put out his hand. "I'm Roger," he said.

I shook his hand, avoiding his eyes. "Alan. I'm glad to meet you." I felt nervous and struggled to find words to keep him there.

"Want to go for a swim?" Roger asked.

"Sure," I said, and we both got up and walked into the sea.

The cold water eased my tension as we swam together. When I paused, Roger did too, his smile making me feel at ease. We left the water, and I shook out my towel to dry off.

"I'm afraid I only have this one," I said.

"Should I bring my things here?" Roger asked.

"Sure," I answered.

"You like O'Neill?" he asked.

"I've only just started, but I've always wanted to read him. Do you like O'Neill?"

"Yes and no," Roger said as he exhaled. "Some of it's a bit pretentious for me, but I think you'll enjoy it. Do you like the theater?"

"Yes, I want to be an actor." It was the first time I'd admitted it out loud.

"I should think you'd do well at it. You're good-looking enough," he said. "Have you ever acted?"

"Not yet. I'm in the dramatic society at school and got an honorable mention in Prize Speaking."

"That's great," Roger said.

The scent of his cigarette mixed pleasantly with the ocean air. "There were six mentions out of ten," I admitted.

Roger smiled. "Still." We sat quietly for a few moments. Then he asked, "Where are you going to college?"

"I'm not sure. I want to go to Dramatic School, but my parents want me to go to college."

"Oh, you're still in high school?"

I panicked at the thought of his not wanting to spend any more time with me if he knew I was only 15. "I'm graduating this year," I said and quickly changed the subject. "Where did you go to college?"

"Mass State, but I don't think that would be good for you if you want to be an actor."

Roger lit another cigarette. "Oh, I'm sorry," he said, "would you like one?"

"No, thank you," I said, pleased he thought I was old enough. The beach was emptying out, and I wished the afternoon could last longer.

He checked his watch. "It's getting late. I'd better go."

"Want to swim tomorrow?" I asked.

"I'm afraid I can only get away on weekends, but we'll see each other on the beach next week."

I stood up. "Well, I guess I'd better be going too."

He turned to me. "You want me to drop you off? I have my car."

"That'd be great, but I have my bike."

"That's okay, it's a convertible. I'll put the top down, and it can go in the backseat."

With the top down, I felt like one of the rich kids who drove past the shop, laughing and carefree. Roger's aftershave drifted on the breeze.

"Your aftershave is terrific," I said. "What is it?"

Roger laughed. "I guess I put it on too heavily this morning. It's called Old Spice."

I had Roger drop me at the store so he wouldn't see the horrible rooming house I lived in. He suggested again that we might see each other on the beach the following weekend, but that was just about when I was leaving to go home. I didn't think we would have any time when we could possibly become friends.

For days, I watched from the store window, hoping Roger would pass by. The maple trees, heavy with rain, were all I saw.

Three

When the sun finally came out, I rode around the town on my bicycle, stopping at all the places where I thought I might run into him. I even went over to Pin Oak Way, where Roger had said he lived. I kept hoping he would step out of one of the doors, but when he didn't, I went back to the store.

Nana was in the back room, reading one of her library romances from the lending collection. I went over to the cash drawer and, very quietly, pressed the first and third keys. The drawer flew open, but I caught it with my hand so there wouldn't be any noise. I took out several dollars and shut it softly. I listened—nothing from behind the curtain.

"I'm going out for a few minutes," I called. I felt guilty about taking the money, but I told myself she owed me for all the work I had done.

I got on my bike and rode over to the Green, where the county fair is held every July. Eighteenth-century houses surrounded the old sheep meadow with its wrought-iron fences and tall elms. On one side were a few stores, and I leaned my bike against a low wall in front of the pharmacy.

Inside, a woman was buying something at the counter. I pretended to browse the postcards until she left. Then I walked up to the old man behind the register and used my deepest voice.

"Have you got any Old Spice?" I asked.

"Which kind?"

I faltered. "I don't know, just Old Spice."

"Well, we've got cologne and we've got aftershave."

"The aftershave is fine."

As soon as I left the store, I ducked into some bushes and opened the box, pulled out the ceramic bottle, removed the metal top, and inhaled deeply. It was just like being with Roger.

By Thursday, I realized it was only five days until Labor Day, when my parents would be coming to take me home. I'd just about given up hope of seeing Roger again and decided to stop mooning over it.

But that evening, as I was carrying in the baskets from the sidewalk, Roger drove up and parked in front of the store. As he got out, I walked over. "Hi," I said.

"It occurred to me," he said, "that next weekend is Labor Day, and I always wanted to do a bicycle trip in Martha's Vineyard. Maybe you'd want to go along."

He seemed so distant and impersonal that I hesitated. I should have been overjoyed, but I felt like a kid being asked by a friend of my father's to go on a camping trip. After all my anticipation, the moment was oddly anticlimactic. Still, I said, "Sure."

"Do you think your grandmother will mind?"

"I don't care what she does," I said.

"Well, we'd better ask her anyway."

Inside, Roger was incredibly charming to Nana, who wasn't used to such attention. He praised her store, telling her that many of his friends thought it was the best on the Byway, and flattered her so much that when he asked if he could take me on a bicycle trip, she said yes.

"Who vas that?" she asked as soon as the door closed.

"Roger," I said. "I just introduced you."

"How'd you meet him?" Her eyes narrowed.

"Through some friends," I lied.

"Who?"

"What's the difference? You liked him."

"He vas all right, but you're not going on any trip with him."

"He works at that big landscaping place near the train station. He knows I don't have any friends here, so I guess he's being nice to me. I haven't asked you for anything else. It will only cost a couple of dollars for meals and a basic room. Can't you give me this one thing?"

Finally, she muttered, "Leave me alone."

A few nights later, I woke up at 4:00, hours before I needed to get up. I lay in the dark, wondering what I'd say to Roger, what it would be like to spend two days with a man twice my age whom I barely knew. I tried to sleep, dozed off, then woke up in a panic, only to realize it was 6:30. Still too early, but I got up anyway, glad to be out of the house.

At five minutes to 8:00, I rode onto Pin Oak Way. Roger was waiting in front of a new clapboard Colonial with hollyhocks in the yard. He greeted me coolly and said we'd better get going.

At the ferry, the sign read: "Martha's Vineyard—$1.30 Round Trip—Bikes Free." I insisted on paying, and for the first time that day, he smiled. His preoccupation had made me wonder if I should have come, but his smile changed everything.

Docking was chaos with tourists rushing off, cars inching forward, porters waving signs, and others boarding for Nantucket. We made our way to our bikes and pushed through the crowd.

Vineyard Haven was picture-perfect: a white-spired church, neat Colonial houses, picket fences. I wanted to explore, but Roger said we had ground to cover. Hours later, we reached Gay Head, where cliffs of red and orange clay dropped to the sea. We changed into bathing suits behind rocks and splashed in the rough surf, cooling off from the long ride.

Afterward, Roger knocked on the door of a farmhouse. A woman in a faded dress brought us ham sandwiches on homemade bread, accompanied by glasses of cold milk. We ate in the shade of a maple, savoring each bite as though it were a feast. Roger split a candy bar for dessert, and we lay in the grass, content.

The ride that afternoon was grueling—scrub pines, flat land, no stores, aching legs. At dusk, we arrived in Edgartown, a town that seemed like a museum, closed for the night. We found a shabby house with a "Rooms" sign, paid $1 each, washed, and went out for supper.

Back in our room, the air was stifling. We opened the window despite the mosquitoes. I tossed for hours until Roger's voice broke the silence.

"What's the matter? Can't you sleep?"

"I don't know. I just don't feel sleepy."

"Do you want to talk?"

"Sure."

He asked about my friends. I told him about my best friend, Irving, and Nancy, as well as the people in Falmouth. Then, cautiously, about the antique dealer Dave Garland.

Roger listened. Then: "Do you wish he were here instead of me?"

"Of course not."

"You know."

"I don't know what you mean."

"You know perfectly well."

I lied about Dave wanting me to go nude swimming. Roger pressed: "Did he ever try to kiss you?"

The word "kiss" froze my heart. "Of course not," I said as flatly as I could.

"You know about him, don't you? That he likes boys."

"No, I didn't."

"Do you think that's so awful?"

"No. Of course not."

"I like boys, too," he said.

"Roger," I whispered, "I'm freezing."

"Do you want to come into my bed?"

I trembled. "Please, you come here."

"No," he said gently but firmly. "You have to come to me."

"I can't. I'm shaking."

"Then don't."

At last, I crossed the space and slipped into his arms. He kissed me, and to my shock, I kissed him back. I climaxed almost instantly, breathless, ashamed.

Roger said. "Just relax."

We lay together, kissing, touching lightly, losing ourselves in a rhythm of breath and silence until we both drifted off to sleep.

Four

When I woke up the next morning, it took me a moment to remember where I was. I got up as quietly as possible and headed to the shower. As I scrubbed myself, I felt nauseous, trying to wash away the memory of what had happened. The night kept replaying in my mind. How could I have let it happen? How could I have let Roger take advantage of me? That was it—he had taken advantage. He was old enough to know better. I wasn't, but even so, I had wanted it. My thoughts went in circles, searching for an escape, but I found none.

Finally, after rubbing my body harshly with the towel, as if I were erasing what had happened, I went back to the room. He was still asleep, so I dressed quietly. As I was putting my few things in the paper bag, I could feel him looking at me.

"Good morning," Roger said.

I glanced at him. His hair stuck up where he had slept on it, and I noticed how thin it was. His ears jutted out like handles on a vase, and he wore a silly smirk. I wondered how I had ever thought he was handsome. I looked at him coldly. "I'll wait for you out on the street."

We ate breakfast in silence. He had taken his cue from me and only spoke when he asked me to pass him the cream and sugar. The tone of his voice was impersonal, and I was careful to keep any warmth out of my voice. We split the check, got on our bikes, and headed to Oak Bluffs to get the ferry back to Woods Hole.

"What's the hurry?" he said as he pulled up beside me. "We're almost there, and we've got two hours before the ferry leaves." I didn't answer him. "Why don't we get some sun on the beach?"

"I want to go home."

"I know you do, but I don't want to sit around in Oak Bluffs for hours." He waited for me to say something. When I didn't, he said, "I'm going to swim. You can do what you want."

There was no malice in the way that he said it. Actually, he looked at me warmly and then took his bike over to a spot on the sand and laid it down. He stripped down to his shorts and went into the water. I thought for a minute about going in by myself, but I didn't want to be anywhere near him.

Roger emerged from the water, dried himself, and then spread his towel neatly on the sand. When he sat down, he looked over at me. I was letting sand pour idly through my fingers.

"Come on," he said, and his voice had nothing but kindness in it. "It's not that bad."

I was afraid I was going to cry. I forced myself to look at him. His body was still wet from the sea, and his shoulder bones protruded from his thin frame. He smiled at me with that same amazing smile I had first seen on the beach. I ran over to him and threw my arms around his neck. "I love you," I said.

***

Clouds gathered in the sky as the ferry rocked on the rough sea. I stood as close to Roger as I could, careful not to touch him in any way that might attract attention. The wind whipped my hair and made my eyes water, but I didn't feel cold. I had a secret, and it filled me with a quiet warmth.

"I'm going to get us some coffee," Roger said.

I saw him walk, as steadily as he could, to the stairs that led below. The boat was pitching, and I had to hold onto the railing. I watched Woods Hole come closer and closer until Roger got back. I took the cardboard cup from him as if he were giving me a precious gift, and I sipped the bitter coffee. We were almost ready to dock. I looked casually at the crowds ready to board. Suddenly, I froze.

"It's my parents," I gasped. "What'll we do?"

"Just leave it to me."

"This is the third ferry we've met," my mother said, glaring at me. "You worried me half to death. I'll never forgive you for this."

"Please, Mother," I said, "everything's okay. This is Roger Alton. These are my parents, Roger."

"I would have recognized you right away," Roger told my mother. "Alan looks so much like you. I'm very sorry—I should have called you both for permission instead of just speaking to Alan's grandmother about taking him to the Vineyard. I thought it would be fine. I've been spending a lot of time encouraging Alan to go to the right college."

"Oh," my mother said, "how good of you. We've been doing the same thing." My parents found themselves apologizing to Roger for having doubted him. He was suddenly in the position of forgiving them, and I just stood by as if I were watching a tennis match. Now that everything was resolved, it was decided that we couldn't get my bicycle in Dad's car, so I would ride back to Falmouth with Roger.

"Don't take too long," my mother said. "We should leave right after supper, and you have to pack."

"What do you mean?" I asked.

"You're going back to Brookline with us. Nana has to have some X-rays tomorrow, so we have to go back tonight."

"I hope you can come to the shop and have coffee with us," my mother said to Roger.

"I'd like to, but I'm afraid I have a dinner date."

"If you ever get to Boston," Dad said, "you must come over and have dinner with us. My wife is a good cook."

"I'm sure she is, and I'd like to," he said.

Roger and my parents exchanged smiles and goodbyes, promising to meet again soon. Then we hopped on our bikes and headed for Falmouth.

As it turned out, my parents were not a problem. Without any argument at all, they said I could stay the week. Roger had won them over completely, and they wanted to know all about him. They were flattered that he had taken such an interest in me. They encouraged me to invite him up to Brookline. We ate the sandwiches Mother had brought and had some soup she had heated on the hot plate. I couldn't wait to see them go, but I tried to act as naturally as possible.

I even managed to say, "Do you have to go so soon?"

Mother grabbed me and kissed me wetly. "Oh, I love you so much."

As soon as they left, I hurried over to Roger's house. The man who opened the door was someone I recognized from the Five and Ten. He directed me to Roger's room at the top of the stairs, on the left. I knew Roger rented a furnished room, but I was surprised by how cramped it was. When he let me in, there was barely enough space for us to stand between the double bed and a small desk.

Roger closed the door and held me for a minute. "I knew you'd be here," he said as he guided me a few steps to a chair. I sat with my knees touching the bed while Roger stretched out. "Don't talk too loudly," he whispered, "the Smiths' room is right across the hall."

"Can I lie there beside you?" I asked.

"Yes, but no distractions," He said as he turned on the record player.

I lay beside him as the record began. I was swept up immediately in the music. "That's the beginning of the Orson Welles radio show," I said, excited that I had recognized it.

"It's the Tchaikovsky 'Piano Concerto,'" Roger corrected me. "Just listen." He turned out the lights and lit a cigarette. He gave me a puff. I didn't inhale, but I just blew the smoke out slowly, copying him. When the theme I had recognized from the radio show was finished, I asked him to play it again.

"You have to hear the whole work," he said, "not just an excerpt, or you'll grow tired of it."

He put on another record. "This is Schubert's 'The Trout,'" he said. "Now just forget that it's classical music and try to imagine a fish jumping and splashing in a brook, alive and free. If you listen carefully, you'll hear it swimming through the water. You may even know when the fisherman catches it."

I concentrated hard, and I was sure I was getting it right. Roger took my hand. "Don't make such an effort. It takes a little time." He stopped the record in the middle. "You need to go home, and I'm exhausted."

The next day seemed interminable. Only a few people came into the shop, and I didn't know what to do with myself. I stood and stared out the front window, hoping that Roger would come by.

I went next door to see Mrs. Goodell. We'd become even more friendly, and I often talked to her. I told her as much as I could about the weekend with Roger. She watched me closely as I kept extolling Roger's qualities. When I'd finished, she said, "Are you going to see him again?"

"Of course," I replied. "We're going to the Cape Playhouse tonight."

"Does he have a girlfriend?" Mrs. Goodell asked.

"I guess so," I said, thrown completely off guard.

"Well, just be careful. I don't think it's good for you to be alone too much with a man so much older. Why don't you introduce him to Liz? It sounds like they might get along."

"Sure," I said.

"He hasn't done anything to you, has he?" she asked.

"Of course not. He's not like that."

"Well, I wouldn't see too much of him, that's all. Even if there's nothing wrong with him, you never can tell what can happen."

"I'm leaving the day after tomorrow, Mrs. G. I probably won't see him again."

"It's better you're with someone your own age," she said.

Roger picked me up at 6:00. I'd gone all the way back to the rooming house to put on my best jacket and a tie. He told me how nice I looked. We went to a restaurant in Yarmouth Port where he had worked ten years before.

At the theater, we sat in the back with the rest of the people who'd gotten in free. The play was *Her Cardboard Lover*, and the star was Tallulah Bankhead. She had a deep, throaty voice and managed to make everything she said have a sexy double meaning. Roger kept roaring with laughter, and I thought people were looking at him.

Once we were in the car and driving back to Falmouth, all of my doubts disappeared. Roger smoked and concentrated on the road ahead. We both listened to the radio. "Indian Summer" was playing, and I felt as if I were in a movie with the perfect background music.

"Would you like to sleep overnight with me?" he asked.

I couldn't believe it. "But what about your landlord?"

"He won't see you leaving in the morning, and if he does, I'll say it was too late for you to go home."

When we were in bed, he reached over and pulled up the window shade so we could see the moon. We lay in each other's arms and kissed. After a moment, I pulled away from our embrace and started to touch my lips to Roger's chest. I then moved down toward his stomach. I felt my head pulled back.

"What are you doing?" Roger whispered.

"I want to kiss all of you," I said.

"No," he said sternly. "Don't!"

"Why not?"

"It isn't right." He sounded annoyed.

"But what could be wrong about it?" I insisted.

"How many other men have you been with like this?"

"None. You know that. I've told you, only the boy at the summer camp, and that was nothing like us."

"Oh, come on, don't kid me."

"But I haven't been with anyone else," I protested. "Can't you tell?"

"You certainly seem to know a lot," he said sullenly. "Why did you want to do that?"

"It seemed so natural."

"Well, it isn't. Let's go to sleep."

I lay awake. I was so frustrated and miserable. What had I done? I thought I was being loving. And then something came to me from my childhood that I had not thought about for years:

I was 7 or 8, and we were living in Falmouth in the little house behind Uncle Louis and Aunt Rae's big house. I was allowed to play on their porch. It was hidden. Heavy vines crawled over three sides of it, leaving just the screen door uncovered. It was a perfect place to hide. They said I was too big for dolls now, but I found some sticks and took silver paper from cigarette packs that I rolled into balls and pushed onto the end of the sticks.

One day, I suddenly heard a cry of "Alan" from the garden. It was my brother. I rushed to the swinging sofa and managed to get up on it as it swayed back and forth. I hid the dolls under the leaves and ran around the house and into the garden.

"Where the hell were you?" Donald demanded as he paced back and forth. "It's bad enough having to mind you, but I'm not going to run all over the place trying to find you."

"I'm sorry. I was right here."

"C'mon." He walked toward the woods. He was five years older than me, so I had to run to keep up with him.

We set off through the woods toward a pile of broken liquor bottles that I thought had pirates' treasure buried beneath them. I'd always wanted to dig there, but I'd cut myself when I tried once. I was just waiting until I had something better than a sand shovel to use.

"Where are we going?" I asked.

"Ask me no questions and I'll tell you no lies," he answered me in a singsong voice.

"I want to know."

"Let's go home, and I'll lock you in the house. I don't want a crybaby with me."

"Please, please. Let me go with you."

"All right, but hurry up."

There was a deer path through the woods, and we followed it. We had to watch out for poison ivy, which was everywhere. We went through a grove of pines. All the lower branches were without needles; I guess from the lack of sun. It was like a dead place, and I felt a chill.

After about ten minutes, we came to a ramshackle lean-to. Only a few slanting rays of sun managed to get through to this place, so it was cold and dark. Donald banged at an old door hanging on one hinge of the shack. Immediately, it popped open, revealing a tall man in his twenties with an ugly scar on his upper lip.

"Where the hell have you been?" he said. Then he glared at me. "What'd ya bring him for?"

Donald said, "I had to mind him, so I had to bring him along."

"I wanted to come," I said, trying to let the giant know that I wasn't a baby.

"Where's the food?" the young man asked.

I noticed for the first time that Donald was carrying a paper bag that he handed over. The man grabbed it, tore it open, and started gobbling some thick sandwiches that were badly wrapped in used wax paper. He went into the shed, and Donald followed him, pushing me in as well. We sat down on the earth floor.

"This is Franklin's secret place," Donald whispered to me. "You can never tell where it is."

I watched Franklin finish the last of the food. He rolled up all the paper in a ball and threw it in a corner. The shed was quite dark, but there was enough light for me to see his eyes gleaming.

"Come here, little boy," he said.

He towered over the two of us sitting on the ground. He was wearing old blue overalls, the type worn by trainmen. He undid two brass buttons on his shoulders and pulled the overalls down. He then pushed his underwear to his knees, exposed himself, and walked over to me.

"Open your mouth," he said. He grabbed a big piece of wood covered with rusty nails. "If you bite me, I'll kill you with this."

Tears poured out of my eyes, and I thought I would choke. I couldn't breathe, and my throat was hurting because he was so big. I was afraid I would throw up. I kept praying that Donald would help me, but he didn't. Franklin pushed in and out, holding my mouth open and hitting me on the head if I moved.

After what seemed like hours, Franklin stopped and pulled out of my mouth. He turned to Donald, who was still sitting quietly. "Take off your pants," he said.

I just stayed where I was, crying softly. I watched Franklin put Donald's tiny thing in his mouth. I closed my eyes and tried to block it all out. After a while, I felt my arm being shaken. I looked up at Donald, who said we were leaving. I wiped my eyes and followed the two of them through the woods.

Outside of a barn, Franklin grabbed me. "You tell anyone what happened today, and I'll take you to the top of this barn and drop you down and kill you."

I think that was the moment when I lost faith in my brother. I saw that he had been as afraid of Franklin as I had been. I always thought that he would take care of me, but now I know that he wouldn't.

Several years later, I did hear my father say that he'd read that Franklin Pease was dead. He had evidently rested his shotgun against his legs, and it went off, killing him instantly. Even knowing that he was gone, I could never tell anyone what had happened. Maybe one day soon, I could tell Roger and how with him, it would have been only about love.

***

In the morning, as soon as I was dressed, I managed to slip out of Roger's house without anyone seeing me. He had acted as if nothing had gone wrong the night before, and I didn't mention it. My father planned to pick me up the next morning, so Roger had said we should spend my last night together. He had a business dinner but would come by the shop afterward.

Roger arrived at the shop shortly after 9:00. He helped me lock up, and we started to go to his car. He stopped and said, "I don't think we should go to my room. The Smiths have seen you there too much. Let's just take a walk."

I tried to hide my disappointment. "Why don't we go up to High Fields?" I asked him. "It's a great place to walk and nobody's ever there."

He said okay, and we set out. The moon was almost full, so we had no trouble finding our way. We turned right at the meat market, crossed the railroad tracks, and went into the woods. The site was once a vast estate, but it has now been converted into a health center. Only the main building was occupied.

"What are we going to do?" I asked. "How will we see each other?"

"I'll come up to Boston every week or so, and we'll go to a museum or a show."

"But how can we be alone?"

"Don't worry. We'll find a way." He put his arms around me. Even though I knew no one ever came there at night, I was afraid someone might see us. But as he began kissing me, I forgot my fear. I grew terribly excited, and he did too. We started to touch each other and, before we knew it, both of us were spent. He took out his handkerchief and dried us off.

"There," he said. "Do you feel better now?"

I thought it was an odd question to ask me, but I answered, "Yes."

When we got back to the shop where Roger's car was parked, I insisted on riding with him to his house. "Please, let me stay with you a few more minutes," I said, hoping I could somehow get him to discuss our future. We drove to Pin Oak Way and got out of the car.

"I'll go back through the fields," I said. "Just come with me to the edge of the grass." We stopped under an arbor studded with late roses. "Please, just tell me it will be all right."

There was a rustle in the grass, and Mr. Smith appeared with his dog. "I was just taking a walk," he said, "I hope I didn't startle you."

"Not at all," Roger said. "Alan was just leaving."

"Goodnight," I said, hesitating for a moment.

"I'll go back to the house with you," Roger said to Mr. Smith. Then he turned to me. "Goodnight, Alan," he said, and they both walked away.

In the morning, I opened the shop as usual. I walked around the tables in the shop. Although a significant amount had been sold during the summer, a substantial amount of merchandise remained. I guess Nana would try to sell it all next summer if she were well enough to have the shop again.

My father would never arrive before noon, so at least I had a few hours left. I locked the shop's doors and got on my bike. When I reached the landscaping office that adjoined the nursery, I decided to take my chances. I put my bicycle against a tree and walked through the front door. The room was filled with desks, drafting tables, and files. There were blueprints tacked on all the walls. Roger, in his shirtsleeves, was pasting down some cardboard trees on a model.

"Hi." Roger said, "How are you?"

"Fine," I said. "Are you busy?"

He stood up. "No, I can take a break." We stepped outside and stood beneath the trees. "Is something wrong?"

I was careful to keep my voice down. "Please don't be angry that I came."

"Of course not."

"I just had to see you. I thought we'd get things straightened out last night, but Mr. Smith ruined it."

He lit a cigarette. "Everything's all right. I'll come and see you as often as I can, and I'll write to you. I promise." His smile told me everything I needed to know. "I have to get back now." He looked me in the eye. "I'll miss you," he said, then walked back into his office.

Five

Since my return to Brookline, I felt like a different person. I saw my old friend Irving, and we talked about our vacations, but I had a secret I couldn't tell him. I read Roger's letter over and over. It was short, and in it, he told me about taking Liz from Mrs. Goodell's dress shop to dinner, so he got that out of the way. He said that Falmouth seemed empty now, and he was coming to visit. He signed it, "Love." I hid it in the back of the clipper ship on the wall, along with my small nude picture collection.

My mother got me out of bed early. There was a lot to do. She seemed more excited than I was and immediately assigned tasks that would take the whole morning. Dad kept out of the way and found a spot far from the line of action to read the Sunday paper. Donald, who was home for the day, pitched in. By noon, everything was ready for Roger's arrival.

I looked around our apartment as if seeing it for the first time through Roger's eyes. The Japanese prints were beautiful, and some of the antiques were truly valuable. Maybe he wouldn't notice that the drapes in the living room were too short or that the pieces of carpeting didn't quite reach the walls.

It was still warm, with just a hint of fall in the air. Roger arrived in a tweed sports jacket and blue sweater. Everyone greeted him as if he were an old friend. No one would have guessed he was closer to me than anyone else in the family.

Mother had outdone herself as she served fruit cups, chicken, four vegetables, and a Jell-O mold. Her famous apple pie with ice cream was the dessert. She kept encouraging Roger to eat more and more. He won her over completely with his praise of her cooking.

Dad, busy with his vegetarian food, must have felt left out. He held out a plate to Roger. "I want you to try some of this soy," he said. "You'll like it."

"Please, Dad, don't make him eat any of that stuff," I said.

"It won't hurt him." He held the plate out again to Roger. "Go ahead, just a taste."

Roger stuck his fork into a substance he had certainly never seen before. "Ha, not bad," he said.

"Doesn't it have a meat flavor?" my father asked.

"Well..." Roger sounded amused.

"If you closed your eyes, and you didn't know, you'd think it was hamburger, wouldn't you?"

"Ralph, please!" my mother interjected.

"Have you ever heard of Dr. Jackson?" My father asked.

"Dad, don't," I tried to stop him.

"No," my father replied, "Roger's interested. Dr. Jackson only eats soybeans, and at seventy-five, he can lie with his head on one chair and his feet on another. And three women can sit across his chest."

"Well," Roger said with a deadpan face, "I guess at 75, you can't be too particular."

My mother let out a shriek and laughed until tears ran down her cheeks. Donald joined her, and finally, even my father laughed as well.

Roger said, "Oh, by the way, on Columbus Day weekend, I thought I'd drive up north and see my mother and look at the autumn leaves. I wondered if Alan would like to come along?"

"Oh, that would be great," I said.

"Well," my father answered, "we're not quite sure of our plans yet."

"Is there a chance you all could come?" Roger asked. "I know my mother would love to meet you."

"Oh no," Mother said, "Donald has too much studying to do, and unfortunately, I can't possibly get away."

I knew she probably had six mahjong games planned since it was a holiday weekend. I turned to my father. "Can I go?"

"We'll see," he said. I knew from his tone that the chances were good.

After dinner, Donald washed the dishes, and I dried them. Mother was on the phone arranging a bridge game for later in the day. Roger and my father were in the living room discussing the possibility of the U.S. getting into the war. Roger said he was sure he'd be drafted if America got involved.

I kept trying to hear what Roger was saying, but the telephone table was just beyond the kitchen, so Mother's voice dominated the others. I did hear her say on the phone that she and my father "would be there in half an hour," so I assumed she'd found another couple for bridge. Suddenly, everybody was saying goodbye, leaving Roger and me alone in the apartment.

We sat awkwardly for a few minutes, making small talk but listening to see if anyone was coming back up the stairs. When we felt enough time had gone by and no one was returning, we went down the hall to my bedroom. It had been so long since we'd been together physically. We lay on my bed, hugging and kissing. Then we touched each other in the way Roger had taught me. The excitement was intense, but what mattered to me was the feeling of being loved.

Later in the day, we went to the museum, and it was a revelation. A world was opened up to me that I had dreamed of but been afraid to explore alone. Roger was the perfect guide. He made me feel comfortable with art for the first time.

"Don't look at the name under the painting to see if it's by somebody famous," he said. "If you do that, you'll make up your mind to like it because you're supposed to." I smiled guiltily. It was what I always did. "Just look at the painting, and say to yourself, 'Do I like this? What do I feel about it, no matter what anybody else says?'"

"I like that," I said, as I looked at a large painting in bright colors of South Sea natives in front of an idol. Then I sneaked a look at the name underneath that said Gauguin. "And it is by somebody famous." We both laughed.

Afterward, we sat on a bench in the Fenway, looking at the river. I was feeling sad at the thought of Roger leaving me to drive back to Falmouth. I wanted to talk about our future, but he put me off.

"You're not even 16," he said. "You have your whole life ahead of you."

"But I know what I want to do. When I graduate in June, I will be an actor. Either I'll go to New York to study and we'll live there, or I'll study in Boston and we can be together here."

He turned to me. "You know how much older I am than you."

"What difference does that make?"

"He smiled and got up from the bench. "It's getting late. I have to drive you home."

***

Roger had to work half a day on Saturday of the Columbus Day weekend, so he didn't get to Brookline until late in the afternoon. I was busy most of the day packing and unpacking a small suitcase Donald had lent me.

Roger came up to say hello to my parents, but they hurried us on our way. They were afraid of us driving in the dark. I grabbed my suitcase and winter coat and ran down the stairs. Once we were in the car, Roger reached over and squeezed my arm. "I can't believe they let you come," he said.

We drove north. The day was gray and surprisingly cold so early in October. There was a lot of traffic as we headed toward Concord. We ran into a crowd leaving a football game and were stalled for a quarter of an hour. We drove through flat farmland that looked like the fields in Kansas that I'd seen when we visited my mother's family.

It was pitch dark when we arrived at Roger's house. We turned into a long driveway, and there, right on the highway, was a white-frame farmhouse. It sat back quite a way, and there was a bright light on a pole in front of it. It was the only thing lit up for miles. It looked fake to me, almost like a stage set.

Roger parked the car near a small, covered porch. Instantly, a light appeared above a doorway, and a woman emerged. She had white hair gathered in a bun, and even in the sketchy light, I could see her resemblance to Roger. She held the front of a cardigan sweater together to keep out the cold.

Roger yelled to her, "Go back inside, Ma. We'll be right in."

We unloaded our two small cases and went into the kitchen. The floor was covered with linoleum, and there was an oilcloth-topped table in the middle with four wooden chairs stained a dark brown. The huge stove still had the old-fashioned iron covers that could be lifted off to put in wood or coal. The overhead light bounced off the shiny, pale green walls. I felt like I was inside a huge meat refrigerator.

Roger kissed his mother on the cheek and introduced me. She didn't move toward me or offer a welcoming smile.

"Pleased to meet you," she said.

"I'm sorry we're so late," he said, "but we ran into terrible traffic."

"Your brother's been waiting to eat with you, so I'll just give him a call," she said as she started out onto the porch.

Through the window, I could see her pull at a large bell hanging from a rafter. It sounded three times, and she came back inside. The table was set, and she told us to wash our hands in the stone kitchen sink. She gave us a thin, worn towel to share between us.

Roger's brother didn't look like him at all. He was wearing overalls and must have weighed 200 pounds. He shook hands with Roger, acknowledged me, and used the same towel after he'd washed his hands.

The supper was tasteless. I wasn't sure if it was chicken or beef stew. It was runny, almost like soup. There was little conversation. Roger asked questions about the cows and the milking. His brother answered in monosyllables. His mother questioned Roger about his draft status, his work, and if he was keeping company with anyone.

After a piece of apple pie with a thick crust that tasted like lard, Roger's brother went back to the barn. I asked if I could help with the dishes. Roger said we both would. His mother washed them while we dried and put them back in the cupboards that ran along one side of the room.

"You have nice manners for a young boy," Roger's mother said to me.

"He does, Ma, and you have no idea how smart he is. He was a salesman in his grandmother's shop all summer, and he sold more than she did."

"No, I didn't," I said.

"Don't listen to him," Roger said, "he's just being modest. He's going to be an actor."

His mother was scraping garbage into the pail under the sink. "Is that right?" she said without much interest.

Roger led me out of the kitchen into the dark hallway, which had a forty-five-degree stairway. Once we were away from the stove, it was cold. We hurried to get to Roger's room. All the walls were white, and there wasn't even a picture to cheer them up. I could see into the living room as I walked up the stairs. It was as drab as the rest of the house.

We undressed quickly. There had been no discussion of separate rooms. I was grateful. At least I would be warm sleeping next to him.

The next morning, as we drove north, the leaves were glorious, but neither of us was able to enjoy them. Roger's mind was somewhere else, and I was afraid to intrude. I wanted to talk about his mother and his brother, but everything I said seemed to antagonize him. I felt as if I were walking on eggshells.

While he drove, I studied the map and tried to find a place for us to spend the night. "What about Bellows Falls?" I asked, having found a name on the map in larger letters than in the surrounding towns. "It must be big enough to have rooming houses."

"Fellow's Balls," Roger said, smiling for the first time that day. "Perfect, we'll stay at Fellow's Balls."

The town was much farther than it had looked on the map. We were exhausted by the time we got there. We found a place to stay and were sent nearby to get soup and a sandwich. Everything else was closed on Sunday. I tried to get Roger to say what was bothering him, but there was no response.

"I wish I could help you drive," I said. "I don't think you're having much fun."

"Don't be silly. I'm having a great time."

The room had twin beds. It was damp and colorless, with faded chintz slip-covered chairs, an ugly stained Oriental rug, and curtains at the windows that had yellowed from all the washing, which I was sure never made them clean. Over each headboard was a hanging lamp with most of its fringe missing, giving it a cockeyed look. When I was in bed, I decided to get things straight.

"What have I done?" I asked.

"What do you mean?" Roger answered as I knew he would.

"You know. Please tell me."

"Nothing."

"If I only knew what I'd done to upset you, I'd apologize, but I don't know what it is."

"You haven't done anything," Roger said as he continued to undress.

"I'm so miserable. Please tell me." I started to cry.

"Now, don't behave like a little boy," he said.

"But you're acting like I'm the last person in the world you want to be with." I somehow stopped my tears. "I thought we loved each other."

"Let's not discuss it."

I steeled myself. "Do you love me?"

"That has nothing to do with it."

"Well then, what is it? It's so awful. I don't know what to do—"

"Alan, you're such a child."

"No, I'm not. Why do you keep saying that?"

"Because you are." He sounded like a kind teacher. "When I first met you on the beach, I thought you were 18. Then, when I heard your real age, you still seemed so much older."

"I'm grown up enough to love you and want to spend my life with you."

Roger walked over and sat on my bed. "We've got to get something straight. You've got to stop talking about us spending our lives together."

"You don't love me."

"Alan, I'm twice your age, and we're the same sex."

"It doesn't matter as long as two people love each other," I said.

"Don't be ridiculous," he replied.

"What does the right sex or age have to do with it? Look at my parents, or Mrs. Goodell and Jim. They're the right sexes and the right ages. It doesn't seem to have made them happy."

"Come on, Alan." He sounded like he'd had enough.

"Or my grandmother, or Liz. She just wants to get married." I was trying desperately to make him understand. "They don't love anybody the way I love you, so why can't we be together?"

He sighed and put his hands on his forehead. "Alan, I need to ask you something. If you really love me, you have to stop bringing this up. I can't keep going over it again and again." He lowered his hands and looked right at me. "I care about you, but if you don't stop, you'll ruin everything."

I knew I shouldn't say anymore, so I just sat quietly. After a few moments, he reached over and kissed me. "Now, let's go to bed."

I started to get into my bed again, but he took me over to his. Oh God, I thought, I just pray that everything's going to be all right now.

***

In November, on my birthday, a package arrived from Roger. It was an etching of people standing on the steps of St. Paul's Cathedral in London. There was a note attached: "Not very much, but at least an original Pennell." I hurried to the public library to look up Pennell and discovered that he was a famous American artist. I owned a real work of art. I immediately made plans to get it framed. The next day, another package arrived from Roger. It was a yellow, cashmere, sleeveless sweater. I didn't let on to Roger that I liked it better than the etching, but it was perfect to wear with the new Hart, Schaffner and Marx sports jacket my parents had given me. I called to thank Roger, and he told me that he'd be in Brookline the first Sunday in December.

He came up to see me as he had promised. To describe what happened on that day, I had to get out my diary again. I felt I had to keep a record of what was going on because it was just too much to remember. Besides, I felt I owed it to posterity so that the world would know everything when I was gone.

Monday, December 8, 1941

Today is an ominous one to start a journal of my life. President Franklin Roosevelt declared war on Japan at 12:35 p.m. Of course, there was school, but everyone heard the President because radios had been set up everywhere. The message was short – just 500 words. He summed up the events that happened yesterday...

We were sitting at Sunday dinner when a friend burst in and almost hysterically shouted, "The Naval Base at Pearl Harbor has been bombed by the Japanese!" We turned on the radio and it was confirmed. Roger was here and he, of course, was worried as the age limit will be up to thirty-five again. He is thirty. Everybody was concerned but not worried. It was said constantly that this was suicide by the Japanese. However, everything is changed today. The record will be left for history, but the seriousness of the situation is now being revealed.

Today, the excitement of war was tremendous. I should have said that the President asked Congress to declare war. The vote was unanimous except for one woman. A great deal of damage is being done to our positions, warships, men, etc. So far, Japan is victorious. It has gained Guam and Wake Island. We are getting allies by the hour – many South American republics.

I can hardly study or do anything with the radio so full of reports. The war is fascinating as well as horrible. The day was very cold. Snowflakes flurried down for a few minutes yesterday. We plan to go to Florida a week from next Friday. Britain declared war on Japan before we did. Many Americans say that Germany forced Japan into war, and that we should declare war on Germany, the true enemy. Farewell, peace.

I put the diary away. I planned to keep track of all the battles until we won the war. But in a few days, it was so complicated I couldn't figure it out anymore. I sat every night at the radio with Mother and Dad. We listened, horrified, to what was going on. I kept worrying about what would happen to Roger. I wished I could tell my parents about my feelings, but it was impossible.

<h1 style="text-align:center">Six</h1>

J uly was very hot. I spent most of my time on the roof, reading until the heat got unbearable. Roger had written that he had gone into the army as an officer and was in training school. I had an address where I could write him, but I realized how busy he was when I heard nothing further from him. I had just come from the library and was carrying my bicycle up the stairs. It was very light but difficult to manipulate around the curve in the wall just before the apartment landing. After I unlocked the door and wheeled it into the hall outside my father's photographic darkroom, I took the books out of the basket on the handlebars and went into the living room. I opened all the windows.

I chose a Walter D. Edmonds book; I was fascinated by the rough-and-tumble world of the Erie Canal. I settled into the wing chair beside the marble-topped table. Suddenly, I noticed an open telegram next to the lamp. I reached over and picked it up. It was addressed to me. My heart pounded as I opened it, worried it might be about Roger. Instead, it read: "PLEASE CALL FORBES THEATER IMMEDIATELY, ROCKPORT 2301 COLLECT." It was signed "Marla Forbes."

I ran to the phone and dialed. It rang and rang. I kept praying that Miss Forbes was there. I felt my stomach turning over and over. Miss Forbes answered the phone, and her voice was warm and friendly.

"Alan," she said, "I got your letter saying you're interested in applying for an acting job in my theater. It turns out I need someone immediately. I will pay you $15 a week. You can rent a room in the house where

all the actors live for only $3, and food is very reasonably priced. You can live quite well on the money. But I must decide right away. Do you want me to talk to your parents?"

"No, thank you," I said. "I'll speak to them and call you in the morning."

Mother was serving the rest of the sponge cake she had baked for the girls—her name for the women she played cards with—when I had an idea. "You're always worried about my health," I said to my father, "but you don't mind me spending the summer in the sweltering heat in Brookline when I could be cool and swimming every day in Rockport."

There was a long silence during which Donald, my mother, and I just looked at my father. We knew his Achilles' heel was to see that everyone was healthy. After what seemed an interminable time, he said, "What about the smoking and the drinking the actors do?"

"I won't smoke, and I won't drink," I said firmly.

Dad got up from the table and went to the icebox. He took out a bottle of soy acidophilus milk and returned. Since he started wearing his glasses all the time, the reflection from the overhead light often hid his eyes.

"I'll tell you what," he said. "I'll let you go to summer stock, but only if Mother goes with you."

I was shocked, but I decided to quit while I was ahead. I was going to be an actor, but my mother was going with me.

***

I couldn't wait to write to Roger and tell him that I was finally going to be a professional actor, and even getting paid for it. I still hadn't received a letter from him, but I kept telling myself he was just too busy to write. Surely this news would prompt him to send a few lines of congratulations.

On Wednesday, my father drove my mother and me to Rockport. He only stayed long enough to help us find a room near the theater. The landlady said she wasn't too keen on "theater folk," but Mother charmed her, and then she admitted we were different. Once we unpacked in the twin-bedded room with its nautical lamps, maple furniture, and white bedspreads covered with tiny balls, we walked into town.

In our second phone conversation, Miss Forbes told me that I wouldn't be needed for rehearsal until Thursday morning. She would leave tickets at the box office for the upcoming play. We walked up the long hill to the theater.

There were just a handful of people in the audience, but at least the theater had been cleaned up. The play was a French farce that was greeted with stony silence. It didn't help matters that the set was flimsy, and every time a door slammed to make a comic point, the flats tottered precariously. There was a certain excitement in anticipating the disaster that was bound to happen. When it didn't, everyone settled down to an interminable wait for the final curtain. My mother wanted to go backstage, but I dissuaded her. I wanted to keep her away from the actors as long as I could.

I was the first to arrive at the theater the next morning. The front door was unlocked, so I stepped into near darkness. Shutters covered all the windows, and I was reluctant to turn on the lights. I sat in the back and waited. After half an hour, others began to arrive, and the lights finally came on.

The huge police dog came bounding in, pulling Miss Forbes on the other end of the leash. She kissed everyone on both cheeks and then disappeared into her office. She came back without the dog and announced the rehearsal would begin.

"Has anyone seen the new actor?" she asked.

Everyone shrugged and said "No."

"Oh dear," Miss Forbes sounded annoyed. "What'll we do?"

I forced myself to stand up. "Here I am," I said.

"Alan," Miss Forbes called out. "What are you doing back there? Come up here." I walked to the footlights, feeling everyone's eyes on me. "Welcome," she said warmly and introduced me to the actors. I made mental notes of each person so I wouldn't get them mixed up.

I shook hands with everyone and mentioned how much I had enjoyed the play the night before. Most were welcoming, except for Rusty, the handsome juvenile lead, who walked off without saying hello and just sat down with his script.

"Where are Alan's sides?" Miss Forbes asked into the air. A girl emerged from the office with a small folder, which she handed to me. "This is Wendy. She does the sets," Miss Forbes said. "Now, where is Alan's wife?" she asked.

Wendy answered. "Lillian had to return some props, so she'll be a few minutes late."

The rehearsal lasted only two hours. The actors, still tired from opening night, mumbled their lines. Miss Forbes, directing, barely looked up from the Samuel French paper copy of Philip Barry's *Holiday* in her hand. She seemed to read her directions straight from the book. Everyone had sides like mine, though the leads had far more pages.

When we were dismissed, Miss Forbes called out to me as I was leaving. "Alan."

"Yes, Miss Forbes?" I was sure I was about to be fired.

"I've told you to call me Marla," she said. "I never want to hear Miss Forbes again! Now, you're not free yet. I have to drive you to Gloucester to rent you a tuxedo."

***

On opening night, I remembered all my lines and all the movements Marla had given me in rehearsal. She hadn't said anything about the character, so I invented one myself. I felt a tense smile frozen on my face, but I couldn't relax enough to let it go. At one point, I glanced out into the audience. A small group of people huddled near the stage, silent.

My mother didn't like *Holiday*. She didn't think much of Trilby, who played the lead, but she praised me. There was to be a party at the actors' house, but Mother thought I should get some sleep.

When we returned to the room, she said as she undressed, "There was someone behind me who said something about the performance that I thought was very good. I wrote it down." She opened her pocketbook and took out an envelope that she unfolded. She read from the back of it. "You can't make a silk purse out of a sow's ear."

I wasn't quite sure what that had to do with the play, but I nodded and went to bed.

After our next rehearsal, we went to dinner, and Mother told me she was going home. We ate fried clams at a candlelit seafood restaurant on Bear Skin Neck. "I really should get home to Daddy," she said. "Everyone in the company seems nice, and I'm sure you'll be perfectly safe."

I tried not to show how overjoyed I was. "I hate for you to leave," I said, "but I know there's nothing for you to do here."

"I'm confident you can take care of yourself," she replied, "but I don't want you living alone in case you get sick. I've spoken to Rusty. He's going to move in with you."

I was stunned. "I don't like Rusty."

"He's the nicest one of all of them. He'll be a good influence on you."

"Can't I just live in the actor's house? I wouldn't be alone."

"I'll feel better if you just stay where you are. I've already settled it with Rusty, unless you'd rather I stayed."

"You know I'd like you to stay, but I know you have to get back. I'll room with Rusty."

I had seen Rusty at the rehearsal, but he'd said nothing about moving in with me. After the performance, he came over to me. "I'll walk to the room with you," he said. When we arrived, I helped him unpack.

He went first to the bathroom at the end of the hall. Then I went, and when I returned after brushing my teeth, I started to get into my bed.

"No," he said, lying down in his shorts. "Let's talk for a while. Come over here so we don't make too much noise." He smoothed a place by his leg. "Look, it's going to be a long summer, and we're going to need sex. We might as well have it together."

I was amazed. It felt so impersonal, as if he had decided everything himself. I'd always thought sex came from love; that was how it was with Roger. "I hate to say it," I said awkwardly, "and I think you're very handsome, Rusty, but I just don't feel anything."

Rusty laughed. "Don't be ridiculous," he said, "I don't feel anything either. It's just a question of getting your rocks off." He pulled back the covers. "Now get into bed, or we'll never get to sleep."

I didn't know what to do. If only Roger was here to take care of the situation, but I still hadn't heard a word from him. I walked back to my bed. I hadn't counted on Rusty's egomania.

"Okay," Rusty said, "I'm tired too. There'll be plenty of other nights."

When I awoke the next morning, he was standing in front of the mirror, sprinkling his thick hair with Vitalis. He combed it lovingly and set a wave in the front with the flat of his hand. As I watched him, I formulated a plan.

Later that day, I went to the actors' house and found a tiny room off the kitchen that was unused since it had no door. There were no other rooms available, but I could put a blanket over the doorway. That night, I waited in the room for Rusty, who had gone to have drinks with friends. When he came in and saw me sitting up in bed, he said, "Hello," and closed the door.

I took a deep breath to get my courage. "Rusty," I said, "I'm moving out. I won't do it until the end of the week, so nobody will think there's anything funny. I don't want anything more to do with you."

He didn't even turn around as he took off his shirt. "Suit yourself," he said.

***

The dress rehearsal of the new play went poorly, but I was told that was traditional in the theater—it meant the opening would be a smash. The curtain went up promptly at 8:30 so the *Gloucester* critic could file her review in time for the next day's paper. I managed to get through the first act, but I was so nervous I didn't wait for my laughs. I talked right through them.

In the second act, all I had to do was wear a gypsy costume and help carry a bathtub on stage. That went all right. But the third act was where I had the most to do. Everyone was trying to coax my character, who had stage fright, onto the stage and deliver the final line of the play. I was so scared I didn't have to act, and the audience laughed hysterically. When I managed to deliver my one line, "People are people, and there's nothing you can do about it," the audience screamed, and the curtain came down to wild applause.

After the curtain call, I climbed the stairs to the dressing room that the men shared. No one said a word to me as I took off my costume and began to remove my makeup. They discussed with each other how much work the play required and how fortunate they were to have gotten through it. I felt depressed. I must have overacted. I had felt so real in my nervousness, but it may have been too much.

Then we all gathered around. Marla tapped her glass to get everyone's attention. When it was quiet, she said, "I'm sad to tell you that I'm closing the theater."

***

Marla scheduled the new play to run for two weeks, so we struggled through until the final performance, often playing to just a handful of people. Mother and Dad came to pick me up. Saying goodbye to everyone felt like the end of the world. Weeks had passed since I'd written to Roger, and still there was no answer. I started to worry that something had happened to him.

When I got back to Brookline, I wrote another letter to him, this time describing my stint at the theater. I tried to make it funny, so he'd be amused. Maybe he had never gotten any of the letters I sent. I hoped he would at least get this one.

After Labor Day, I read that the Tributary Theater in Boston was holding auditions for *Much Ado About Nothing*. I memorized a Shakespeare monologue, waited hours for my turn, and finally stood on a nearly dark stage. Since I couldn't see the judges, I wasn't nervous. I launched into Hamlet's "Oh that this too, too solid flesh would melt" and, to my surprise, finished without interruption. Instead of "Don't call us, we'll call you," they offered me a role on the spot. Rehearsals were at night, so I found a day job at Filene's department store as a stock boy, earning $13.31 a week.

There, I noticed a blond man in his 20s—Mr. Black, the assistant buyer. The salesladies warned me to obey him instantly. One day, instead of barking orders, he said pleasantly, "I've been noticing you. I think you could be more than a stock boy." He recommended me for a clerical job with better pay. Although I wasn't interested in merchandising, I accepted the position under pressure and received a raise. Soon after, Mr. Black—Leslie, as he insisted that I call him, invited me to lunch now that I was "respectable" enough. Always immaculate in a pin-stripe suit, he spoke about his Harvard background and the joys of department store life.

When I admitted I wanted to be an actor, he brushed it off: "With your good looks, you belong here."

We lunched together often, but always away from the store so "people wouldn't talk." His interest grew more personal, and though I tried to avoid him with rehearsals as an excuse, he cornered me one Saturday with tickets to the theater. I didn't want him to see my family's modest apartment, so I met him outside. We dined at an elegant Beacon Hill restaurant where I felt out of place. When the bill came, he split it; I was short $2, which he magnanimously covered.

At the play, Leslie became loud and drunk. On the drive home, he bypassed my street, insisting we "talk" by the reservoir. His jaw was set as he pulled onto a dirt road, a known lover's lane. Suddenly, he exposed himself and begged me to teach him, claiming he was going crazy. Before I could react, headlights flared. Two policemen got out of a car. A man's deep, rough voice shouted, "Look at that cock. He's really hot. And look at the jail bait."

They ordered us out of the car. Leslie wept and blamed me while they asked if he'd forced me. I could have said he had, and I'd be free. But I immediately thought of men going to prison for molesting minors.

Even though I had nothing but contempt for Leslie, I answered, "No, he didn't force me."

The officers sneered at Leslie, scolded him, and finally ordered him to drive me home, with their car trailing us. They said they'd pick me up in the morning. On the way, Leslie said it was all my fault and that I'd ruined his life by resisting him. I walked into my house knowing that my life was destroyed.

I let myself into the apartment. The night-light they'd left on told me my parents were asleep. I went straight to my room and sat by the window, waiting for the police to return. All I could think about was suicide. My mind raced: We're on the second floor. It's high enough that I could kill myself if I jumped. However, I couldn't muster the courage. I just sat and waited. When dawn came, and the police still hadn't arrived, I got undressed and got into bed. Every time I heard a car, I jumped up, sure they had come for me.

I awoke with my mother shaking me. "It's 9:00," she said. "Are you going to sleep all day?" I immediately remembered the night before and started to tell her, but she was out of the room before I had a chance. "Come and have your breakfast," she yelled. I leapt up and rushed to the window. There was no police car parked there.

My father nodded to me as he sat at the kitchen table, reading the Sunday papers. He looked so formidable that I couldn't say anything to him. I nibbled some food so they wouldn't question why I wasn't eating. I just waited for the doorbell to ring with my stomach in knots.

Around 4:00 in the afternoon, the phone rang, and my mother sang out, "Alan, it's for you."

I picked up the phone, holding my breath. "Hello," I said.

"Hello," Leslie said brightly, "how are you?"

My mother was hovering nearby. "Fine," I answered.

"Can you go for a ride?"

I could hardly speak. "Sure."

"I'll come right over," he said and hung up.

"I'm going for a ride with Leslie," I said as if I were an automaton.

After what seemed like an eternity, Leslie's car pulled up, and I got inside and shut the door. "We'll just drive around," he said. He was freshly shaven and in one of his pin-stripe suits.

"Leslie, what happened?" I begged.

"Oh, have you been worried about that?" Leslie asked flippantly. "For God's sake, they wanted money. I knew that. I had to give them $50; you'll have to pay me half."

I was stunned. "You mean we don't have to go to jail?"

"Of course not," Leslie said as if he were talking to a child. "I just had to find the money for them, and believe me, that wasn't so easy at 2:00 in the morning; but I did, and I fixed it all."

"But Leslie," I tried not to let him see how upset I was, "why didn't you tell me earlier?"

"I never thought you'd take it seriously," he scoffed. "Anyway, it's all over, and I've decided that I'm going to get my own place," he said triumphantly. "We can't go through anything like last night again."

I steeled myself. "I don't want to see you anymore."

"Well, you're going to," he said fiercely.

In the days that followed, I was able to put Leslie off by saying I was rehearsing for *Much Ado About Nothing* in every spare minute, but I'd see him after the play opened. When it opened, I had already given my notice at Filene's, so I wouldn't have to see Leslie. I just didn't tell my parents I'd quit until I could find something else.

Seven

The director told me that, with so many young men drafted from radio stations, I might have a chance as an announcer. I had a deep voice for my age and was willing to try anything. I auditioned whenever I could.

One windy day by the Charles, I climbed the stairs to a reception room with plastic furniture and a window looking into a studio. A large man in a blue suit appeared and asked if I'd been helped. When I said I wanted an audition, he smiled broadly. "What about me?" he said, introducing himself as John Kiley, head of the station.

He ushered me into a studio, handed me some copy, and listened from the control room. I read commercials, news, and music intros, feeling no nerves, just talking as if to someone I knew. When he returned, beaming, he said, "You're very good. One of the guys may be drafted. I'd like to give you a try." That night, he called to confirm. I was amazed. I had the job, with $10 more a week than at Filene's. I never saw Leslie again, but I repaid every cent I owed him.

The next week I went on the air for the first time. "Alan, you're about to be heard by over a million people," Kiley said. Instead of fear, I felt a rush. When I finished, he clapped me on the back and said, "Alan, you're a born announcer!"

The work, however, was far from glamorous. I spent 8 hours alone in a padded booth, reading news, spinning records, and filling airtime with talk on almost anything, as long as it didn't require too many facts.

Every 15 or 30 minutes, I alternated with another announcer—a small man in his 40s who fussed constantly with his thick hair. Otherwise, my only contact was the engineer behind the glass.

A month passed without any routine changes. One night, Mr. Kiley got me a job introducing speakers at a banquet he was attending. I would be paid $25. He said he'd be by to pick me up at 7:00. I was both excited and nervous as I sat at the kitchen table with my parents. I picked at my food and continued to glance at my watch.

"Finish your dinner," my father said.

"I'm just not hungry."

"You eat everything on your plate, or you're not going out."

"I'm just too excited to eat," I explained, "and Mr. Kiley will be here any minute."

"I told you; you're not going anywhere unless you eat that food."

I was upset and suddenly stubborn. "I don't have to. I'm going to go to work, and I'm going to make $25. I don't have to eat anything more."

My father got up from his chair, walked over to me, and slapped me hard across the face. I ran to my room and slammed the door. I sat there, trying to calm down. When the doorbell rang, I grabbed my coat and left without saying goodbye to my parents.

I had to find a way to get away from them.

***

Once a week, the radio station would broadcast a live mystery program featuring actors from Boston's theater scene. The show was late at night, long after I finished work, but I always made an effort to listen to it. I had recently been assigned to an interview program where I spoke with some of the same actors, so listening helped me discuss their performances when I met them. It immediately broke the ice.

I had heard a particularly gruesome thriller entitled *The Fog Drips Blood* starring Guerita Donnelly, who was playing a small role in a touring company of the Broadway hit *Junior Miss*. I laughed as she used her husky, British-accented voice to wring every bit of melodrama out of the amateurish script.

The next morning, I was alone in the studio playing records, with only the engineer behind the glass partition to keep me company. I sipped my stale coffee and occasionally answered the phone if anyone called with a request. The air conditioner was barely adequate, and the room had a stale, cigarette-smelling odor. At the end of the day, I always had a slight headache from the lack of oxygen.

The phone lit up, and I finished my introduction, put the needle on the record, and signaled the engineer to bring up the volume. I then picked up the phone. A smoky, slightly drunken voice said, "This is *The Fog Drips Blood.*"

"Good morning, Miss Donnelly," I said without the slightest hesitation. There was no mistaking the voice I had heard the night before.

"You see," she said seductively, "you can't get away from me."

The interview went very well. Gerry, as she insisted I call her, turned out to be a dumpy, middle-aged woman with smeared makeup and rumpled clothes, but she had the speaking voice of a duchess. Her words, though, sounded as if they were trying to walk a straight line for a sobriety test. With her was Louis Beachner, a handsome young actor several years older than me, who played the juvenile lead in the play.

The three of us chatted amiably, and I asked all my usual questions about their careers. When I offered them coffee afterward, we sat down, and they began to question me. I confessed that I wanted to be an actor and was planning to go to New York as soon as I could save enough money.

"Don't," said Gerry imperiously. "It could be five years before you get a role in a play on Broadway."

When it was time for them to leave, they invited me to their show. I said I would be free the following night.

"We'll leave a ticket in your name at the box office," Louis said. I noticed that he had the slightest British accent, too, though he'd said in the interview that he was from Jersey City.

After the show, I went backstage to see Gerry and Louis. She had been superb as a tough, wisecracking maid, and he had been appropriately handsome and charming as the boy who takes out the girl when she has turned into a beautiful young woman. Over sandwiches at a delicatessen, I spoke again about my dream of going to New York and becoming an actor. They were both sympathetic but told me I would be crazy to try New York until I had enough money to support myself while I waited for something to happen.

"Remember what I told you at the radio station," Gerry said. "It could be five years before you ever get a play on Broadway."

A week later, Gerry called the radio station. When she got me on the phone, she said, "You won't believe this, but one of the boys in the show has been drafted, and you're going to get the role."

I was flabbergasted. "What are you talking about?"

"I've already spoken to the stage manager," she said, "and you're going to get a reading and, no question, you'll get the part."

For a moment, I thought it might be possible, but I didn't dare believe it. "Which part is it?" I asked as I held my breath.

"The football player," Gerry said. "It's the best part of any of the boys."

My heart sank. For a moment, I had escaped my family and finally become an actor, and now the fantasy was shattered. With my mound of brown hair and thinness, a poet's frame, no one would ever believe me as a loutish football player. "Thanks," I said, crestfallen, "but I don't think I'm right for that."

"What's the matter with you?" Gerry shot back. "You want to be an actor, don't you? I'll coach you. You'll see the play tonight, study the scene, and you'll get it. Come on, cheer up."

That night, I watched the play again, dread tightening my spine when the football player appeared. He stormed onstage, slapped the hungover father on the back, and mimed bowling with a roar. The audience roared too, especially when he sampled a candy, spat it out and said "cream" in disgust, and smeared the rest onto his spotless camel-hair coat. They loved it. I was revolted.

Later, I told Gerry and Louis, "I just don't see how I can do this."

"You want New York, don't you?" Gerry pressed. "Here's your chance." She handed me a couple of pages. "Learn them. I'll rehearse you. You'll be fine."

On audition day, I was paralyzed with fear. I had memorized the lines, copied every move the actor made, but felt grotesque. Gerry had been too ill to coach me, and I longed only for it to be over. Still, I couldn't be ungrateful.

At the theater, the doorman gave me a message: Miss Donnelly wanted to see me. In her dressing room, Gerry held out the camel-hair coat and yellow scarf the football player wore.

"I stole these from wardrobe," she said with a grin. "Put them on."

The coat swallowed me, the scarf garish against my neck. In the mirror, I looked like a poster for needy children. "Perfect," Gerry said, rolling up my sleeves.

She led me onto the stage, dimly lit by a single bulb. From the wings, a little man peered at me like an old leprechaun.

"What do you think, Bill?" Gerry called. "Doesn't he look the part?"

He squinted. "Yuh. Could save money if he can do it. Let's hear him."

As he shuffled toward the house, Gerry whispered, "Yell loud. He's hard of hearing." Then she hurried after him.

I noticed the stage manager stagger and wondered if he was drunk, but there was no time for that. "All right, go ahead," came the voice from the dark.

I burst through the door, bellowing lines and mimicking every gesture I had studied. No one read cues, so I barreled on, a whirlwind in that heavy coat, until I stood panting and drenched. Silence. Then the little man approached the footlights.

"Not bad," he said, pursing his lips. "You could use some rehearsal."

"He was great!" Gerry hollered from her seat.

The stage manager turned to me. "You open in Hartford on Christmas Day."

***

I walked into the kitchen where my parents were listening to the war news on the radio. I had a trump card: the actor's minimum salary for a road show, $55 a week, five more than my father's new salary as an insurance instructor. He had finally given up photography after years of struggle.

I made them turn down the radio so they could hear my good fortune. My father hit the ceiling. "Absolutely not! Under no circumstances."

My mother chimed in: "You're only 17. You should be going to college."

"You have a good job as a radio announcer," my father pressed. "There's a future in radio. And the people aren't awful the way they are in the theater."

I fought desperately. "I'll never forgive you if I lose this chance. I could never buy this kind of experience, and they're paying me a fortune to do it." But this time, nothing moved them. Because of my age, one of them had to sign the contract. Without it, the one-way ticket to Hartford the stage manager had given me was useless. I told no one, not even Gerry or Louis, afraid they'd tell someone else about the job if they knew.

The days that followed were agony. Mr. Kiley at the station was kind, holding my job in case I couldn't go. My brother refused to help. My wealthy aunt and uncle were as opposed to acting as my parents were.

Before closing night in Boston, I saw the play one more time. The role still felt foreign. I had been reading Stanislavsky, who insisted you must find something of yourself in a character. I hadn't yet, but I believed I would if I could just get to Hartford. Backstage, Gerry and Louis told me she was leaving the show for a minor operation. It was a blow; I had counted on her coaching. Louis suggested we share a room in Hartford so he could help me with lines. I agreed. As we said goodbye, I considered telling them the truth, but I held out hope.

I hadn't heard from Roger in eight months, though my letters to Officers Training School weren't returned. I wrote to him one last time.

I told him I had to escape from my parents—that he knew well my father's coldness and my mother's indifference. Once I had loved her fiercely, but now she cared only for her clubs and card games. I tried to amuse Roger with her latest obsession: writing lyrics to honor the 20 past presidents of her club, set to popular tunes. She paraded through the house singing lines like "Dora Wyzanski, we all love you" to "I Love You Truly," and "Sadie Margolis always lends a helping hand" to "Bei Mir Bist Du Schoen." I hoped Roger would write me that it made him laugh.

In the middle of all this, my mother began confiding in me about her failing marriage. "Your father is not a sexual man," she said. She claimed she still loved her childhood sweetheart in Kansas and expected to hear from him any day. I was sure it was all fantasy.

I poured everything into my letter to Roger: my dream of acting since the day we met, my summer in Rockport, Shakespeare, and the radio work. Writing to him felt like talking to him. I ended, "If you're ever in a city where *Junior Miss* is playing, find out if I'm in the cast."

As Christmas approached, I tried again to change my parents' minds. They were immovable. Then the unexpected happened: I fell ill. Fever, cough, laryngitis—I went to bed. My father, who related more to illness than to ambition, finally relented. Seeing me sick with despair, he signed the contract.

On Christmas morning, I rose from bed, packed my bag, and left with my parents for Back Bay Station. My father never gave me verbal permission, but I didn't need it. With a temperature of 101° and barely a voice, I boarded the train. I was finally on my way to Hartford and on the cusp of my debut as a professional actor.

***

I slept most of the train ride. When I woke, I pictured my mother begging me not to go and my father warning me to get plenty of sleep and not to smoke. The gray New England light chilled me through the window, even though fever sweat still ran down my back. It felt less like the start of a career and more like a march to prison. I kept pulling the sides from my pocket, repeating lines I'd known for a week but now forgot in new places every time. Detached, as if it were all happening to someone else, I thought: If only they had rehearsed me in Boston.

At the Bond Annex Hotel, I floated through arrival, barely aware of the cab or my suitcases. Louis was already in the room. Through my clogged ears, I gathered he'd take me to the theater for rehearsal at 2:00. On the way, my nose began to bleed.

"What if it happens onstage?" I asked.

"That would never happen," Louis said. But how could he know?

A telegram from my parents was waiting at the theater: 'Hope you feel well and were a success.'

I only wished it were already over. Alone on the vast stage, I looked into the darkened auditorium that seemed endless, the orchestra pit yawning like a swimming pool. "My God," I thought. "They'll never hear me."

The stage manager appeared. "Let's get started. I only have a few minutes."

"Are the other actors coming?"

"Of course. Just walk through it till they arrive."

I barreled in, shouting my lines, miming bowling at the back of the theater.

"No, no, no," he snapped. "That looks like you're giving someone a triple goose."

He mounted the stage, demonstrating with a twisted, claw-like gesture. I copied desperately, not knowing he was missing a finger. My imitation would make no sense to anyone who'd ever bowled.

The actors arrived, warm and welcoming, but I forgot my lines after two speeches. My nose bled again. When we resumed, I blanked in another spot.

"I can't hear a word you're saying, and you don't know your lines," the stage manager barked. I stammered about aspirin and a cold. He relented: "If you don't know them tonight, the understudy goes on."

An actor whispered, "If you don't go on tonight, you'll never go on."

Louis spent the afternoon cueing me patiently as I drifted in and out of fevered naps. Before curtain, the stage manager listened to me recite. This time, I remembered everything.

"All right," he said, "I've got my fingers crossed."

In the dressing room, I opened a Christmas present from Louis—a beautiful makeup kit, a tradition for opening night gifts. I felt ashamed that I had nothing for him, but he brushed it off. "I hear we're almost full tonight," my roommate said. "Place seats 3,500."

I moved through it like a dream, walled off from the world. In the camel-hair coat, sleeves shortened but still absurd, I waited in the wings, muttering my lines faster and faster. At my cue, the doorbell rang. I burst through: "Happy New Year, Lois, old girl, old girl!"

Guided toward the footlights, I whacked her "father" on the back. The audience roared as he grimaced in pain. Their laughter jolted me awake. I became a whirlwind, shouting, slamming doors, riding wave after wave of guffaws. When I exited, the applause followed me.

"The boy before you never got a hand," Lois whispered. The others crowded around, congratulating me.

But something felt wrong. I went to the stage manager. He studied me.

"It was okay," he said at last.

"Can we rehearse tomorrow?" I asked.

"Tomorrow's a matinee day. What's the difference? You got a hand, didn't you?" He turned away.

I returned to the cast uneasy. Maybe they laughed because I'd made a fool of myself. Yet the company treated me as though I'd triumphed.

Eight

Several weeks later, when we were playing in Philadelphia, I arrived at the theater to get ready for the evening performance. I found a letter in my mailbox. My first thought was that my mother had forwarded it, and finally, I was hearing from Roger. I opened it and saw it was from the producers of *Junior Miss*. It was typewritten and read as follows:

In accordance with your contract, this is a two-week notice. Your last performance is on February 6th.

I ran up the stairs to Louis's dressing room. He was sitting in his shorts reading *Variety*. I couldn't speak, so I just thrust the letter in front of him. He took it, and his mouth fell open.

"I don't believe it," he said. "You've been doing so well."

He got me to sit down, and we went over the weeks since the opening in Hartford. We tried to find an incident that could have triggered the firing. The performances had gone well, and I had gotten all my laughs. I never did get applause on my exit again, but the other actors told me the part never did. If anything, there seemed to be a shocked silence after my scene. I attributed it to the character's obnoxiousness.

By the time we left Hartford, I had lost my voice completely. Taking so much aspirin, I was barely aware of dragging my bags through the railway station. With the wartime crowds and no red caps, I just managed to board the train for New Haven, where we had to change for Philadelphia.

Louis suggested we continue to room together, so he got us into the Ritz-Carlton hotel. It sounded grand, but it was a small place, only $15 a week. I went to bed as soon as we arrived and spent the next several weeks there, except when I was doing the show or seeing a doctor for my throat. Eight performances a week irritated it, so my voice never sounded quite right. The stage manager criticized something I did wrong almost every night, but eventually he stopped, and I felt more confident. Still, I never believed I truly became the character.

After we had talked about all this, Louis said, "There must be some mistake. Go downstairs and speak to the stage manager. After all, he hired you."

I stood in front of the tall desk in the wings where the stage manager ran the show. The little man sat on a high stool, his face in darkness, since the only light was a small clip-on illuminating the script. He didn't even try to be kind.

"You had bad luck," he said. "Somebody from the New York office came to see the show and thought you were wrong for the part."

"But you knew that from the beginning," I said.

"Well, I thought you'd work into it, but you just didn't get better."

I was relieved in a way. I hated the character I had to play. Every time I went onstage, I had to grit my teeth, take a deep breath, and scream my way through the scene. I knew the laughs were built into the script. Anyone could have gotten them. As for the applause, it was probably just shock after seeing a maniac running around the stage for several minutes. At least I'd only have to endure 16 more performances. Now, though, I'd have to face the embarrassment of everyone knowing I'd been fired. I also needed to figure out what to do next, but I was determined not to go back home, no matter what.

The actors were wonderful. They all said it was terrible and unfair. They told me how much I'd improved in the part and came up with elaborate excuses to help me feel better. The leading lady offered a perfect explanation—maybe management had closed another show and needed to find a job for someone under contract. Everyone reminded me that I was now a member of Actors' Equity, so finding another job would be much easier.

I was sitting in my dressing room, feeling almost triumphant from what everyone said. The boy who shared the room with me said, "You're a wonderful actor. They never should have fired you." I thanked him. "By the way," the boy said, "can I have your makeup kit since you won't be using it again?"

I rushed out and slammed the door. I leaned against a yellowed hallway wall, harshly lit by bare bulbs in metal cages. The tears I'd held back all night poured down my face. So that's what they all think—that I'm no good and I'll never act again. Well, they're wrong. When I finally stopped crying, I went back into the dressing room to get ready for the performance.

***

After the show, Louis stepped into the role of the older brother I'd always wished for. "You're going to New York to be an actor," he said. "That's what you've always wanted." He outlined a plan: we'd travel together after the performances, stay with his parents in Jersey City, and take the tube into New York to look for work. "You're not draft age and there are lots of jobs opening up," he said. Louis made it all sound easy, but I worried about telling my parents I'd been fired. Perhaps I could find a job before they discovered it.

Wednesday after the show, Louis and I took a train to Jersey City. His parents lived in a small, neat house outside town. Even at 2:00 in the morning, they were up, greeting us as if we were only a little late for a party. His mother was a petite woman, her hair dyed jet-black, who bore a resemblance to her idol, Mrs. Arthur Murray. His father, a large, quiet man in the construction industry, seemed fascinated by his wife.

"Let's have a drink," Louis's mother said as soon as we met. We went to the basement, which was decorated like a South Seas bar. After a few drinks, Pinky—her nickname—danced and sang, "Arthur Murray Taught Me Dancing in a Hurry." Her voice rattled, but her dancing was impressive. I felt as if I'd landed on the set of *You Can't Take It with You*.

The next day, Louis took me to Greenwich Village to look for a cheap room. First, we visited his friends, Marie and Madeline, both recent Smith graduates who shared an apartment across from the New School. Marie was a pretty, old-fashioned actress; Madeline, a writer, was tall and plain behind large glasses.

They swarmed Louis, fussing over his hair and appearance, until he introduced me. I felt shy, but soon they had me on the sofa with tea, beneath a print of picnickers by a river. As they disappeared into the bedroom to talk, I wondered if Louis and Marie were involved. I took in the delicate, antique furniture and shelves of books in French and English.

When they returned, I was the center of attention. Louis must have told them I'd been fired, and they were eager to help. They'd seen a room for rent on 10th Street and urged us to check it out.

"You'd be right near us," Marie said. "Everyone comes for dinner and chips in. We could make sure you eat enough."

After we left, Louis said he was glad Marie took to me so quickly. He explained Madeline was from a wealthy New York family, hence all the antiques.

We found a "For Rent" sign in a window of a shabby house. An older woman led us up several flights of dark stairs to a cramped room with a cot and a lamp. The heat gave off an acrid smell. I wanted nothing more than to get back outside.

"How much is it?" I heard Louis ask.

"Four dollars a week, two weeks in advance," the old woman muttered from the hall.

I pulled up the shade, hoping for sunlight, but found only an air shaft. "You should take it," Louis said. "You'll be near Marie and Madeline. You can always move later."

I paid $8 and said I'd move in on Sunday, February 7th. She barely glanced at me. I suspected no one stayed long if they could help it.

On our next trip, Louis took me to Times Square to buy *Show Business*, the weekly paper listing acting jobs. The wind made it impossible to read, so we ducked into Nedick's for coffee and mapped out my rounds. We managed to visit several offices before heading back to Philadelphia. At the agencies, crowds of actors waited, and a receptionist told us, "Nothing today." I thought it all seemed easy—surely it was just a matter of time before I got a job.

I knew I had to tell my parents I'd left the play, so I wrote a letter putting the best spin on everything. I described my new room as if it belonged in a magazine and mentioned being promised a reading in *Life with Father*. "I know I will be a success," I wrote, reminding them how much I wanted this.

For the first time, they seemed to truly grasp the concept. They must have realized how much I needed their support. They wrote back, agreeing I should give acting a try, and included a high school newspaper clipping titled "Mr. Cinderella." It said I was on my way to stardom. If I'd considered going home, I certainly couldn't now.

On my last night, Louis and two girls from the show took me to Stouffer's for dinner. I had a fruit cup, steak, vegetables, and Dutch apple pie with ice cream—all for $1. They insisted on paying. It felt like a last meal before execution, so I ate every bite.

My scene went better than ever. As I left for the dressing room, the stage manager called me over. He looked at me and said, "If you'd done it that way when the office was here, they wouldn't have fired you."

I thanked him and walked away. That night, I tried to comfort everyone as they offered condolences. After the show, we packed our makeup kits in a communal trunk for the move to Washington. I carried mine to the stage door. Two boys, placing theirs in the trunk, looked up, embarrassed to see me still holding mine. I walked out with my head held high.

Back at the hotel, Louis was waiting, nervously smoking, a rare habit for him. He looked uneasy, probably unsure what to say about my leaving the play.

"Don't worry," I said. "I'll be fine. I have friends, and I know I'll find work."

"That's not what's on my mind," he said.

"Well, then what is wrong? Did I do something?"

"I love you," Louis blurted. "I couldn't say it before because you were ill and struggling with the play. I don't expect you to feel the same, but I had to tell you before we parted."

I was stunned. I'd never thought of Louis that way. Too much else was on my mind. He'd been a great friend, and I didn't want to hurt him. Roger kept coming to mind. After months without a word, I thought he must want to end things, but why hadn't he just said so? Or had something happened to him? I wasn't free to think about anyone else, and I couldn't explain it all to Louis.

"Louis, you're wonderful, but I just feel numb. It's not that I don't care for you. I just don't feel anything for anyone right now."

"That's all right. I just wanted to let you know before we parted. Maybe when the play closes, and I return, we can live together, and maybe someday you'll love me."

I hugged Louis. "We'll be apart for a while. Let's write and get to know each other better. Who knows what might happen?" Louis seemed satisfied, and I was off the hook.

***

I lay on my back, eyes closed, hoping to fall asleep again. I gripped the stiff top sheet and tried to calm myself, but anxiety lingered. It was my first day in New York, and I was alone with almost no money. It was only 6:00. I barely slept; the bed was too small, and it felt like a board. The oil heat clogged my sinuses but did little to warm the freezing room.

I got up and headed to the communal bathroom, afraid a shower would wake everyone. I filled the stained tub with lukewarm water and tried to clean it, but the grime wouldn't budge. As I soaked, I stared at a black-painted window. With my room's window facing an air shaft, I realized I'd never know the weather until I stepped outside. I needed to find a better place to live.

When I stepped outside, a rush of wind blew open my coat. I shivered and buttoned it. The herringbone tweed was meant for fall, not February, but it was my only decent coat. Louis had told me to always dress up to see agents, so I wore my best suit and thin-soled black shoes. Dirty snow lingered in the gutters, but the sidewalks were clear.

At 10th Street and 6th Avenue, I tried to get my bearings. I spotted the Empire State Building and knew that way was 34th Street. On the subway, I only remembered two stops, 14th Street and Times Square at 42nd. To go uptown, I'd get off at 42nd and walk. Later, I learned about the subway system, and life became easier.

At Times Square, I bought *Show Business* at a newsstand, but it was only 8:00, and the theater offices weren't open yet. I went to Nedick's for a 10-cent breakfast—orange drink, doughnut, and coffee. I underlined job notices until the counterman asked me to order more or leave, so I wandered Times Square until 10:00. There was no movie glamour here—just dirt, crowds, and people rushing everywhere. I paused at the *Times* building, surrounded by winds from every direction. At a newsstand, I found *The Boston Globe* and felt a sharp wave of homesickness. I pushed it away and went inside to get warm.

By 3:00, I stood in line at the Playhouse Theater stage door, grateful just to be somewhere work might exist. All day, I'd heard "Nothing today" from secretaries behind glass. But *Show Business* listed auditions for *Janie*, so I waited, numb from the cold. After an hour, a man looked me over, then told a younger man with a clipboard, "Okay." I gave my name and number, amazed at my luck. It looked like I'd get a reading.

"Be here at 8:00 tonight," the younger man said. I wanted to ask about the script, but didn't want to seem inexperienced. I returned to my tiny room and waited until it was time to go uptown again.

I arrived 15 minutes early. The old stage doorman greeted me with a surly, "What do you want?"

"I was told to be here at 8:00," I said. "I'm a little early."

"You can go down to the basement," he said and pointed, "through that door."

Beneath the stage was a cavernous room lined with benches and lockers. I sat and waited as other young men arrived, joking and playing cards, ignoring me.

The stage manager walked in with a clipboard and made a beeline for me. "You were early," he said. "I thought I told you 8:00."

"I had to be in the neighborhood," I said, afraid of seeming too eager.

"Come with me," he said, leading me to a rack of army uniforms. He found one my size. "Try this on." I looked for somewhere to change, but he said, "Nobody's going to look. Change here." The uniform fits perfectly. "Looks good," he said. "Be here every night at 9:00. You go on at 9:20 and get $1 afterwards.

"What do I do?" I asked.

"You've seen the play, haven't you?" the man asked.

I was afraid that if I said I hadn't, they'd pick someone else. "Oh sure," I said.

"Good. Just follow the others and make a lot of noise." He wrote my name on the costume tag. "Put this in your pocket," he said, then disappeared upstairs.

I sat in uniform, waiting. More young men arrived, changed into uniforms, and put name tags in their pockets. I couldn't believe my luck. It was my first day in New York, and I'd be on a Broadway stage. But what was I supposed to do?

At last, the stage manager's assistant called, "Let's go, guys." I followed, thinking, What do I say? What do I do? I'm going to make a fool of myself.

We gathered at the backstage door. Before I could ask what to do, the stage manager gave a signal, and everyone began yelling and laughing. The door opened, and I was swept onstage with the others. The spotlights blinded me for a moment. The curtain was already coming down. We were onstage for less than a minute, then applause erupted.

Afterward, I lined up for my dollar. The stage manager said, "Make more noise tomorrow. Act like you're at a party."

I smiled. I've just made my Broadway debut.

***

It was my second night in a dingy room that hardly qualified as furnished. With no bureau, I kept my suitcases under the bed and pulled them out whenever I needed something. Even though the window was sealed, I felt a draft as I lay awake. My father's warnings echoed in my head: What if I got sick? Would I have to go home?

Louis called from Washington, having jotted down the pay phone number on the first floor. The landlady yelled for me, but instead of a complaint, it was Louis, surprising me with good wishes. He said he missed me and told me my name was still listed with the other actors on the theater's front.

"So, in a way, you're still appearing in Washington," he joked. I laughed and updated him on *Janie*, assuring him everything was fine.

After another sleepless night with the furnace clanking, I knew I needed to move. With $8 a week from the play and some war bonds I'd sent home, maybe I could afford more than $4 a week.

The day before, I'd seen a rental ad in *Show Business*—$40 a month. After that awful night, I decided to investigate further. I called, made an appointment, and spotted the building's awning with "Forty" in white on a dark green background. I took a deep breath and told myself to act like I belonged. I squared my shoulders and walked in.

"Good morning," said the doorman.

"I'm here to see Mr. Broner," I replied.

"That's the penthouse," the old man said, "go right in." He held open the door, and I walked through. An elevator man stood waiting.

"This gentleman is for Mr. Broner, Fred," the doorman said as I got into the elevator.

I wondered if there was a mistake—$40 seemed too cheap for a doorman building on 55th Street, just off 5th Avenue. The elevator gate opened, and I stepped into a narrow hall. "That one there," the elevator man said, pointing. I rang the bell.

A huge man greeted me. "You must be Mr. Shayne. Come in." I entered a vault-like room with a big window overlooking the skyline and a grand piano covered in sheet music. I started imagining how I'd clean the place up, but he quickly said, "Needless to say, this isn't the place I'm renting. It's next door."

I followed him, noticing he was in stocking feet. "This is it," Mr. Broner said, showing me a large white room with a black cement floor and two windows facing a balcony and the side of another building. "That's the Rockefeller Apartments. Gertrude Lawrence lives in that one with the terrace."

I was stunned. I'd once waited an hour in freezing Boston for her autograph. Now I could almost reach out and touch her if she stepped outside. The room had a studio couch with a blue cover and a white dresser. "Is this all?" I asked.

"I haven't shown you the kitchen and bathroom yet," he said, leading me into the hall. One door opened to a tiny toilet, another to a shower, and a third to a kitchenette. I'd have to wash in the kitchen and walk into the hall in pajamas, but at least I wouldn't be sharing with six people. "I'm a musician and practice all day," he explained. "That's why I'm charging so little."

It wasn't the penthouse of my dreams, but it would get me out of that filthy room. "How about $35 a month?" I asked. "There isn't any furniture."

"I can get you a few more things," he said. "You can have it."

That night I had dinner at Marie and Madeline's with several older guests discussing Kafka and Eliot, writers I knew nothing about, so I stayed quiet. Sensing my discomfort, Marie asked about my day. I described my apartment hunt, and everyone laughed. Madeline offered to show me the furniture she had in storage after dinner.

I had to be at the theater by 9:00 for *Janie*, so we quickly looked at the furniture. I picked out blue-striped draperies, a gate-legged table, a chair Madeline claimed belonged to Napoleon's son, two French maps, and mismatched dishes. Marie offered to bring them over if Broner agreed. I paid for dinner, and we said goodbye.

I called my parents after the show and shared the good news. They seemed pleased and said they'd send me $20 instead of cashing two war bonds. Mother also said she'd send several heavy sweaters that I could wear under my thin overcoat.

Within a week, I settled into my new place. The room was warmer, so I wasn't cold at night. Being closer to the theater offices made it easier to make the rounds. To save money, I walked instead of taking the subway and ate cheap meals: a ten-cent breakfast at Nedick's and a hot-dog-and-bean dinner at the Automat.

The package arrived from my mother. Inside, wrapped in my sweaters, was the cut-glass decanter I had managed to wheedle out of my grandmother. There was a note from my mother saying she knew I planned to have it in my penthouse in New York and she wished me well. I put some Welch's grape juice in the decanter (since it was cheaper than wine) and set it on the dining room table.

I left Louis my new number and news about the apartment. On *Junior Miss*'s last day in Washington, Broner gave me a note. Louis wanted me to call after the matinee. I could use the room's extension phone if I paid for calls, and Broner offered to take messages, knowing I was job hunting.

When I called, Louis said he missed me and that Marie and Madeline thought I was charming. I discussed seeing agents and hoping for auditions, although things felt bleak. Still, I didn't want to burden him.

"Listen," he said, "I have something funny to tell you. Remember, I said your name was still on the theater poster?"

"Yes," I said. "They forgot to list my replacement. Why? Is someone making trouble?"

"No, nothing like that. Two army officers came backstage before the show, asking for you. The doorman said you weren't with the company. They were drunk, and one kept insisting, 'You've got to see this kid. He's so talented, and he can sing too.' He couldn't believe you'd left, so an actor came and got me, knowing I was in touch with you. I told them you were in New York and offered your address, but the officer got annoyed, and they both left. Any idea who they were?"

"No, probably friends of my brother's. Did he take my address?"

"No," Louis said. "He didn't want it."

We returned to discussing casting in New York. There was nothing promising. I thanked Louis again for connecting me with Marie and Madeline, and we promised to speak soon.

I hung up and sat in Napoleon's son's chair. So, Roger was alive. Relief washed over me. I'd often prayed he was safe, just unwilling to contact me. Now I finally have an answer. But why didn't he write? Did he think I couldn't handle it?

Louis said he called me a kid—he'd last seen me at 16. Now, almost 18 and on my own in New York, I'd changed. I felt sad realizing that my feelings for him were gone. He'd killed them by staying away. Maybe he just wanted to show off that he knew someone in a Broadway play.

I didn't feel angry; I was just grateful to Roger for opening doors I never would have found on my own. But I no longer needed his help, guidance, or love. It was a good feeling to close the curtain on that part of my life.

Nine

I collected my dollar from walking on in *Janie* and went straight to the "penthouse." It was warm and comforting, despite the concrete floor and harsh lighting. I couldn't sleep, so I got up and grabbed my Stanislavsky book, thinking I'd read for a while. I noticed a note on the table from my landlord. I shared his phone, and it said "Call Louis" with a number in Washington, where Junior Miss was still playing. I quickly called, figuring Louis might still be awake.

"I was just falling off to sleep," Louis answered.

"I thought you might have some news about a job for me," I said.

"Better than that," he replied, "I've just quit the show. I can't be away from you any longer."

I was shocked. "Louis," I said, "why didn't you tell me first. It's not good for your career."

"You don't want me," Louis said.

"No, of course I do, but you have a good job—"

"I'll get another one in New York. I just have to be with you. I don't expect you to love me. Just so I can be near you. I had to give them four weeks' notice, but can we at least be together?"

Louis had been such a good friend to me, I couldn't turn him down. "Of course," I said. When I hung up, I looked around my little room. It was bare even with Madeline's few pieces of furniture. But it was mine, alone. Now I'd have to share it.

I wrote my mother two letters. The first brimmed with hope. I told her a top agent gave me a reading, called me talented, and would submit me for three roles—including *The Eve of St. Mark*. "So, you see," I wrote, "things are turning out just the way we hoped. Keep your faith in me. I know I'll succeed."

By month's end, every lead had vanished. I had to have a tooth taken out, and I couldn't afford a new one. I practiced smiling, careful not to show the gap. In my next letter, I couldn't admit the truth. I apologized for not sending an anniversary card, told her I was trying for radio announcing jobs (one station said I had "a beautiful voice"), and I ended with a plea for money if they could afford a little.

Louis returned in April and moved into my "penthouse." I hadn't realized how small it was. We squeezed onto the studio couch. If people asked us, we called ourselves roommates. Back then, even a rumor of homosexuality could ruin you, so Louis gave his family's New Jersey address in offices.

Despite the strain, Louis lifted my spirits. Irreverent and quick to mimic, he made our endless rounds feel like a party. With him, and with the help of Madeline and Marie, I was brought into their circle. The girls adored Louis. Their brownstone, lined with books and centered on a grand piano, felt alive. Marie sang often with Louis while Madeline went every night to the theater where she worked for the actress Eva Le Gallienne.

Sometimes Jacqueline ("Jackie"), another Smith alumna, joined us. She was very attractive but she somehow frightened me. Her piercing stare made me uneasy, as if she were about to pin me in her collection.

Regaining confidence was harder. Being fired still gnawed at me, but Louis' praise helped. He also filled our ears with stories of Broadway legends: Tallulah Bankhead, Bea Lillie, and Dorothy Parker. His anecdotes were like a night at a show. One about Bankhead at a Harlem sex show had us roaring with laughter. A woman was going down on a man with a huge penis. She was nervous in front of the star, and the penis slipped out of her mouth. She bowed to Talulah and said, "Excuse me, Miss Bankhead." It was one of everyone's favorites.

Louis' affection deepened, but I just couldn't return his love. My body responded even if my heart didn't. I told myself that this might be the way I had to live if love never came again.

By summer, the girls left to go to Nantucket, so Louis moved us into their Village apartment. Leaving my uptown "penthouse", a step away from the theaters, put a pall on things. Louis had replaced the actor who had his role in *Junior Miss,* so he paid most of the rent.

The days blurred in oppressive heat. Louis and I sat in our underwear by the windows, rum in fruit juice, sweating in our glasses, Noel Coward on the record player. We drifted into drunken naps before rushing to our theaters at night. Got a job announcing at WNYC for $37 a week but still walked on in *Janie* to stay afloat. My life felt stalled; the dream of acting was slipping away.

Louis, meanwhile, was radiant at the piano, Jersey roots vanishing as he sang Coward and Gertrude Lawrence with clipped London tones. I admired him, but I couldn't fall in love. I felt he was my closest friend.

As summer dragged on, the work wore me down. At the station, I spoke for hours—news, music, civic programs—until my voice felt mechanical. Fatigue made me careless. Once, I announced "seven and a half people" lived in New York, leaving out the word "million." Mayor LaGuardia called, furious. Dame Myra Hess phoned mid-broadcast to scold me for misplacing a movement in her concerto.

I was exhausted doing the two jobs, so I quit *Janie.* I needed sleep to function. One morning, while an older announcer covered a segment, I stepped out for some air. An elderly man with a henna hair dye and powdered skin waited for his lunch date—Tommy, the veteran announcer I alternated with. Seeing them startled me. Was this what long partnerships between men became, husband and wife, no matter how they began? I wondered which role Louis and I would fall into if we ever got together.

Soon after, we found a furnished room near Abington Square, owned by Mr. Dorn, a prim German. Spacious, with a Van Gogh print, a king bed, and shelves of Thomas Hardy novels, it felt like home. On Sundays, we wandered the Village, ate at the Beatrice Inn for a dollar, and tried not to think about the future.

Then a young dancer, Carolyn, appeared, who had moved next door. One night, she brought wine, and we laughed until 2:00 a.m. Later, she knocked on our door in her nightgown, asking to stay because she was lonely. She slipped between the two of us in bed, body tense beside mine. I couldn't resist touching her and getting more and more familiar. Louis kept stopping me, pulling my hand away. Carolyn left without a word and soon moved away.

When I turned 18, the draft notice arrived, and I quit my job at the radio station to get ready for the service. I told myself I'd serve, return with the GI Bill, and finally learn to act. Louis took me to a class with Phoebe Brand of the Group Theater. She had us imagine a concentration camp. The others bent into fear and hunger; I stared at the bare room, unable to feel anything.

During my physical, the doctor spent a considerable amount of time examining my ears. I told him of my childhood mastoids. He said they had been damaged. I was unfit for service.

I stepped outside, shivering in the cold, unexpectedly free. With that freedom came my promise: I would learn my craft, no matter how long it took.

Spring arrived in the city. I spent days job-hunting, rehearsing auditions in front of mirrors, and reading at night. Louis was happiest at the theater, coming home humming and sharing stories from his fellow actors. I admired his joy and envied his certainty. Would I ever feel like that?

I tried to embrace the actor's life, joining Louis at Madeline and Marie's apartment, now a hub of chatter, books, and coffee. Marie's warmth filled the space while Madeline's seriousness added gravity. Occasionally, Jackie arrived, sharp-eyed and laughing, making me feel exposed, as if she saw what I wanted to hide.

Louis told stories, sang at the piano, and filled the room with laughter, making everyone feel alive. I sat back, half participant, half observer, acutely aware of how little I contributed. Still, their gatherings eased my loneliness.

Privately, Louis urged me to open up. He never hid his feelings; his love was patient but persistent. I tried to reciprocate, but my heart wasn't in it. I told myself I was saving my passion for art, but I knew I was still haunted by my lost love for Roger.

I kept my promise: I would finally study. I would master my craft, learn The Method, and build the life I dreamed of. It felt like fate. I earned a scholarship to The New School of Social Research, just across from Madeline and Marie's apartment. The drama department was prestigious; the judges applauded my Shakespeare audition. They found me a cafeteria job with free meals and tips. Louis and the girls were thrilled. For the first time, I believed I'd learn real acting instead of waiting for inspiration.

On my first day, the registrar, Miss Van Bynam, handed me my schedule: Drama Technique, Fundamental Acting, Theater History, Fencing, Modern Dance, and Makeup. After paperwork, she led me to my group. Ten students sat in front of mirrors, applying makeup. All paused as she introduced me like an honored guest.

"He's joining your class. I hope you'll make him feel at home."

Several boys shook my hand; the girls greeted me. One handsome boy, his face only half made-up, stared at me with open hostility. I offered my hand, but he glared and walked out.

Everyone giggled. Miss Van Bynam said, "Don't mind him. That's just Marlon showing off."

A boy lent me makeup, and I sat by the mirror, hoping not to make a mistake. I reminded myself I was a professional with an Equity card and

I had been in summer stock—yet here I was, learning makeup basics. I knew I needed to study or I'd never be great.

The next weeks were as hectic as my WNYC and *Janie* days. Classes filled my days; evenings I waited tables for demanding, often unpleasant guests, many refugees from Europe, still hard to please. I smiled, even when they left no tip.

The Orozco murals in the cafeteria lifted my mood: brooding browns and blacks, figures of workers and the oppressed. Another waiter said the artist was a Communist. Guests often huddled, talking politics. I wondered if they were, too.

Classes were interesting, if not focused enough on acting technique. The fencing master claimed it would help us mingle with high society on ocean liners, like a scene from an old movie. Looking at my classmates, I doubted we'd ever test his theory.

Theater history was a highlight. I devoured stories of great actors, designers, and costumes and marveled at a time when theater dominated entertainment. I loved reading about Fanny Kemble, Sarah Bernhardt, Ben Greet, and Henry Irving, as well as listening to old recordings of actors singing their lines. Ben Greet's *Macbeth* soliloquy, delivered like a musical scale, was my favorite.

"Is this a dagger that I see before me?" sounded like do, re, mi, fa, so, la, ti, do. Greet crashed down at "Come let me clutch thee." I enjoyed imitating him for Louis, along with our speech teacher who resembled Leslie Howard in *Pygmalion*.

But when would we actually learn acting technique? Finally, Stella Adler, the country's most famous acting teacher, was coming. I was thrilled. She had studied with Stanislavsky, whose book I reread like scripture, though I still couldn't grasp The Method. I was sure Adler would make it clear. She arrived half an hour late, but no one seemed surprised. The room fell silent as expensive perfume drifted in. Miss Adler entered. Hands rushed to take her umbrella, bag, and fur coat.

"Darlings," she cooed, kissing and hugging nearby students. They led her to the only armchair. She removed her hatpin and asked, "What do you think of my chapeau?" Her black cap was crowned with feathers that danced with every movement.

A girl said, "It's beautiful, Miss Adler."

Miss Adler ignored her, shed her jacket to reveal a satin blouse, and suddenly looked at me. "You must be the new boy," she said.

I felt her eyes examining every part of me. "Yes, Miss Adler."

She reached out, and I stumbled over. "I hope you're very talented," she said in a surprisingly British accent. I had always heard of her as an acclaimed actress for older Jewish mothers; this glamorous figure surprised me. "Sit down, darling," she said, and I returned to my seat.

She spent half an hour talking about her clothes, debating which suit—green or blue—matched her Gibson girl red hair. Finally, as if we'd delayed her, she said, "Let's get to work. Marlon, you lazy boy, get in that chair," addressing the actor who'd ignored me.

I hadn't seen him in other classes, but I often spotted him playing bongos in the hall, surrounded by admirers. A friend said his last name was Brando, rumored to be kept by a wealthy older man, and dating a girl named Blossom Plum. The class watched as Marlon slumped theatrically into the chair.

"Now, Marlon," Miss Adler said briskly, "peel an apple." Marlon pantomimed, the peel magically unbroken, curling to the floor. "Now, Marlon, I'll say some words. React: Cold... Hot... Hungry... Tired... Depressed..."

I couldn't believe it. Marlon kept peeling the apple, subtly transforming with each word: cold, hot, hungry. I thought, I'll never be able to do that. My doubts faded as the class applauded and Marlon slouched back to his chair, indifferent.

"Ooh," Miss Adler sighed, "our time is up. Every actor should have a second skill—singing, storytelling, dancing—so you're never caught unprepared onstage. Next time, bring a story, poem, or anything to perform as if you're in a cabaret."

Actors murmured in agreement and scrambled to help Miss Adler with her coat. I lingered, deciding to perform *The Devil and Daniel*

Webster, my prize-winning piece from high school. I wanted to show them Marlon wasn't the only talent in the class.

When the next class with Miss Adler arrived, the excitement matched that of opening night. No one revealed their act; everything was a surprise. A guitar was tuned, props arranged, and a girl paced and mumbled. Then, on cue, everything stopped—the perfume, fur coat, hat, and "darlings." Miss Adler entered, transforming a plain basement room into a salon.

Once settled, Miss Adler said, "Today I'll just be the audience, and you'll amaze me." Laughter rippled. "Stuart, begin."

A studious boy with glasses and a big nose stood before the semi-circle of chairs. "I really can't sing," he began.

Miss Adler stopped him. "Don't explain or complain," she said. "We're here to learn, not judge."

Stuart closed his eyes, clasped his hands, and spoke with emotion: "Without a song," he paused, looking upward, "the day would never end." He wandered the room, acting out the song, pointing to "that field of corn." When he finished, the class waited for Miss Adler's opinion before reacting.

"Very good, Stuart," she said. Everyone applauded.

After a show of hands, Miss Adler chose Elaine Stritch, a lanky blonde in trainman's overalls. She sat on the floor and strummed her guitar. She sang in a haunting, simple voice, "I wonder as I wander out under the sky, how Jesus the Savior did come for to die?" Her talent was obvious. The class applauded loudly without waiting for Miss Adler.

Afraid the class would end before my turn, I waved at Miss Adler. "The new boy is eager. All right, darling, you go next."

I stepped onto the platform, eager to stand out. Marlon had left, which relieved me. It felt like performing for royalty. Two years had passed since I'd won Prize Speaking, but I remembered every word of Benet's story. Nervous at first, I found authority. I played 20 parts, shifting accents and characters, telling the Devil's battle with Daniel Webster, growing more impassioned as Webster won.

I'd barely finished when Miss Adler declared, "Excellent," and the class applauded. For the first time, I felt camaraderie. As soon as I sat, Miss Adler gestured my way. "Now, let's not be confused. That wasn't acting. He told a story and used voices. That's fine for cabaret, but not real acting." Everyone agreed. I didn't see why Miss Adler criticized me publicly.

Suddenly, the curtains closed, and the lights went out. Someone played a record. The curtains parted, revealing a striking woman in a velvet dress and white gloves— it was Marlon in a blond wig. The class gasped.

Judy Garland's "Zing! Go the Strings of My Heart" played at double speed. Marlon lip-synced, turning Garland's voice comic, like Betty Boop. The class erupted; some slid off their chairs, rocking with laughter. Marlon continued, deadpan, as Miss Adler collapsed with laughter. My performance was immediately forgotten.

Auditions began for the year's big play, *Twelfth Night*. I was excited. I'd acted in *Much Ado* in Boston, knew some Shakespeare, and earned my scholarship with a soliloquy. Every boy wanted Duke Orsino, the role I coveted. We read for Erwin Piscator, the school's director, a slight, elegant man once famous in Germany for Epic Theater, now in New York after fleeing the Nazis. He sat hunched near the front as we took the stage.

I was surprised to see Marlon, who'd been absent. Word was, he was obsessed with John Barrymore's antics in *Good Night Sweet Prince*, especially the outrageous stunts. It was sad that such a talented actor resorted to tricks, but it fit Marlon's show-off nature.

As always, Marlon ignored me as we waited in the wings. I couldn't figure out why he disliked me, but pushed it aside. The other boys' readings were bland. Marlon's was worse; he mumbled and mangled the verse. Still, he was a faculty favorite. When my turn came, I lost myself in performing. Piscator simply said, "Thank you." Days later, the cast list went up: I was the coveted Duke Orsino.

On the first day of rehearsal, nerves ran high. Piscator, who'd worked with Europe's greats, sat in the front row. "Alright, begin," he said. I started, but he jumped up. "No, no, no! You Americans are afraid of the poetry." He came onstage. "You have one of the most beautiful speeches in Shakespeare. It must be a rhapsody. Your voice should sound like a cello. Begin again."

I sat in the Duke's chair, imagined the musicians, and said, "If music be the food of love, play on," as if cueing the orchestra.

Piscator bounded back onstage. "Listen to how I do it." He demonstrated, elongating every vowel, then turned to me: "You understand?"

"Of course," I said, determined not to lose the part. I mimicked his style, skipping the accent, and nearly sang the line.

"That's it! Now you've got it. Go on." I continued, channeling Ben Greet, varying tempo and melody, almost singing an aria. Piscator applauded. "Perfect. Now do that with the whole part." If I did, I'd be the biggest ham onstage.

After weeks of rehearsal, I prepared for the first of two performances. My hair was long, my costume striking: red doublet, tights, blue blouse, and silver cape. There'd be a school matinee and an evening opening. As I finished combing my hair, the director entered.

"Good afternoon, Mr. Piscator," everyone greeted him. "I just came to say merde," he replied, wishing us luck. Then to me: "There's been a problem, but I think we've solved it."

"What is it?" I asked.

"Stuart's mother is ill, so he had to go to Washington and can't make the matinee. He'll be here tonight, but we needed someone to fill in. It's only eight lines."

That was the Priest—the hardest moment for me, when the Duke discovers his beloved has married his servant. "Who's playing it?" I asked.

"Marlon's helping out, even though it's a small role," Piscator said.

"Can we rehearse before curtain?" I asked.

"No time. He's in costume and knows where to go. He'll be fine."

Of all the actors. I pushed it aside. There was a whole play before the Priest's scene. I sat onstage, savoring the pre-curtain excitement. After applause for the set, I delivered, "If music be the food of love, play on." The opening scene balanced emotion and poetry. As I exited, applause thundered.

The play went well until near the end, when I learned Olivia had married Cesario, my servant, and the Priest was called. As I acted out my turmoil, the audience began laughing. I turned and saw the Priest.

Marlon's tights were stuffed with a drum to look pregnant. As the crowd caught on, he pounded the drum and mumbled his lines. The audience went wild laughing, applauding, urging him on. The other actors broke up, but I was furious. It felt like they were laughing at me; the play forgotten. Marlon left to an ovation. I waited for silence to deliver my line. The audience laughed again, but we managed to finish.

I stormed to the dressing room, thinking of my year in New York: hungry, losing a tooth, always cold, taking menial jobs—all for the theater I loved. But this was not the theater I'd dreamed of.

In the dressing room, Marlon lounged, face covered in cold cream. "How dare you ruin this play?" I said. He stayed silent, looking away. "Aren't you even sorry?" Nothing. "I'll do everything I can to keep you off Broadway," I said, feeling defeated as Piscator entered.

"Wonderful, wonderful," he said.

I walked over. "Will you say anything to Marlon?" I asked.

"My dear," Piscator said, "it was wrong, but just high spirits. Tonight is what matters. Stuart will be here."

He no longer seemed like a great director. "If you don't reprimand him, I'll leave the school." Piscator just raised a hand and left.

I did the evening performance and never returned to the school. Marlon Brando was on Broadway within months.

Ten

The cabaret night was the last time I saw Stella Adler. She took a role in *Pretty Little Parlor,* which closed after a short New York run. My parents saw it in Boston and met her backstage, mentioning I was her student. She told them I was talented but hoped they had a business for me at home; a reminder of her cabaret put-down. I felt no sadness when her play closed after five performances.

Years later in Positano, I ran into her. She said she'd seen me star in *The Infernal Machine* and called me "brilliant." I didn't ask why she hadn't told me then, when it mattered. I simply thanked her and left her with her admirers.

Stella Adler's brother, Luther Adler, a renowned Group Theater actor, had taken over the class when she had gone into rehearsal. We were excited. He was all business, but warm and helpful. I was finally going to learn The Method, now the foundation of good acting.

On his first day, Luther Adler had us improvise as chickens in a barnyard learning of war breaking out. We had to choose who was to be married, single, coward, or hero. The class clucked and acted out scenes, but I still was uncomfortable with improvisation. I played a loner and paid no attention to anyone. I just sulked.

Next, we paired off to rehearse scenes. I was assigned Phyllis, rumored heir to a pickle fortune, but down-to-earth. We chose a scene from Noël Coward's *Still Life* and agreed to meet at my place since she lived with her parents.

Louis was at the movies; his show had closed, so I had the room to myself. I tidied up, making the place look its best. Books lined the shelves, patterned pillows matched the couch, and green drapes framed a Van Gogh print. I hoped Phyllis would be impressed, even knowing I was broke and waiting tables. I planned we'd read the scene, maybe improvise, then get serious next time.

When Phyllis arrived, she complimented the room and took off her coat. She was confident, maybe due to her wealth. After reading the scene, we discussed how the doctor's talk of his practice was really a confession of love. We decided to improvise: I'd talk about acting, but really be telling her I loved her.

We sat on the bed. She took my hands. Her heart-shaped face and knowing eyes made it easy to follow Adler's advice, find something specific to love. But all I could focus on were her breasts, straining against her blouse. I tried to talk about acting, but my mind wandered.

She encouraged me. Soon, I had my arm around her, unbuttoning her blouse. She let me, then undid her bra herself when I struggled. I kissed and fondled her; our improvisation forgotten. She kissed back, and I undid her skirt and she removed her stockings. Reclining with a Cheshire Cat smile, she let me pull down her panties and touch her. A fluid traced down her leg.

"Please let me put it in," I begged.

"Do you have anything?" she asked. I'd never had reason to buy condoms, but I didn't want her to know.

"Not at the moment," I said. "I'll just put it in and take it right out."

Phyllis straightened her clothes. "Accidents can happen. Some other time."

Frustrated, I hoped she'd suggest something else, but she just dressed. "I have to get home," she said.

I felt like a punished child. "When will we meet next week?" I asked.

"I have family coming in," she answered. "Maybe we should just rehearse at school before class." Suddenly, she seemed older and in total control.

"Okay," I said. "I'm sorry you're leaving so soon."

"I think it's better," she said, putting on her coat and leaving, more matron than student. I sat on the bed, aching and wondering if she knew about Louis. I felt no guilt. I wasn't cheating with another man. One day, when Louis accepted I didn't love him, I'd leave. We both knew it wasn't permanent. Still, I wished I'd gone further.

A positive outcome from my New School days: Madeline left for a writer's colony to finish her novel, *The Small Rain*. Marie befriended actress-director Miranda d'Ancona, whose mother funded a Nantucket summer theater. Marie would star, Miranda would direct. After seeing me in *Twelfth Night*, they invited me to join. I was thrilled. Louis had already signed on, so we'd be together. Soon, I'd be acting again and my summer was secure.

The registrar at the New School sent a note, saying she was sorry I'd left and mentioning a plastic surgeon who needed help in his office. I jumped at the chance. The doctor's office was high in the Squibb Building, overlooking Central Park. He was handsome, in his 50s, with a touch of gray. I told him I couldn't do secretarial work and would leave for summer stock in May, but he didn't mind. He needed someone for errands and offered $35 a week, enough until Nantucket.

"What time is it?" he asked. "I'm sorry, I don't have a watch," I replied.

He looked at me, pushed up his sleeve, revealing two watches. He handed me one. "Take this. I don't need two. Be here at 10:00 tomorrow. We'll find things for you to do." I felt odd accepting it, but he insisted.

When I told Louis about the watch, he asked if the doctor had come on to me. I said no, but we both thought it odd. "Just be careful," Louis warned.

The job was easy; the doctor barely noticed me, and the watch seemed a whim. I sat in a small cubicle, occasionally taking slow dictation and retyping letters when I made mistakes. He didn't seem to mind. A few times, he took me to lunch at the Hotel Pierre or the

Sherry, always insisting on a full meal. He seemed to know everyone and introduced me as his assistant. I sensed he didn't want to eat alone. Sometimes he sent me with a gift to his mistress at the Sherry-Netherland; I only saw her maid. Rose, the nurse, said she was a beauty.

Rose, the nurse, and I became friends when she wasn't assisting the doctor. She looked like a prairie pioneer but had raucous, party-girl energy and a stevedore's vocabulary. Rose told wild stories about being drunk during surgeries, using coffee grounds in her mask to hide liquor, and sometimes getting sick. Her tales made me doubt the medical profession, but I enjoyed our talks. They filled my empty hours.

Months passed as I watched Central Park turn from white to green. Louis and I often visited his parents in New Jersey. His tiny, cheerful mother loaded us with food, and the family swapped stories about quirky Irish relatives—making Grandma jump from a slow-moving car, or Uncle Paddy, the panhandler. Their world fascinated me.

One night, Louis' parents surprised us with tickets to an ANTA theater benefit. I watched legendary stars perform: Jane Cowl reprised *Smilin' Through;* Judith Anderson performed a scene from *Come of Age.*

All evening, I watched in awe as legends brought down the house. It revived my love for theater. Real actors like Jane Cowl and Judith Anderson relied on talent, not stunts. That's how I wanted to perform. By the end, I felt reborn.

***

In Nantucket, on the opening night of Ibsen's *The Master Builder,* I finally felt I was learning to act. The play follows an aging contractor, inspired by Hilda, a young woman who convinces him he's still vital. She urges him to climb his latest building and hang a wreath. Though frail, he tries. I played the young man in his office who idolizes him and watches as he climbs.

When he falls to his death, Hilda cries, "My master builder!" and the curtain falls. For the first time, I was so lost in my character that I burst into tears during the curtain call. The other actors comforted me, but I could tell they resented the attention I drew from the audience. I didn't care; I finally felt like a true actor.

Another incident turned the cast against me. During *Lady Windermere's Fan*, I played a charming young man. After the show, a movie scout offered me a Universal contract and said I was the only one fit for film. Word spread, and the others grew colder than ever.

My life changed with *The Animal Kingdom* by Philip Barry. It was my first lead, a real test of whether I could carry a show. The play centers on a man torn between his wife, Marie, and his mistress, Miranda. Both women were wonderfully supportive. Opening night was a hit; audiences, tired of heavy drama, welcomed something contemporary. At 19, I seemed older onstage, and the cast dynamic worked. Whenever The Animal Kingdom played, the house was packed.

"You were both very good," said a voice from the wings. It was Jackie, who often visited Marie and Madeline's apartment in New York.

"I didn't know you were in Nantucket," Marie said.

Seeing Jackie always made me uneasy, as if she were dangerous. "Why did you have to be here tonight?" I said. "The audience seemed asleep."

"It didn't matter," Jackie said. "You were excellent. Get ready. I'll buy you all a drink."

On the way to the bar, Jackie told me she now worked for a theatrical agent and would introduce me in New York. I was glad she'd seen me in a lead, not a minor role. Jackie always made me nervous and excited. She was sharp and full of energy. "I have a theory," she said. "Actors need a caricature-able face. That's why you'll succeed. You're not just handsome; your features will end up on Sardi's wall."

I was flattered. At the smoky, lantern-lit bar, Jackie ordered a martini with bitters and onions, chain-smoking with a short holder. Her huge diamond ring reminded me that Miranda had said she came from money.

Jackie asked about the season. Marie said weekends sold out, but weekdays barely broke even. Miranda noted they'd return to New York with little to show except the satisfaction of performing Chekhov,

Wilde, Ibsen, and modern plays for summer tourists. Louis laughed. "A lot of them hate The Seagull, but there's nowhere else to go."

Miranda was quiet, but Marie kept the conversation going. We said goodnight to Jackie and walked home down deserted Main Street. Miranda hung back to walk with me.

"What do you think of Jackie?" Miranda asked in her contralto voice, her Italian accent clear.

"I like her," I said, "but she makes me uneasy. She's so sure of herself."

That night, Louis jolted me awake, turning on the light. "We need to talk about this," he said.

I rubbed my eyes. "What is there to talk about?"

"Well, I don't know about you," he said, "but I can't go on this way."

I sat up, hugging my knees. We'd had so many discussions, always ending the same way. We knew we had to separate, but it was easier to drift along than face breaking up, dividing belongings, and splitting friends.

But something had changed that summer. I'd grown more confident as an actor and less dependent on Louis' approval. Our relationship reminded me of an etching I'd bought, two princes, in the Tower of London, clinging to each other before their deaths. I'd clung to Louis out of fear, failure, hunger, or going home. Part of me hesitated, but another part longed for independence.

"Maybe we should think of living apart when we get back to New York," I said.

"Maybe we should," Louis replied.

For once, Louis didn't say, "I don't know what I'll do without you." Panic hit me. One step more, and I was on a road I'd never traveled. I thought, I'm not ready. Just a little longer.

"Let's not do anything rash," I said. "Let's see how we feel in the city."

"No," Louis said. "We're not living together anymore. I'm moving in with Sam."

I was stunned. Sam was only an acquaintance. "You don't have to do that," I said.

"You don't understand," Louis said. "I want to live with Sam. He's everything you aren't."

I felt slapped, as if it were my fault. I couldn't help not loving Louis, but guilt washed over me. "I'm sorry," I said.

"Don't be," Louis said, smiling. "I'm happy. It's a relief to have this out in the open."

"We'll still be friends?" I asked.

"Of course," Louis said. "Miranda and Marie are raising money for a winter repertory—we'll both be in it."

"Yes," I said, but I worried Sam might take my place. How would I pay the rent by myself? I lay awake, anxious about returning to New York. I was no further along as an actor, broke, and on my own.

Eleven

It was my third cold winter in New York, and I was barely getting by. The plastic surgeon let me return to his office, where Rose told her gruesome hospital stories. Money was tight, so I ushered evenings at the Alvin Theatre. Without Louis, I couldn't afford our old room, but Mr. Dorn rented me a tiny one for $4 a week. It had just enough space for a bed and a narrow place to stand to change clothes. Maybe being cramped kept loneliness away. I had no time for self-pity, rushing between office, auditions, and theater.

The first play I ushered at was Margaret Webster's *The Tempest*, on Norman Bel Geddes's elaborate revolving island set. The producer, Cheryl Crawford, had given an interview saying that "Miss Webster was so upset by the dress rehearsal, she climbed up on Mr. Bel Geddes' beautiful erection and wept." It became part of Broadway lore.

The theater was fun, crowded with ushers, mostly out-of-work actors, swapping stories. One night, I held the door for Greta Garbo. She said "Thank you" in the *Anna Christie* voice, unforgettable, and she was as beautiful as ever.

The Tempest itself was a mixed bag. Canada Lee played Caliban, Vera Zorina was Ariel, but the production felt ponderous. One night, as Prospero's lines "Our little lives are rounded with a sleep" brought the curtain down, a loud snore was heard from the audience.

Next came *The Firebrand* of Florence, with music by Kurt Weill and lyrics by Ira Gershwin. I saw all 43 performances. The show flopped.

Lotte Lenya, Weill's wife, played the Duchess but wasn't convincing. Still, I learned to critique theater with a sharper eye.

Eventually, I landed a leading role, still not on Broadway, so the *Junior Miss* actress's prediction held. The Equity Library Theater let actors perform for free in New York libraries, with simple sets and no pay. I played Kostya in Chekhov's *The Sea Gull*.

We'd done *The Sea Gull* in Nantucket, with Louis as Kostya and me as Medvedenko. I was on stage all of Act Two, but I only had one line to speak the whole time. I used Method acting to stay engaged, imagining I always wanted to speak but was constantly cut off. Now, as Kostya, the sensitive, struggling writer, I finally had the lead. Audiences joked about the endless Russian names, especially when the play ended with, "Konstantin Gavrilovich has shot himself" and no one could remember which one had been Konstantin Gagrilovich.

Rehearsals were in the afternoons, right after work. The uptown library was off the beaten path, but I'd mastered the subway. Our director, Iza Itkin, daughter of a Moscow Art Theater member, was young, short, and confident. She'd been raised in The Method.

The cast was strong, with several Broadway credits, and I finally felt among professionals. My onstage mother was striking, with a square jaw and broad forehead; Iza said she'd once been Garbo's studio standby. Now married, she'd helped fund the show to showcase her talent.

I related to Kostya, an aspiring writer, as I was an aspiring actor—both penniless and frustrated by others' success. My real challenge was exhaustion: doctor's office, rehearsals, lines, ushering, and little sleep. During breaks, I napped on the library floor. My only regret was wearing a fancy blue blouse; Kostya should have been in rags, but vanity won out. In the end, hardly anyone came. Maybe we were too far uptown, or maybe no one wanted more Chekhov.

I was back to making the rounds, scanning *Show Business* for casting. Marie and Miranda couldn't raise enough for a repertory, so they focused on next year. I saw them when I could. Louis was busy with Sam, and we rarely saw each other, probably for the best.

With spring approaching, I saw an ad for the USO and felt guilty for not contributing to the war effort. I went to their headquarters and discovered that a *Junior Miss* company was forming to go overseas. The director thought I was perfect for the football player, the same role I'd been fired from in Philadelphia. Now two years older and heavier, I felt I could do it well. We'd be gone six months, somewhere in Europe. The war was still on, but looked nearly over.

The following weeks were filled with rehearsals and fittings for cold-weather uniforms. Mr. Dorn, impressed by my new job entertaining soldiers, moved me back into my old room that I'd shared with Louis at no extra charge. I earned a salary plus a little extra as the stage manager. I sent a third of my pay to my parents, a third to Marie and Miranda for their summer theater, and kept the rest.

The days flew by. I took a quick trip to Boston to see my parents, paid with a salary advance. Before I left, Jackie wanted to celebrate and took me to Tony's, a former speakeasy on 52nd Street. It was hard to get a table, but Jackie was a favorite of the star, Mabel Mercer, so the maître d' always squeezed us in. Jackie and I had grown close since she introduced me to her agent. She was often free in the evenings, and we became regular companions. She always paid, insisting money meant nothing to her and she valued my company.

When we arrived, Tony was standing on his head, singing Italian opera. The chic crowd found it ridiculous but tolerated it since he owned the place. I loved the glamorous crowd—elegant women, suited men, cloaked in perfume and confidence. Jackie fit in perfectly in a pleated silk dress, gold chain, and her signature diamond ring. She wore just a hint of Chanel's Russia Leather, smoked constantly, and blew impressive smoke rings. With her long hair and knowing smile, she had Lauren Bacall's style and husky voice.

As our martinis arrived, Jackie's always on the rocks with both olives and onions, Mabel Mercer was introduced to wild applause. She spotted Jackie and joined our table, dressed simply in black with a red scarf. Her voice captivated the room as she sang, "Remind me not to find you so attractive…" The club went silent. With Mabel at our table, I felt important. I envied this world, wealthy and confident, never worrying about jobs or frayed collars. Mabel's songs lingered: "Now all my efforts to forget you remind me I'm in love again."

As Mabel sang, "Just One of Those Things," I noticed a man at the bar. Only Billie Holiday sat nearby, listening between sets, gardenias and rimless glasses at odds with her dress. The man and I locked eyes, then looked away. When Mabel belted, "HOT, not to cool down," the crowd erupted.

I tried to look disinterested, but he was still watching. Handsome, dark-haired, olive-skinned, in a sharp suit and gold bracelet, he smiled; I half smiled back and turned to Jackie.

"You've been watching him a lot," Jackie said.

"Sorry, I didn't mean to be rude."

"Don't be silly. He's great-looking. Should I ask him to join us?" I felt dizzy.

"You can't do that," I protested.

"Why not?" Jackie said. "You don't have many nights left. Don't miss an opportunity."

I felt out of control, warm from the crowd and drinks. For a moment, anticipation and attraction made everything feel perfect. As Mabel sang, Jackie spoke to the man, who smiled and joined us.

After Jackie introduced Cass Stevens, I barely spoke while she peppered him with questions. Cass, with a soft Southern accent from Texas and working in publishing, hit it off with Jackie. I felt left out until Cass asked, "Can we take you home, Jackie?"

Jackie replied, "I'll join friends across the room. Good night." She insisted on paying the check.

Outside, Cass said he was staying at a friend's place but wished we could be alone. Hesitant, I offered, "I have a room in the Village. It's not much."

"I don't care," he said. "As long as we're together." In the cab, Cass held my hand out of sight.

Inside, my room looked shabbier than ever. As soon as the door closed, Cass kissed me, and everything unraveled. I'd never felt so natural making love. Afterward, we lay beneath the barred window, moonlight shining down as Cass propped himself on one elbow and looked at me.

"You're so handsome," he said. "I love you and want to live with you forever." I thought of the love potion in *Midsummer Night's Dream*. Had Cass bewitched me? I'd never felt so honest, and so myself.

"I love you too," I said, "but I'm going overseas in a day or two."

"No," Cass said, "it can't be."

"I signed up with the USO for six months. We leave any day. That's what Jackie and I were celebrating."

Cass sat up. "Can you get out of it?" he asked.

"Of course not," I replied. We lit cigarettes and stared into the darkness.

"It's all right," Cass said. "I'll wait until you come back."

The next days were frantic. I packed and handled stage-managing duties for the tour. Whenever I could, I rushed to Cass's apartment. He was between jobs, staying in a composer friend's room and helping with lyrics. I never knew exactly what Cass did, but it didn't matter. We wanted every minute together before I shipped out.

With my salary advance, I bought tickets for *Carousel* and *On the Town*. When Nancy Walker sang "Some Other Time," all I could think about was living with Cass after I returned. We talked about our future and past. Cass didn't know his real parents but was close to his sister. Since I couldn't write to him freely, we decided I'd address letters to her. I had arranged a third of my salary to go to Marie and Miranda for their theater, so I told them to help Cass if he needed anything. Questions about his fine clothes and jewelry occurred to me, but I let them go. Everything had to be settled before I left.

I packed, visited Jackie, Marie, and Miranda, stored my few things, hurried to see Cass, and went to Tony's for a farewell. Then I was on the train to Seattle, feeling like I was in a war movie.

***

After breakfast, everyone went up to sunbathe. Sated from a huge meal, we lounged on the top deck, forgetting the war except for the ship's zigzagging and lifebelt warnings. The sea was hypnotic, erasing thoughts of where we were headed. With no pool, the main activity was suntan oil; books were quickly abandoned. We were farther from land than anywhere on earth, with deep blue sea and pink-tinged sky.

There were 14 actors in our USO group: five young men (including me), three young women, and six adults. After a month of rehearsing in New York, I knew them well. In Seattle, I roomed with Bill, a handsome ex-model worried about losing his hair, who sometimes asked me to leave when he brought back a sailor. The other boys were also gay: Eric, the all-American type; Merrill, flamboyant and dramatic; and Johnny, a prudish Midwesterner shocked by the others.

The girls were a mix: Peggy, playing the lead, was wide-eyed but older than she looked; Dana, her "sister," tried to seem sophisticated but couldn't hide her country roots; Dodie, the friend, was lively and fun. Among the adults, Brandon, the vain company manager, and his much younger wife Alice often fussed over each other. Nancy, the elegant mother, stood out. The older character man was deaf and heavyset; Liz and Paul played the lovers. We mostly got along, except for Merrill, who'd caused a scene in Grand Central, brandishing a bottle of perfume that he didn't have room to pack.

I started to question if joining this tour was right, not just because of Cass. I'd wanted to contribute to the war, but always felt distant from it. My father was an air raid warden, my brother in the Coast Guard, but not overseas. I hadn't been touched by the war, and my prayers lacked urgency. I joined the USO to grow as a person and actor, but now, lying in the sun, I wondered what our play could mean to men headed for combat.

The ship's engines lulled me to sleep. When I woke, some of the cast were playing shuffleboard, the only real activity besides cards. There was no lounge, and space was tight, so everyone mingled, at least among the officers and USO troupe. The enlisted men remained crammed below. I went to our cramped cabin to wash up, grateful for a rare moment alone.

I thought about writing to Cass, but waited since I couldn't mail anything until landfall. I wanted to tell him about Seattle: endless shots, new ID photos, luggage searches, being issued heavy uniforms, and constant physical exams. Cass would laugh at the "short arm" inspection. I replayed it in my mind so I wouldn't forget.

A doctor told a roomful of soldiers, "Take it out and milk it down." I was horrified to realize what he meant, but the room was already roaring with laughter.

Seattle was mostly waiting and wondering where we'd be sent. In my free time, I wandered the market or listened to the Warsaw Concerto in a record store booth, the music that Cass and I had adopted as our own. Hearing it again, I thought about patience and the reason we'd found each other, only to be parted.

Now I understand that happiness has to be fought for. If it comes too easily, people lose it without knowing. Cass and I were being tested; if we passed, we could have a lifetime together.

The loudspeaker announced lunch. I sat up, ducked my head, and slid to the floor, happy and ravenous.

Twelve

The volcanic mountains of Oahu rose sharply from the sea, not the flat, lush island I expected. After a week at sea, I was ecstatic to see land.

On deck, a loudspeaker played Armed Forces recordings. As we neared Honolulu, Dinah Shore's voice sang numbers from current Broadway shows. When she reached "If I Loved You" from *Carousel,* a show Cass and I had seen together, I felt a brief, sharp longing.

Near the Aloha Tower and the Dole factory's giant pineapple, people said goodbye. The night before, the crew held a send-off with opera arias and sing-alongs. Under a star-filled sky, we joined hands for "Auld Lang Syne." The ship had felt safe, but now our duties were about to begin. From shore, an army band played "Lay That Pistol Down, Babe." I had hoped for "Aloha Oe."

The actors and I waited as troops disembarked. They looked heartbreakingly young, buried in gear and nearly faceless. A brief round of applause faded to silence.

USO personnel rode trucks to Camp Schofield. Honolulu disappointed us, with hot dog stands and bowling alleys, while barracks and airfields dominated the landscape. Outside the city, sugarcane and pineapple fields stretched for miles. Clouds hung over jagged hills, and Pearl Harbor's locks looked like pressed fingers in the earth.

We were billeted in cottages opposite the camp. I shared with Paul, who played the romantic lead. Minutes after arriving, I was whisked off to meet our Special Services officer, a stern Captain with matinee-idol looks. He wanted performance dates and sets arranged immediately, and we headed back to Honolulu.

At the University of Hawaii, we toured Special Services. Maurice Evans, the famed Shakespearean actor, had built a professional theater workshop: shops for costumes, makeup, props, and even dyes. Photos of past productions made me worry *Junior Miss* would look amateurish, since Evans's *Hamlet* with GIs was a triumph.

"See?" the Captain said, showing a photo. Next to Evans stood a blond Horatio, the Captain himself. "I was Horatio," he said, pleased.

I realized his hair had once been blond for the stage. On the ride back, he invited me to see a play that evening, and I quickly accepted.

At the theater, I was stunned to see Gertrude Lawrence and Mildred Natwick in *Blithe Spirit.* Years earlier, I'd waited in Boston for Lawrence's autograph after *Lady in the Dark.* Now she was just a few feet away in Honolulu.

But the thrill faded once she began to act. She exaggerated every line for the soldiers' amusement and forced every double entendre. Her drawn-out words made me hold my breath in sympathy.

Afterward, Carl took me backstage. Lawrence was glamorous, surrounded by a chic crowd, including a Hawaiian of royal birth. I felt I'd stepped onto Broadway, not the Pacific.

The curfew had just been lifted, though bars still closed early. Carl took me to Kau Kau in the Crossroads of the Pacific, a lively spot of diverse people. The air buzzed with energy.

On the drive back, Carl was quiet. He pulled onto the sand and suggested we swim. The Pacific was cold at first, then warmed, phosphorescence sparkling around us. This was the Pacific I'd dreamed of.

"It's glorious," Carl said. "Can you smell it?"

"What?"

"My cologne. Jean Patou's *Moment Suprême.*"

I swam away, unsure of Carl's intent. Soon we were back in the Jeep. Later, alone, I wondered if this whole trip had been a mistake.

I sat in the Moana Hotel dining room with the cast, grateful to be in Waikiki. We watched surfers, canoes, and crowds on the beach. The crowded beach and rough coral disappointed me at first, but the shifting blue water and mountains created a stunning view.

Carl joined us, praising the show. Schofield's 800-seat theater was packed all week. Paul said I deserved much of the credit, but I insisted it was a group effort.

When rehearsals faltered, I stepped in to direct. The cast followed, and the show was a success. The audience applauded like a Broadway crowd. Stage-managing, I skipped my own bow, realizing there's more to theater than acting.

On my day off, Carl drove me into the mountains for dinner at a friend's. From a hilltop, we looked over Manoa Valley, then arrived at a modest house. Our host, Doc Wyman, greeted us with his dog. He had a kindly face, reminding me of H.B. Warner in *King of Kings*.

"This is Doc Wyman," Carl said. Inside, the view from the lanai revealed the valley, mountains, and distant Waikiki surf—this was the Hawaii I'd imagined.

We changed into Hawaiian shirts, settled on the lanai, and listened to Beatrice Lillie records. More guests arrived, and we ate dinner by candlelight, the room fragrant with gardenias.

Doc, a longtime university professor, had directed shows for Maurice Evans. Bookshelves lined the walls, filled with plays. I couldn't resist browsing.

"Borrow as many as you want," Doc said. I thanked him and promised to return them.

We talked of theater, military intrigue, and Honolulu's nightlife. When it was time to leave, I told Doc it was my happiest night on the island.

"Do you work tomorrow?" Doc asked.

"No, I start at 4:00," I replied.

"Stay overnight," Doc said. "Watch the sunrise over Manoa Valley."

After everyone left, Doc and I watched the city lights and the moon over the mountains. We talked about love, his past, and my hopes for Cass. I admitted I worried about Cass meeting someone, but we'd promised not to feel guilty about temptation. I hoped to stay faithful, though six months was a long time.

Later, as I lay on the veranda, Doc entered in a bathrobe and slippers.

"I was thinking about what you said," Doc said. "You'll need some relief. I'd be glad to help."

I lay still, surprised by the casual offer. "I'll be all right," I said, closing the topic.

Doc walked back into the living room. From the dark, I heard, "I'll take my teeth out."

Too stunned to reply, I listened as Doc went to his room. I lay awake with cicadas buzzing, feeling only sympathy for him. How sad to be old and alone. I resolved that my life would be different. There must be a way for two people to grow old together. I fell asleep planning a long letter to Cass.

***

A pounding on the door woke me. At first, I thought I was still at Camp Schofield, but the other bed reminded me I was at the Moana Hotel. Paul's bed was empty. The knocking persisted until I opened the door to find Paul and Carl grinning.

"Get dressed," Paul said. "The war is over." Still half-asleep, I tried not to wake up completely. They were obviously drunk.

"What time is it?" I asked.

"Four a.m.," Carl said. "We're waking everyone up with the news."

"Are you serious?" I asked.

"The war with Japan is over," Paul repeated. "Come on."

In the hotel lobby, Navy men huddled around a radio. We drove down the boulevard, people waving from cars. At the university, we woke the barracks. When the men heard the news, they shouted and joked. We all made a beeline to the Hambs Club, a beer bar named after New York's Lambs Club.

Inside, we turned on the radio. It wasn't official yet, but promising enough for beers and talk of going home. Someone played piano, and we all sang; a few men danced together. By 5:00 a.m., we were groggy but afraid to sleep in case it was all a dream.

I barely had time to shower before my driver arrived. At Bellows Field, I supervised loading sets, costumes, and props for the truck. At Pearl Harbor's submarine base, I trained a crew to assemble the set. We moved bases daily, each time with a new crew. Once the set was up, I'd hunt for furniture, usually at the Officer's Club. By early afternoon, I was done. On the way back, I marveled at Pearl Harbor and its ships.

At 4:00, we went to the theater. The actors bickered about dressing rooms and food, now viewing me as staff since I handled sets and logistics. After each show, I packed everything away, which distanced me further. I worked on lights while the others attended the Commander's cocktail party. The officers' club felt like a movie set, excitement buzzing with rumors the war was ending.

Midway through the second act, sirens blared, the signal for the war's end. Paul was onstage when the Commander told him to announce Japan's surrender. Two thousand sailors roared, cheering for five minutes. The actors, tears in their eyes, forgot their arguments. Guns fired, and flares lit up the sky above the outdoor theater.

I remembered the war's start: Roger at dinner, a neighbor bursting in to announce Pearl Harbor's bombing. Now, I was at Pearl Harbor for peace. The audience's call to continue the play broke my reverie. At last, there was time to think about the future.

The next day, at 1:30 a.m., we piled into a carry-all for the airport. The flight wasn't until 3:00, so we spent the time getting customs slips signed and weighing in. The women had overpacked, and we were 100 pounds over. After a group effort, tossing shoes, books, and clothes on the scale, we finally cleared.

A soldier who'd grown close to one of the girls came to see us off. He was resting on Oahu before returning to Saipan. Tired and limping, he spoke of traveling and still finding prejudice. "What's wrong with men who go through all this and still hate?" he asked. The loudspeaker announced our flight, and we gathered our things. The soldier hid a bottle of rum in my bag, and we promised to meet on Saipan.

As we dashed through the rain, the soldier called, "Sit up front! The tail gets knocked around."

I boarded the plane and was surprised by the cramped, submarine-like cabin packed with luggage. A single row of canvas benches lined one wall. We strapped on Mae West life vests as the engines roared to life. After a long taxi, the plane finally lifted off, and Honolulu's lights sparkled below.

Once airborne, exhaustion hit. We took off our vests, spread blankets, and tried to sleep. I squeezed in beside a snoring soldier and, unable to rest, wandered to the cockpit for a sandwich and canned apricots.

A sleepy sergeant warned, "Better save that for the long flight from Johnston to Kwajalein. You only get one."

At sunrise, I pressed my face to the window, gazing at clouds below and above, like valleys, lakes, and mountains. Nancy, who played the mother in our show, caught my eye. She'd been looking out, too.

"See how easy it is to get into heaven?" she whispered. I smiled.

***

Rain slashed through the screen door, nearly reaching my army cot. I dreaded a cold saltwater wash that never left me clean. I thought about writing Cass, but out here, I felt detached from home. Cass's letters were vague; I realized he wasn't working and hadn't contacted Marie or Miranda. In his last letter, he mentioned an argument with his composer roommate and said he'd gone home to Texas.

I wondered if there was something between them. Being so far away made every letter raise new suspicions. I fought the fear that Cass had lost interest, but there was nothing I could do. Any question would take a month for a reply, so I chose to send love letters and wait.

For the first time, I was enjoying the tour. Oahu had been easy, but the men there didn't need us. Kwajalein, though, was a barren coral island with little but palm trees and Quonset huts. The sun was nearly unbearable. Here, the show was a real break for the men.

It was hard to imagine men enduring the island for 20 months. Our show gave them a taste of home: family, girlfriends, holidays. I talked with the men who helped set up scenery, fascinated by their stories, like the sailor who'd crewed the first submarine into Tokyo Bay, gathering information for Doolittle's raid.

I was busy all day setting up, only seeing the actors during the show. I was focused on props and cues. The women, except Alice, often found officers in each new place and partied late into the night.

Bill, my former roommate, kept me updated on the boys' adventures. They found interested men everywhere, even on Kwajalein. Bill was involved with a married soldier and claimed they'd found a hidden spot on the island.

I checked my watch: "One in the afternoon Tuesday here, 10:00 p.m. Monday in New York." I grabbed soap and stepped out into the rain.

***

The smell was nearly unbearable, but I followed the soldier through the tunnel, scraping my fatigues on the floor. My flashlight swept over holes in the walls, like kennels for small dogs.

"What are those?" I asked in the darkness.

"They were the bedrooms," the guide replied. "Two Japs huddled in each one."

I couldn't imagine anyone fitting in such a cramped space. The tunnel was only four feet high and three feet wide. My flashlight caught skeletons in an adjacent tunnel, surrounded by bones and the stench of decay. I crawled past, stopping short of a skull with enough skin and hair to seem alive. Nausea hit me.

"Let's go back," I yelled.

"Don't want a souvenir?" the soldier asked. Many competed for the goriest relics, but I found the practice disgusting.

"It's OK," I answered. "I've got enough."

Back at the Jeep, the soldier said the island was riddled with caves like the one we'd explored: tiny holes where the enemy could fight unseen.

"The Marines rarely saw a live Japanese soldier," he said. "There were so many, it took 24 days to advance less than a mile."

I took deep breaths to clear the cave air from my lungs, but Iwo Jima dust made me cough. Doctors warned that coral ash was bad for the lungs; no one should stay more than six months. We'd be there for only ten days, but many men spent over eight months.

We drove toward the volcano, passing sunken Japanese ships and wreckage. The road up Mount Suribachi twisted and turned as the soldier recited statistics like a tour guide. "The Japanese spent 40 years trying to build a road up here. The Seabees did it in 27 days," he said.

He floored the Jeep, and we reached the spot where five Marines raised the flag. I got out and saw Iwo Jima spread below—like a kitten curled by the fire. On the ocean side, the crater still smoked, an everlasting memorial.

***

I stood in the outdoor shower, scrubbing dust from my body. Sun-heated saltwater stung my skin. In my room, a thick layer of coral powder already coated the sheets I'd just cleaned. I gave up trying to keep them clean.

I wondered if last night's meeting would change anything. The actors were shocked when I threatened to quit, but quickly blamed each other. Just a few gave us a bad name, but it affected us all. If only we didn't have parties every night, maybe they'd stop getting so drunk and sleeping with anyone who asked.

Working closely with the men, I heard their resentment toward USO groups, especially the women always with officers. Soldiers watched actresses get so drunk they could barely walk to their rooms. Their behavior made us a laughingstock and hurt our reputation. I needed support.

Moving the show nightly meant long days. After acting and running the show, I tore down the set while others removed their makeup. Sometimes there weren't enough men assigned, and I needed the actors to help, but they acted like prima donnas. If last night's meeting got them to pitch in, it was worth it.

Bill and Eric helped with the set, and everyone skipped the Officer's Club for an early night—a silent apology. I knew things would return to normal soon. Lying in bed, I thought about going home, but I wouldn't leave in disgrace.

In less than two months, I'd be 20. I'd always wanted to act, but until now I'd been floundering, afraid to seize opportunities. The tour changed me; I'm ready to do everything I can to get where I want to go.

A flash of heat lightning reminded me of Cass. We'd exchanged letters and planned to get an apartment. But I started adding up expenses: classes, a gym, new clothes. My $18 a week unemployment wouldn't go far. What if I spent it all and Cass and I didn't get along? I used to think love mattered more than career. Maybe I was just getting island crazy like the men stuck too long out here.

Two soldiers paced outside. There was no longer any danger from snipers. The women across the road still needed guards, so the men kept watch. As I closed my eyes, I saw the silhouette of a helmet and gun.

***

"Pennies in a stream, warbling of the meadowlark, moonlight in Vermont."

A woman's voice over the loudspeaker was pure and rich. I lay in the sun, letting the music wash over me, plunging occasionally into the pool carved from rock. After Saipan, Tinian felt like a vacation. Special Services gave me a Jeep, a driver, and a truck for props. With work done in two hours, I could be at the beach by noon.

On Saipan, we'd been treated poorly, crowded into a leaking Quonset hut with dozens of USO groups. Rumors of scandals didn't help. An older concert performer was caught servicing soldiers in a shed, so they sent his whole company home. Each disgrace reflected on all of us. Even though *Junior Miss* drew thousands each night, the Navy gave us no favors. Tinian, by contrast, was paradise: real mattresses, flush toilets, and occasional warm showers.

As I stretched on my cot, a small lizard scurried up my leg. I flicked it away and turned toward Gordon, who was determined to deepen his tan. How odd to see a B-29 flight officer with 28 missions over Tokyo, worrying about suntans and swimwear. Yet it was oddly comforting.

From the start, Gordon and I agreed to spend my days on the island together, not as lovers but as companions. Carl in Honolulu had told me to look him up. Gordon had a partner in Minneapolis; I had Cass. Romance wasn't the point. I'd been desperately lonely, and simple closeness felt like oxygen. This was release, not betrayal. I hoped Cass was giving himself the same mercy.

War was full of contradictions. Tinian held the world's largest airfield and more B-29s than anywhere. I met many pilots, but admired the bomber crews most; their courage seemed extraordinary. Many were gay, flying with their lovers, drawing strength from being together. And yet here they were, lounging on beaches, trading bracelets, stitching parachute silk into bikinis, passing time until they could go home.

"Let's go for a ride," Gordon said, breaking my reverie. "I'm bored."

We pulled on clothes and climbed into his Jeep. Yellow Beach was crowded with his squadron, and he waved as we left. At the wheel, Gordon looked like a movie star. We'd clicked right away. On my first night off, he took me to North Tinian Field to watch B-29s land. The sheer size stunned me—giant shadows swooping from darkness, prehistoric birds thundering onto the runway. Gordon's stories fascinated me, like old sailors' tales. He was only 22, like most of his crew, and I wondered if youth itself gave them such reckless courage.

The island itself was small and flat, more like Pennsylvania than the tropics. Unlike Saipan, there were no caves for Japanese holdouts, though rumors lingered. Some Japanese soldiers blended into chow lines or slipped into movie theaters undetected. I even wondered if they had seen *Junior Miss*.

Gordon and I spent every free hour together, swimming, lounging on the beach, drinking beer after shows, riding late at night. We found a hidden cove for midnight suppers, surf glittering with starlight. For me, it was pure release, a chance to stop worrying about Cass, the future, or responsibility. For once, someone else took care of me.

But Cass was never far from my mind. Sporadic mail strained us. In one letter, he said he hadn't heard from me in weeks and wanted to break it off. I hoped my missing letters would arrive, and all would be forgiven. I couldn't brood. Life here felt oddly preordained, thousands of miles from home, death possible, yet I believed I was protected. Hamlet's words echoed: *"There is a special providence in the fall of a sparrow... The readiness is all."*

"You look serious," Gordon said, pulling me back. "What are you thinking? I'm hungry."

"Let's go get something to eat," I said, and we climbed back into the Jeep.

***

Guam was so close that we barely got off the plane in Tinian before landing again. The island was huge and lush. We stayed in Quonset huts above a pristine bay. The days were easy: helpers set up, audiences packed the house, ovations came freely. We'd finish on a high note.

One afternoon, my driver took me to a native village to meet some of the Chamorros. An elderly woman introduced the villagers and, gesturing to a young man, said, "He's not married. He likes his own kind." She said it simply, as fact.

On my day off, I sat at the Officer's Club terrace, watching dusk fall over the bay. The next day, I waded to a hidden strip of sand at the cliffs' base. Alone in the sun, I finally found relief from the actors' complaints. That spot became my refuge.

We didn't know our final performance had already passed. We were scheduled for another island, but Brandon, who played the father, could no longer manage his false teeth, so the production shut down quietly. We'd waited so long to celebrate the "last show" that it slipped by unnoticed. Now we sat idle, desperate to leave, but space on ships and planes was scarce.

I suspected the real reason for the delay: Peggy, our lead, had fallen for a high-ranking officer. He wouldn't let her go, so neither could we. Tensions rose. Merrill, impatient, stowed away on a plane to Oahu, only to be caught and sent back.

With no work, the tropics drained me. Guam was beautiful, but all I wanted was home. I lay on the beach, rereading Cass's letters, which had grown more tender once mine reached him.

His latest read:

Dear One,

To start with, I can never begin to tell you how much I love you...even a lifetime won't be enough. Last night I played gin rummy with friends, but I keep thinking about us. I wonder if you'll be content to stay in more—I must with this new job as Assistant Production Manager of Homemaker Magazine. *It will take all my strength, but I'm overjoyed at the responsibility. I bring it up because you've been working hard, yet still running about, boozing. I'm afraid I can't keep that pace, at least for now.*

Have I told you I love you? Yes—completely and wholeheartedly. I always think of your return. But I'm frightened too. Will you still find me attractive? Will I live up to what you desire? Will I be able to control my temper, to avoid rashness that could damage us? Can I tame my jealousy and settle into peace with you? God give me strength.

Still, I know happiness takes more than sex or attraction. I'm willing. How about you?

Yours, Cass

***

The platform was teeming with people as I dragged my luggage out. I saw cast members with relatives and felt relieved I'd told Cass not to meet me. I'd already said goodbye to those who'd ridden east with me. It was amicable, but none of us wanted to see each other again. The tour did not make us friends.

Shivering, I stood in the cab line. In the taxi, I gave the driver the hotel name, leaned back, and tried to relax. New York felt strange, as though I'd never lived there.

The Wellington was on a busy side street in the jewelry district. A torn awning drooped toward the curb, and there was no doorman. The driver helped me haul my bags into the cramped lobby. Behind a partition, a woman spoke into a phone. She covered the receiver and looked at me.

"Yes?" she asked.

"Mr. Stevens made a reservation," I said.

She pushed a pad toward me. "Fill this out," she said.

The form asked for a name and address. I realized I didn't actually live anywhere. I finally wrote down my parents' address and was given a key.

The room was dingy: twin beds, a scarred chair, thin drapes. I shuddered. I didn't unpack, just pulled out underwear and a shirt. The shower was rusty, the water faintly brown but hot. I stood in it a long time, trying to calm my nerves about seeing Cass.

I lay on the bed waiting for 6:00. Cass had been too busy with his new job to find us an apartment. In all our letters, we'd planned for a home together, and here I was in this shabby hotel. I told myself not to blame him. I'd find us a place soon.

At last, I heard a key in the lock. Cass entered, closed the door, and looked at me silently. For a moment, I feared he was disappointed in me. Then he crossed the room, pulled me up, and held me.

"I'm so glad you're finally home," he said. I buried my face in his neck. He drew back. "I'm filthy—I've got to shower."

I watched him tear off his clothes and disappear into the bathroom. I sat waiting. Cass returned in a towel, helped me undress, and we crawled into one of the twin beds. I felt wrapped in a cloud that separated me from him, even as we made love.

Afterward, Cass sighed. "That was wonderful. Now get dressed. We'll grab a bite—I'm exhausted and need to be up early."

Sitting on the bed to tie my shoes, I rubbed below my ribs. An ache radiated through me. *It'll go away*, I told myself.

We'd been in the car for no more than five minutes when the discussion began. My mother started: "Well, dear, I know you're older now, so I'm sure you'll go to school."

I was blindsided. I thought I'd returned as a successful actor after months overseas, yet they came at me with the same old arguments, as if I'd failed. Even my brother's new wife, whom I'd just met, joined in, urging me to leave New York and return to Boston. By the time I gathered myself to respond, my father was pulling up in front of the apartment.

From the moment I saw them waving at the airport, I'd felt a strange detachment. My mother kissed me with tears in her eyes, and I felt nothing. The change in our relationship had crept up over the three years I'd been away, but I was still startled by my lack of emotion.

Inside the apartment, everything looked smaller and cheaper: short drapes, scraps of broadloom pieced together to mimic wall-to-wall carpet, the marble-topped table, and Japanese prints. I remembered living here, but with no fondness. On the table sat a cake with "Welcome home – USO" written in icing. I was embarrassed.

The next morning, my mother let me sleep until noon, "late enough for anyone," she declared. As soon as I sat down to breakfast, they started again. Since it was Sunday, my father unleashed his full arsenal: my age, lack of a degree, and failure to advance in theater. My brother and his wife piled on, as though tearing me down was a family sport.

Finally, I snapped. "How can you treat me like this? I've been gone seven months overseas, working harder than any of you, without any of the pleasures you take for granted. And this is my welcome home?"

I'd promised myself years ago, after my father struck me for not finishing dinner, that I'd never let them upset me again. Yet here I was, retreating to my childhood bedroom to hide the tears. *This is not my home, and they are not my family*, I thought.

That evening, relatives came by. They asked about my trip, but as soon as I answered, their eyes glazed. When I mentioned Honolulu, one uncle launched into a fifteen-minute story about a sister he hadn't spoken to in twenty years. No one listened. I thought of the thousands of GIs I'd spoken with overseas, how even their gripes and hopes had seemed more alive than this.

I tried to describe the Marshall Islanders, segregated by the military, but my father interrupted with a joke: "Did you hear about the Texan who was greeted at the Gates of Heaven with, 'Well, you can come in, but you won't like it as well'?"

I drifted to a cousin I'd once liked. Now he flaunted his success and mocked me, saying he'd heard I was starving in a Greenwich Village hovel. I forced a laugh, but I knew he meant it. Why so much resentment? Was it because I hadn't followed their path?

When they finally left, I sat in my old room and wrote to Cass. How strange that I hadn't been able to talk to him when we were together, but away from him, I knew exactly what to say. I wrote that there was no home for me unless we were together, and promised to find us an apartment as soon as I returned to New York.

Cass told me over dinner he'd grown close to Marie and Miranda while I was gone. They were trying to secure a summer theater, and he might have to leave his job to manage it. I'd blurted out, "Oh, no," then regretted it. I wanted him to be the stable one, the anchor, while I was the "artist." Now I tried to amend it, telling him I'd be happy if he joined the theater, just so we could share the summer.

I wrote: *This has been my first moment alone to write. Even now, I half expect my mother to burst in and snatch the letter from me. But let her—I'm too tired to care. I love you more than any of these "acceptable" people around me love each other. Kiss the girls for me, and tell them that when I come to New York on Saturday, there'll be no sentimental 'I've just returned from the Pacific.' I'm back, steady, ready to get us settled and to work.*

I hid the letter in a book and turned out the light.

Thirteen

While Cass and I wrote letters, our plans seemed perfect. Living together was different. Money was tight. Cass hadn't saved much, and most of my tour earnings were gone. Every penny mattered. I was back in a $9-a-week furnished room, worse than the one I'd shared with Louis.

At first, we tried to make the place livable. Cass fixed up a table from the street, but soon we gave up "playing house." Money was too tight for dinners out, and his friends drifted away. We spent time with Marie and Miranda planning their theater, but Cass felt out of place with Louis and his circle. Jackie never warmed to him, so I stopped seeing her. Tension grew until something unexpected shifted it.

One icy day, trudging through auditions, I heard about replacements for Maurice Evans' *The GI Hamlet* at the International Theater. The audition was open. I joined the line and was told, "You'll need a Shakespeare soliloquy. Otherwise, don't bother."

That was no problem. I'd memorized plenty of them. Hamlet was too obvious, John of Gaunt too stiff. Then I chose Richard II's speech that moves from defeat to strength.

When my turn came, I was led onto the set and began:

"I have been studying how I may compare this prison where I live unto the world."

I faltered, then rallied and finished the soliloquy. Silence followed.

Finally, a voice said, "Thank you. That was very good. You know you sat in Mr. Evans' spot, where he does 'To be or not to be'?"

I had no idea. "Thank you, that's all we need," the voice added. I stumbled off, mortified.

The next day, the stage manager called: I had the job. He congratulated me on my "courage" in choosing Evans' sacred place; everyone else had avoided it. My obliviousness amused them all.

***

It was so hot and humid that Miranda stopped rehearsal early. "Let's all go home and rest," she said.

I slipped out of the theater and walked toward the Pig and Whistle. I loved Arden, with its cottages hidden by greenery, but I couldn't focus at rehearsal, forgetting lines I never forgot. At the house, Hazel, the cook, waved me over, but I shook my head. The forest was quiet except for birdsong. At our house, I pulled down the Murphy bed, lay still, and tried to clear my head.

The summer hadn't worked out. I should have trusted my instincts and asked Cass not to come, but by then he'd quit his job. Our letters during my *Hamlet* tour had been full of hope. But even with a charming house and food covered by the theater, Cass was unhappy. He said Marie and Miranda didn't recognize his work. The more restless he grew, the more he took it out on me.

Meanwhile, I was thriving onstage. In Benn Levy's *The Devil Passes,* I played the Devil stirring up the people in a country house. My voice and old Prize Speaking flair returned. I loved it, as I loved my role in *Dame Nature.* Both plays were successful. But while I was onstage, Cass began driving into Wilmington, returning late, smelling of liquor.

A wasp buzzed in; I swatted it away. Cass entered, clearly upset. "What's wrong?" I asked. He threw his briefcase onto a chair.

"Can't you make up the bed?" he snapped.

"I was just resting," I said, straightening the sheets. "Do you want to talk about it?"

"Yes. Marie's brother is coming. Did you know?"

"No," I said. "But what difference does it make?"

"Only that he's coming for my job," Cass said.

"Cass, that's not true," I said.

"What else could it be?" He ripped off his shirt. "There's nothing for him to do but my work. Am I supposed to sit around while he does everything?"

"There must be enough work for two people, or they wouldn't bring him."

"They're bringing him because he's Marie's brother. Don't be stupid." Cass paced. "I've taken the last licking I'm going to. I'm not going to do all the hard work so they can bring along dead wood."

"I'm sure if you talk to Marie and Miranda, it can be worked out," I said.

Cass stopped. "The only smart thing Jackie ever said was that you have infinite trust in people."

"But you love the girls," I said. "And they love you."

"I've quit. I'm going back to Texas."

I exhaled. "Don't you think we should have discussed it first?"

He softened, taking my shoulders. "I can't stay any longer. I thought I could protect you, but you don't need me. You're doing fine."

"But I do need you," I protested.

"I need a job where I'm respected and can make money," Cass said. "I hate living like this."

"What about us?"

"I just don't think it's in the cards," he replied.

"We have to work at it."

"Look," Cass said, guiding me to the sofa, "I waited seven months while you were overseas, then we were together for two, then apart for two more while you were on tour, and now you're going to be away with the Hamlet tour."

"They just asked me," I interrupted. "It's not settled."

"No," Cass said quietly. "But it will be."

"Then I'll refuse to go."

"You're an actor. You can't turn down an important role. I wouldn't want you to. But you can't expect me to sit around while you build your career. I can get an ad job in Houston, find a place, and live a little."

"Without me," I said.

"Then give up the theater and come with me," Cass replied.

I said nothing. No matter what I said, it would end the same way.

***

"Be delicate and tender," said director George Schaefer as we rehearsed *Hamlet*. Those were Hamlet's words about my character, Fortinbras, but I thought it was a ridiculous direction. Still, I nodded.

Cass had been right: Maurice Evans himself had offered me the part. Evans, the great Shakespearean, was forming a company to tour *Hamlet* across America. I jumped at it. A year of one-nighters and constant motion suited me. After two failed attempts at love, I was ready to focus on work.

Stage manager Bud Williams, a close friend from my spring tour, had touted me to Evans. My two scenes were small, but one mattered: the ending. As soldiers lifted Hamlet onto his bier, I raised my sword and ordered the tribute: "Take up the bodies... Go, bid the soldiers shoot." That final moment was mine, and I never tired of it.

Billy Nichols, who played Guildenstern (or Rosencrantz, I never knew which), teased me for how I pronounced "bodies." I had to project over organ music while moving downstage, and clarity was everything. My father said I sounded like Colonel Stoopnagle yelling in the vastness of the North Pole. The company teased me for my odd Boston-Shakespeare accent, but I didn't mind.

One night, the joke became legend. The crew hadn't been able to set the spotlight, which was my cue to stop walking toward the footlights. I searched for the spotlight and kept walking, finally stopping when I sensed something wrong. I then raised my sword and spoke the last line. The curtain dropped...right on my head. I crawled under it, then back again to retrieve my cap. The cast was in hysterics, Maurice Evans loudest of all. From then on, I was nicknamed "Schnook."

Despite the nickname, I loved my costume: red uniform, shiny sword, black boots, and fur-trimmed cape.

I shared a dressing room with Emmett Rogers, who played Laertes and lived with Evans. Emmett said that on their cross-country drive, Evans had made him crouch in the back seat to avoid suspicion. Evans couldn't risk being seen with another man. It might invite whispers, and hurt his leading man appeal.

I learned much from watching Emmett's elaborate makeup. Thinking it was his secret, I copied every step until my face looked like a patchwork quilt. My friend Billy gasped, "Schnookle, are you crazy? Just use pancake and you'll be fine." He was right. I was learning.

The tour also gave me another friend. On the first day, I noticed her—striking, self-possessed, with perfect features. Cast as the Player Queen, she sat alone between scenes, her haughtiness saying, "Keep away." But once we broke through her shyness, she became the life of the party. That was Neva Patterson, who would go on to a long career on Broadway and in Hollywood.

We started out and, thanks to Maurice Evans' fame and his pared-down *Hamlet*, the tour was a huge success. Theaters filled, especially with young people seeing Shakespeare and live theater for the first time. The only problem: kids talked through the show, distracting the actors.

Maurice Evans solved it by stepping in front of the curtain, telling the students, "At the movies, the actors can't hear you talk. But we're right here, and it's hard to give our best if you're making noise." The crowd was always surprised, then silent for the rest of the show.

The tour settled into a routine: train travel at night, new city by day, evening show. On matinee days, there was little time to explore. When I could, I worked out at the YMCA or visited museums to fill the hours in towns we'd never see again.

Whenever we stayed overnight in a hotel, we partied. Bud, Billy, Neva, and others would gather to drink, sing, and swap theater stories. One night, the police knocked on my door about the noise, and I greeted them with a nervous "Are we making too much 'noisey'?" It became a running joke. After always being in charge, it was nice to be coddled for a change.

Another night, our group went to a club. At the bar, two heavily made-up women asked if I was in the *Hamlet* show. I was pleased to be recognized and chatted with them. Later, I told Billy and Bud about it. They exchanged looks.

"Are you kidding?" Billy said. "You really are a schnook. They were men, drag queens."

I couldn't believe it. I'd never seen a drag queen before. The next day, roses and an invitation to meet them arrived at the theater. I was relieved we had to rush to the train after the show.

Billy was my voice of reason on tour. He was witty, imaginative, and later produced award-winning TV specials. If there was a piano, Billy would play and sing Gershwin or Rodgers and Hart. Sometimes Neva joined, singing with sultry nightclub style.

Neva was funny, too, singing "down home" songs from her Iowa roots. One night after a party, we ended up in bed together. I'd never been with a woman but felt comfortable, maybe thanks to Neva's experience. It was enjoyable, and I felt very grown-up at 20.

It didn't lead to anything. We slept together a few more times, then went back to being friends. Later, Neva was seeing another actor, which was fine with me. I found sex with men more exciting and continued my own brief encounters on the tour.

I learned more about Neva when our tour took us to Iowa, close to her hometown, and her family invited us for Thanksgiving. Our group set out on a crisp winter day, snow covering the farmland, barns, and farmhouses,

Neva's parents could have stepped out of Grant Wood's *American Gothic*. Her mother was sweet-faced and welcoming, her father gray-haired and weathered. The house was simple but spotless. Neva tried to be the dutiful daughter, but to me, she seemed more like a glamorous visitor checking in.

The meal was hearty—turkey, relishes, her mother's jams, and home-made cider. After dinner, I climbed the water tower beside the house. For years, Neva said her parents remembered me as "the boy who climbed the water tower."

As the tour wound down, I was ready for it to end. Even good actors tire after a year in the same role. Still, I earned good reviews, and Maurice Evans praised my work. Most importantly, I had solid acting credit and lasting friendships. I returned to New York hopeful to find an agent or land a reading for a new play.

***

Traffic crawled, and my excitement got the better of me. I jumped out at 6th Avenue into crisp autumn air. It was a magnificent October day, and I tried to recall a poem about October's bright blue weather.

I hurried into the bar, past the crowd and the sound of the piano. I spotted Jackie, punctual as always. We'd been seeing each other again since my return from the tour and Cass's exit from my life. I kissed her cheek and sat down.

"You're only 15 minutes late," she said, dimples deepening with annoyance.

"Wait till you hear why," I replied, signaling for a drink. I ordered a Rob Roy; she had her martini with onions and olives.

"Okay," she said. "Don't be coy. Out with it."

She looked more beautiful than ever—long dark hair, burgundy suit, gold earrings, diamond pendant. She was the picture of New York success, and I was proud to be with her.

"Well," I began, "I had a reading for a replacement in the Katharine Cornell show yesterday."

"You got it!" she burst out.

"Let me tell the story," I said. "I was dressing to meet you when the hall phone rang. A voice said, 'This is Guthrie McClintic. Can you come right over now?' He gave me his Beekman Place address. I tried to call you, but no answer, so I figured you'd forgive me when you heard."

Jackie leaned in. "Go on."

"I worried all the way in the cab. Why his home and not the theater? But it was 7:30. McClintic let me in, took me into the dark garden, and handed me a book. 'I've marked the roles you are to play,' he said. 'Be at rehearsal at 10:00 a.m.'"

Jackie grabbed my head and kissed me. "That's the best news. Congratulations."

"The funny thing," I said, "is the actress who got me into *Junior Miss* once said it would take me five years to get a Broadway part. That's exactly how long it's been."

"No," Jackie reminded me, "you went on once in *Hamlet* before the spring tour."

"It doesn't count. That was as an understudy. This is my own role and a famous speech."

Jackie stubbed out her cigarette. "Perfect time for what I wanted to say. I think we should get married."

Mabel Mercer began to sing at a nearby table, and the room fell silent. I kept staring at Jackie, realizing she was serious. When Mabel finished, Jackie went on. "It makes sense. We both want companionship and a home, and we can't seem to find them elsewhere. Cass didn't work out for you. We love each other as much as we're ever going to. Think of the relief from our families' matchmaking."

At the mention of Cass, I glanced toward the bar where we'd met. For an instant, I thought he'd appear, but I didn't want him to. We'd seen each other once since our separation—an awkward dinner and a worse evening. I wasn't that boy anymore. I'd toured the country with a star, made Broadway friends, and found my footing.

"You're thinking about Cass," Jackie said.

"You always know," I replied.

"He was a kept boy," she said. "First the composer, then the older man, while you were away."

"I think he tried. We both did. But it's not possible for me anymore."

"So," Jackie said, as if resting her case, "let's get married."

"What if one of us falls in love with someone else?"

"We'll all live together until it's over—it always is—and then we'll still have each other. I do love you."

"I love you too," I said simply.

"We can live in my apartment, use our gift money to fix it up, and entertain theater people—good for your career. And remember, I've worked in an agent's office. They won't send you out if they think you're homosexual."

I slipped off the signet ring Louis had given me and held it out. Jackie slid a small gold ring with a tiny diamond from her finger.

We exchanged rings. "Jacqueline, will you marry me?" I asked.

"You bet your ass," she said.

***

Suddenly, chaos. I had to be in Buffalo for the pre-Broadway tryout of *Antony and Cleopatra*, set to open in New York on November 27. Jacqueline, never "Jackie" now, was in Boston, assistant to Irene Selznick on *A Streetcar Named Desire*, opening a week later.

Our wedding was set for Sunday, November 30, wedged between two Broadway openings. We had only weeks to pull off two debuts and a marriage. Jacqueline's mother, bedridden but commanding, orchestrated everything: food, flowers, guests, even Jacqueline's outfit and jewelry.

Meanwhile, I was living with Bret Morrison, a radio star and voice of *The Shadow*. Kids everywhere imitated him. We'd met at a party, and I went home with him to a stunning duplex overlooking Central Park. He seemed dashing and charming, but alone, I glimpsed the loneliness beneath the surface.

Bret asked me to move in for company, not romance. There was a spare room, and it saved me rent. He even decorated it in 18th-century New England style—after years of shabby rooms, it felt like a fantasy.

Sometimes I worried I was being "kept," but I went on auditioning. Bret encouraged me to bring friends over, so I invented a Sunday Hunt Breakfast: bikes in Central Park, then brunch and champagne. The apartment filled with laughter after Bret's years of loneliness. I paid him back by joining his *Shadow* appearances at New Jersey fairs, introducing him in my announcer's voice as he swept onstage. Crowds adored him.

When Jacqueline and I decided to marry, I told Bret. He was sad but gracious. As a wedding gift, he had luggage made with my name—for a honeymoon Jacqueline and I never took.

Rehearsals for *Antony and Cleopatra* went beautifully. The sets were magnificent, no expense spared on costumes. Miss Cornell was breathtaking in a Valentina-designed uniform. Only one problem plagued rehearsals: Cleopatra's handmaidens. The younger actress annoyed Cornell, pawing at her during the death scene. She was quickly replaced by a bold young discovery: Maureen Stapleton.

Legend had it that Maureen once called Guthrie McClintic about *The Playboy of the Western World*. When told the role was cast, she replied, "I don't give a fuck who's playing it, if I'm not doing it." He was so charmed, he made her the understudy. Now she was brought in to play Iras.

On her first night, she called me out of the blue: "This is Maureen. I'm in your hotel. Room 316. Come right over." Click. Worried she was in trouble, I went. She opened the door in pajamas, face dotted with pimple cream. "Sit," she ordered. "We've only got a couple of weeks before New York. I need to know who the homos are in this cast. Nothing against them, I just don't want to waste time. I'll never get laid." I told her what I knew; she jotted down names. She was rarely without a man afterward.

Later, in Detroit, she cornered me: "Why can't I get that laugh in the scene with Eli Wallach?" You know when he says our fortunes are alike, and I say I don't want my fortune in my husband's nose. I suggested, "Deliver it like what it is, the punchline of a dirty joke." She tried, but never landed the laugh. Years later, as a celebrated actress, the first thing she asked was, "Why couldn't I get that laugh in *Antony and Cleopatra?*"

At last, we returned to New York for the dress rehearsal. My opening scene went smoothly, then Katherine Cornell and Godfrey Tearle entered as lovers. Suddenly, from the darkened orchestra, came a roar: "You're all terrible! This isn't acting! I'll cancel the play if this is the best you can do!"

It was McClintic. His tirades were legendary; fear-sharpened performances, and it worked. Opening night began beautifully, until disaster struck. As Cornell and Tearle embraced, the massive columns framing Egypt began rising too soon. The audience gasped. The columns jerked back down and trembled, but Cornell and Tearle pressed on. Reviews were strong, and the show became the longest-running *Antony and Cleopatra* ever.

With Jacqueline still out of town, her childhood friend Eleanor Vaughn stood in as my date. Eleanor taught psychology at Hofstra College, but she was a beauty as well as a brain. I was proud to walk into Sardi's with her. For the first time, I was on the inside, looking out.

***

"Wake up. We're getting married in four hours." Jacqueline shook me until I focused. We were sleeping in separate beds, but it still felt wrong to be under the same roof before the ceremony. I was about to stand before family and friends and promise myself to her. I should have taken a hotel room.

"There's coffee," she said, already composed beneath her robe.

By the time the maid ushered us into her parents' apartment, the scent of lilies already filled the air. Every surface was covered with blooms, their perfume heavy in the stifling heat that was always turned up for Jacqueline's bedridden mother. Her father, jovial and barrel-chested, appeared with his doctor's bag and gave his wife an injection. Within minutes, she was smiling dreamily.

Guests soon arrived —just 20 to keep things calm: family, relatives, and a few actors—Eleanor, Billy Nichols, Bret Morrison, and Neva Patterson, carrying her present: a toaster. Louis was on tour; Marie and Miranda had drifted away. Jacqueline's old agents were there too; I hoped they might open doors for me.

Jacqueline wore a brown dress with white orchids pinned to her shoulder and a lace handkerchief tucked in the belt. I wore a matching brown suit; my mother insisted on a carnation for my lapel. We looked solemn, more like mourners than newlyweds.

The minister, a family friend brought down from Boston, pulled us aside before the ceremony. My stomach lurched. Had he guessed the truth—that it was a marriage of convenience? Would he refuse to marry us? Instead, he explained that he wasn't licensed in New York. He could perform the ceremony, but a colleague would have to sign the certificate later. "The only problem," he said, "is that you won't really be married on your wedding night."

Relief rushed through me. "That doesn't matter," I blurted.

Soon, we stood before our families. I looked into Jacqueline's steady green eyes and said, "I do." Her gaze was resolute, almost defiant.

After the vows came champagne, toasts, and tears. My mother wept. Jacqueline's mother had another injection. Our fathers swapped jokes while actors got drunk. When it was time to leave, Bret drove us in his two-seater MG. Jacqueline perched on my lap as the cold wind cut through us. By the time we reached the Pierre Hotel, the orchids had wilted, and our bodies ached.

The bellboy smirked as if he'd just delivered a pair of blushing newly-weds. Jacqueline unpacked our few things and handed me my pajamas. I stared at the king-sized bed uneasily. Should I do something? Would she expect it? I thought of Neva, of how simple it had been with her, and of the vague idea that Jacqueline and I might one day have a child, the one subject we had never dared touch on.

Jacqueline drew the curtains, poured champagne into water glasses, and handed me one. "Cheers," she said. "Cheers."

She sat beside me, and the bed collapsed with a crack, sinking to the floor. For a moment, the day's solemn weight lifted, and we laughed until tears came. Whatever else our marriage would turn out to be, that night we slept like children.

In just a few days, Jacqueline would open in *Streetcar,* and she was so consumed with preparations that I hardly saw her. Meanwhile, I had developed a monstrous stye on my right eye. It throbbed, looked dreadful, and felt like a visible mark of all my frayed nerves. Still, I performed. The audience didn't seem to notice, though offstage I wore a patch and looked like the man in the Hathaway shirt ad. Oddly enough, that patch brought me my first real moment with Miss Cornell.

She had always been cordial but distant, as though surrounded by an invisible wall: *Don't disturb me, I'm busy creating.* Actors from her former shows gathered around her like guards, calling her "Miss Kitty." The rest of us, more timid, said "Miss Cornell." We shared the opening scene, so I always saw her as she wandered the stage before curtain, studying the columns and stairs as if she were willing Egypt into existence. At most, I'd get a nod or a clipped "Good evening."

But when she saw my stye, she came straight to me. "You have a stye!" she said, alarmed.

"I'm sorry," I stammered, as though I'd failed her. "Is it very painful?"'

"Just uncomfortable."

"You poor thing. It will go away. Imagine, when I was in *The Green Hat,* I had styes on both eyes and still performed."

"How did you manage?" I asked.

"I pulled the hat lower over my face."

She wasn't joking. Humor was not her strong suit. Just then, the stage manager signaled, and she gave me a parting, almost maternal glance. "I hope you'll feel better." That was the most animated I'd ever seen her. I would come to know her peculiar fondness for illness.

Streetcar opened to rapturous reviews, the kind that set careers aflame. I couldn't attend the performance itself, but Jacqueline insisted I accompany her to producer Irene Selznick's party afterward. My stye throbbed under its patch, and I felt ridiculous arriving half-blind among Broadway royalty.

It wasn't a large gathering—just the cast, a few backers, close friends—but that only heightened my discomfort. Jacqueline disappeared at once to confer with Irene, who looked exhausted. The atmosphere was strangely muted, like a wake rather than a triumph. Marlon Brando sulked in a corner, already hailed as the future of American theater, but he barely looked at me. He never did. I remembered threatening to keep him off Broadway, a ridiculous promise. His talent was undeniable, even if his presence was insufferable.

I stood awkward and silent, grateful when Jacqueline, pale from her own exhaustion, finally said, "Let's go home."

The weeks that followed were the happiest of our marriage. We were young, attractive, both in hit shows, and for a brief moment, sought out as a golden couple of the stage. Invitations poured in. Jacqueline sifted through them, discarding what "didn't make sense." Her ambition was never subtle. She wanted to make it big in New York, and together we seemed halfway there.

With wedding money, we transformed her fourth-floor walkup on 53rd Street. The address was good, a block from 5th Avenue, though the apartment was cramped. The bedroom was barely big enough for storage, so we lined the living room wall with two studio couches in bold yellow and gray stripes. At night, we slept head-to-head, feet nearly touching, bodies set apart as though by design. Bright yellow draperies matched the couches, pride of place given to a Noguchi coffee table, the most extravagant piece we owned.

The marble fireplace was broken, so I filled the gaps with plants, a clumsy but cheerful repair. By December's end, Jacqueline was ready to launch her campaign to conquer the theater socially as well as professionally. She accepted multiple invitations for New Year's Eve, promising to pick me up after my show.

As I left for the theater, she called after me with a grin: "I've made up something very witty, 'It sure was heaven in '47, but we're going straight in '48.'" She repeated it again and again as I went down the stairs, her voice following me like a refrain.

Fourteen

Jacqueline waited at the stage door, and for once, I hurried, knowing she hated standing in the hallway. *Don't keep Jacqueline waiting,* topped my New Year's resolutions, just below *give up smoking and promiscuity*. With my makeup already off, I was out quickly, and we made our way from the Martin Beck Theatre through Times Square toward 45th Street.

Billy Nichols, my closest friend from the *Hamlet* tour, lived near the Lyceum. Jacqueline called him "just an actor," but I adored him; he was sharp, funny, and his home felt like an oasis.

Billy's commercial loft was a haven: flea market finds, walls lined with books and paintings. Touring friends greeted me, some calling me "Schnookle." Neva appeared, kissed me, and Jacqueline shot a frosty glance.

At midnight, we crowded onto Billy's balcony. The roar of Times Square rose. I kissed Jacqueline, and she whispered, "We're going to go straight in '48, and you'll be mine in '49."

We caught a cab uptown to a party at the Wickham Arms. The apartment was packed, and I lost Jacqueline in the crowd. I sipped my drink, left hers untouched, and wandered, wishing I were home. Suddenly, Jacqueline burst in, pulling a young woman by the hand. "This is Mary," she announced. "She's an actress." Mary, a blonde, smiled warmly. "She's coming home with us," Jacqueline said.

By the time we climbed to our walkup, we were exhausted. Mary's theater gossip kept us laughing. Our apartment had two studio couches and a tiny bedroom with a cot. I offered to make up the cot for Mary, but neither answered. Jacqueline fixed drinks while I laid out sheets.

When I came back from the bathroom, Jacqueline and Mary sat, arms around each other. "I think I'll just sleep in the storeroom," I said. Jacqueline kissed me on the cheek, then Mary did too.

I closed the door, telling myself nothing was wrong, though I felt like an intruder in my own home. Soon, I heard Mary's voice through the wall, soft moans rising until I buried my head under the pillow and drifted into uneasy sleep.

The next morning, Mary moved in.

Jacqueline declared we were a family, she the mother, I the father, Mary the baby. "We are a unit," she insisted, "no one can break us up."

We were a unit, but the roles weren't so clear. Jacqueline left early for work, leaving Mary and me to our own devices. Mary's new show closed within a month.

When Jacqueline left for work, the apartment shifted. Mary and I drank coffee, talked theater, and sometimes walked around nude. But the idyll ended when Jacqueline returned, inspecting the apartment for signs of neglect and scolding me for not putting tops on the toothpaste.

Still, when *Antony and Cleopatra* closed and prepared to tour, I wrote Jacqueline from the train, telling her how much I missed our family.

But Jacqueline changed. Her bond with Mary deepened, her ambitions for us faded, and she stopped caring about appearances. When I brought her mascara for her lashes, she painted a mustache under her nose. After that, I said nothing more.

At home, nights were filled with moans from the next room, a reminder of the women's intimacy. I distracted myself with casual affairs, though my cramped quarters made it all very awkward.

The theater gave me camaraderie. Our dressing room was crowded with men swapping jokes. One tall, talentless actor bragged about getting so many fan letters. We voted him the least likely to succeed. His name was Charlton Heston, and he became as famous as Marlon.

A snowstorm blanketed the city during the run. After the show, we escorted Miss Cornell home through the empty, glittering streets. We laughed and sang, and for once her isolation vanished, replaced by a youthful radiance. I never saw her so alive again.

On tour in Boston, I stayed at my parents' house. It was a mistake. They unleashed all the old disapprovals. I wasn't saving, wasn't planning for children, had promised stardom and delivered mediocrity. My father's words cut deepest: "You've been in New York for five years, and you're nowhere near a star." I left relieved to move on.

Backstage, I got to know Katharine Cornell. We often waited together before the curtain. One night, I mentioned a piece of news, and she recoiled: "I don't want to hear about it. I can't read the papers. I get so upset I can't act."

When Ted, the actor who shared my opening scene, was hospitalized, I accompanied him. Before the matinee, Miss Cornell summoned me to her chaise, pressed me for details, then handed me a small wooden dachshund. "Give this to him," she said, "and tell him I'm thinking of him."

The next evening, she called me to her dressing room before the show. "They said Ted will be all right. Did you give him the dachshund?"

"Yes," I told her. "He held it all through the operation."

Great tears rolled from her eyes. In that moment, Katharine Cornell was more real, more human, than I had ever seen her on stage.

***

The four flights of stairs to Jacqueline's apartment, though I still couldn't bring myself to call it mine, felt steeper than ever. I stumbled into the room and collapsed into the one comfortable chair, staring at the unmade beds and the breakfast dishes scattered across the table. The mess was proof of the morning's rush to get Jacqueline and Mary to the ship. I told myself I'd clean it all up, but for the moment, I just sat, breathing heavily.

A scrap of tissue paper peeked out from under one of the beds, leftover from our packing. I pulled it out and crushed it in my hand, as though I were closing a chapter of my life. Perhaps, in a way, I was. Maybe this was the beginning of something new. I told myself I'd sleep in that room now, on the better mattress, and start over.

The image of the ship still floated in my mind, drifting toward the Narrows. I could taste the champagne they'd served in paper cups, its sweetness clashing with my growing melancholy. Nine months. That was how long the three of us had lived in each other's pockets. Despite Jacqueline's new role as the imperious one, ordering Mary and me about, I would miss her. I had grown to depend on her, not just emotionally, but financially as well. Sharing bills had brought a sense of stability. Now I faced the rent alone, except for the half Jacqueline promised to keep sending. Abandoned was too strong a word, but the silence of the apartment made me feel it all the same.

At first, I had thought Jacqueline's talk of Europe was idle fancy. But she never let it go. "I want to live in Rome with Mary," she told me again and again. "It's the only time in our lives we'll be able to do it. I want to learn Italian and write a book."

One day, she simply resigned from her producer's office and set her plan in motion. Her parents disapproved, of course, but Jacqueline barreled past them, determined to live the life she had imagined. I didn't argue. What right had I? If people asked, I smiled and said I was thrilled she was finally going back to writing. I told them she had real talent. I had read her earlier novel, never published, which began with the line: *In New York City, no matter what you are doing, somebody else is doing it at the same time.* A sharp observation, I thought. The book was about her affair with a married woman, not easy to publish at that time.

Still, I wondered if I had somehow driven her away. Perhaps Europe wasn't an adventure but an escape. That thought returned as I remembered our summer on Fire Island. The stage manager from *Antony and Cleopatra* had asked me to perform two light comedies, *The Male Animal* and *The Vinegar Tree*, at the Robin Hood Theatre. I relished the roles, particularly the Thurber play, which had me teasing a man of forty: "Oh, that time when all is over and love has turned to kindliness." At 22, age 40 felt like the end of the road. When the run ended, Jacqueline insisted we share a cottage at Cherry Grove for August. "We can make it work," she said, her favorite phrase.

Cherry Grove was already attracting a certain crowd—gay men, artists, the fashionable Avedons. Our roommates included Irene Selznick's assistant Irving Schneider, his current and former partners, and Clinton Wilder, another producer, now coupled again. A strange mix, almost like a farce. The four rooms held two couples, Jacqueline and Mary, and me alone. Doors stayed shut. The household felt secretive, partitioned. I drifted between them, lonely even in company.

Jacqueline ran into Brando one day and, of course, he ended up on our couch. He was as aloof and filthy as ever, and I ignored him. Meals with Jacqueline and Mary were worse; their bond only deepened. When they took me to the local bar, a converted barn with music and dancing, I felt even more on the outside. I told Jacqueline I wanted to leave early. Her answer was to fling her martini at me. Glass shattered across the floor. Conversation stopped. Our roommate, Clinton, rushed to demand an explanation, but I had none to give. I only knew Jacqueline wanted me gone without admitting it. Europe was her escape route.

Back in the city, I returned to the grind. The weather was colder now, but my new coat with its cheap fur collar softened the rounds of rejections. "Nothing today" was the refrain from every office. The only respite was the Liebling-Wood agency, where Jacqueline had once worked. They were among the few who showed me warmth. Bill Liebling was wiry, energetic, with the look of a retired jockey. Miss Wood, elegant but stern, addressed everyone by surname as if to keep the world at arm's length. Tennessee Williams was her client, enough responsibility for anyone.

Usually, I had to plead my way in, but this time Liebling greeted me with unusual warmth. "Just the man I wanted to see," he said. My heart leapt. He handed me a thick script, a rough translation of the French play *The Madwoman of Chaillot* by Jean Giraudoux. "It's a big hit in Paris. De Liagre is producing it here. He'll direct, too. They're adapting it, but there's a boy in it you might be right for."

The translation was stiff and dull, but I saw the possibility. I auditioned, then auditioned again. Five times I was called back, each reading opposite the stage manager, who spoke in a lifeless monotone. My most important scene was meant to be with the star, where her character convinces mine to embrace life after a suicide attempt. Against the drone of the stage manager, I struggled to summon emotion. But my desperation to prove myself—five years in New York and little to show for it—poured out. Tears came easily.

Still, De Liagre dismissed me with the usual, "Thank you, we'll be in touch." Each time, those words stabbed like knives. Why keep calling me back if they meant nothing? It felt like torture. On the way home, I stopped to tie my coat belt and noticed a man selling bittersweet, the bright orange berries glowing in the cold air.

"How much?" I asked.

"Thirty-five cents," he said.

I walked away. Thirty-five cents was dinner at the Automat. I couldn't afford a handful of bittersweet. My eyes filled with tears. After five years, this was where I was: alone in a walkup, waiting for the phone to ring, unable to buy even the cheapest symbol of nature.

***

The Belasco Theatre always struck me as eerie, even with actors and crew bustling. Its shadows whispered of a grander time. People said David Belasco haunted the place, drifting about in his cassock. Some claimed to see a ghostly woman in the wings. I didn't believe in ghosts, but as I waited for the star, I kept glancing into the gloom, expecting judgment from the rafters.

We'd been called back from lunch, but rehearsal stalled. The work light swung above the stage, too dim to make anything feel real. Actors sat scattered, waiting. Martita Hunt had yet to appear. Yesterday, too tired from the ship, the stage manager read her lines. We slogged through the play, hoping the star would electrify it.

I sat beside Leora Dana, cast as my love interest. She was delicate and understated, her beauty never fully captured in photos. Her husky, sorrow-tinged voice could mesmerize. I noticed her restless fingers worrying at her nails.

"What's the matter?" I asked softly.

She gave me a sidelong look. "I'm terrified Martita Hunt won't like me. She can have us fired in five days."

The thought struck me cold. Until then, I'd been relieved to be cast, imagining myself secure. Martita hadn't seen any of us; if she didn't approve, I could be gone by tomorrow.

"Why wouldn't she like you?" I tried to sound confident. "De Liagre hired us; he knows what he's doing."

Leora shook her head. "She was frightening in *Great Expectations*. Brilliant, but frightening."

I bent over my script, hiding my unease. Leora had her soliloquy, but I faced greater risk: two pivotal scenes opposite Martita. If she decided I was wrong, there'd be no appeal.

The air shifted, like leaves before a storm. A door creaked open. A low, unmistakably British voice rang out: "I'm Martita Hunt." It wasn't loud, but it carried through the theatre.

De Liagre sprang up to greet her. She entered, draped in black, every movement deliberate. She pulled back her veil, revealing her famous, sharp profile. She was younger and more vital than Miss Havisham—tall, straight, and red-haired.

We paraded before her. Each actor announced a role. "Ah, yes," she murmured, moving on. When she stopped before me, her eyes fixed on mine.

"You're my little Pierre." The words, simple and almost tender, hit me like a reprieve.

We began reading. She sat stiffly, spine straight, eyes darting from actor to actor. I stumbled through my lines, terrified. At the break, I fled to the stage edge, lit a cigarette, and tried to steady myself. A sharp scent drifted toward me. She glided closer, eyes cool, lips set in disdain.

"I'm at the Stanhope Hotel," she said. "Be there after rehearsal." She was gone before I could respond.

Her suite smelled of smoke and Scotch. She paced, wrapped in a blue dressing gown, hair in a kerchief, face slick with cold cream—stripped of glamour.

"I won't do it," she burst out, pacing faster. "I'll take the next boat back to England!"

I sat in silence, afraid to speak, afraid her fury would turn on me.

"How dare they?" she whirled, glaring. "They've given me actors who mimic my tone. I can't perform like this. I'm not a star." She paused, waiting for contradiction. I considered saying, "But you are, Miss Hunt," but held my tongue.

"If they wanted a star, why didn't they get Peggy Ashcroft?" she demanded. "I'm a character actress! I need strong actors opposite me. Where did they find this lot?" Her eyes locked, daring me to answer.

"They auditioned many people," I said carefully.

"Auditions," she scoffed. "That director wouldn't know a good actor if he tripped over one. They all must go." Then, seeing my stricken face, she softened. "Not you. You're terrible, but at least they didn't give me some little queer boy. I can teach you."

The words struck. I bit my tongue. Part of me wanted to shout the truth—*I am that queer boy*—but I couldn't risk it.

She moved toward me, voice lowering. "There's something wrong with your back. Acting begins in the coccyx, propelling you forward. Stand up."

I obeyed. Her hands pressed my spine. "We stand on two feet, head lifted toward heaven, a breath from the angels." Her touch grew intimate. "Do you have a girlfriend?"

"I'm married," I said.

She withdrew her hands. "How sweet." She poured another Scotch. "Now go. Call me Martita. Not a word."

Outside, the cold air slapped my face. I looked up at the Stanhope. Her window glowed faintly. I could almost see her shadow.

"You're terrible," her voice echoed in my head.

I hailed a cab, still shaken, and returned to 53th Street and the apartment's silence.

***

I sat behind the Chez Francis set, trying not to hear the play. Lines leaked through, each one closer to my entrance. I told myself to focus, recalling yesterday's walk to the 59th Street Bridge to see what my character faced with a suicide attempt: just cold wind, the churn of the East River, the edge where despair might tip a body forward. I tried to touch that feeling, but instead, I now saw the house full of people waiting to judge me. Fear pinned me in place.

A low buzzing cut through the stage murmur. I opened my eyes: Martita stood in the wings, waiting for her cue, dressed as the Madwoman. The buzzing came from her half-open mouth—a sound she said could steady the soul. She looked both present and far away.

She must be as nervous as I am, I thought. The cue came. Applause. Her voice: "Year-ma. Are my bones ready?"

I had only moments left. Four weeks of rehearsals and no out-of-town tryout. Every day I expected to be fired. Leora muttered the same fear until she hired a press agent. Martita never fired anyone, but directed everyone, saving her longest lectures for me.

When she couldn't talk to me in person, Martita wrote notes: "My sweet boy, imagine you are lying on the back of a seagull. Do nothing, or remember, do not fight your boring Martie. Lie back in the arms of Jesus. Count sheep. Do not act." Still, the notes arrived.

I began to dread the doorman's message that Martita wanted to see me. The director seemed to hope the play would stumble into failure. I couldn't avoid Martita, so I stood by while she made up, complained, then circled back to my faults. The lectures paused only when she sipped Scotch. At dress rehearsal, I used pancake makeup. She took one look and snapped that I looked like one of Bebe Bérard's little boys. The makeup came off.

Two nights earlier, as she coaxed me back to life, tears streaked her face. The moment was written as joy, but liquor tipped it toward grief. The preview audience loved it. Now I heard laughter—she must be feeding her invisible birds. It was time.

The actor playing the policeman lifted me and carried me on. I closed my eyes, trying to forget the audience and be the boy who had failed at dying. He laid me on the bench. I aimed for quiet inside myself and was close to it when I heard my mother's cough—her signal at every performance.

The cue came. I opened my eyes and saw the grotesque figure beside me. I raised myself on one arm, as if waking in another world. Martita stood farther upstage than usual, and my neck cramped from angling toward her.

She began the speech that would become famous. To be alive is to be fortunate. The words rolled out in her deep voice as she spoke of mornings that did not feel gay, of hair from a drawer, teeth from a glass, of how out of place a body can feel. I breathed with the rhythm and let the sound reach me. When she ended with How does life seem to you now, my eyes filled. It seems marvelous, I said, and I meant it. Later, I learned that much of the audience had seen only the back of my head.

The rest of the act lurched forward. Martita was flustered. Props fell like hail. She thumped my back as I spoke, pointing at the floor, and I bent to retrieve whatever landed next. When she took my arm and we walked off to strong applause, I knew the ovation was for her.

After the final curtain, I changed quickly, and my mother rushed in with my aunt from San Francisco, both thrilled, both talking at once.

"I have never seen so many stars," my mother said.

My aunt held up a hand. "Wait until you hear. At intermission, your mother went up to Mary Martin and said, 'May I shake your hand?' Mary Martin shook it. As your mother backed away, I stepped in and said, 'That was the boy who is playing Pierre's mother.'"

I groaned. "What do you mean?"

"I'm sure she was glad to meet your mother," my aunt said.

Eleanor appeared, and my mother remembered her from the wedding, so she embraced her. Eleanor crossed to me and put her arms around my shoulders. Her collar brushed my neck, and a trace of perfume cut through the dressing room scent.

"You were wonderful," she said.

For a moment, I forgot the opening night, the clatter of props, and even Martita. "Thank you for coming," I said.

"I wouldn't have missed it," she replied.

Fifteen

I woke to the smell of smoke. Eleanor sat nearby, smoking and watching me.

"You slept well. You were exhausted," she said.

I pushed myself up. "What time is it?"

"Almost 8:00."

"I've got to get home," I said, starting to get up.

She held my arm. "Why? You have all day."

"Jacqueline's calling from Rome around ten for the reviews," I said. "I have to be there."

Eleanor looked disappointed. I touched her face. "I don't want to go," I said, pulling her close.

It felt natural to make love to her. After opening night at Sardi's, we were giddy. The play was a hit, and I had good reviews. I'd finally made it to Broadway in an important role, with enough money for rent and classes.

After we dropped my mother and aunt at their hotel, Eleanor said, "It's silly for you to go all the way downtown and then back to 53rd Street at this hour." Jacqueline made me promise to see her often while she was away, calling her the perfect sounding board.

During rehearsals, Eleanor and I often had dinner together. She helped me weather storms with Martita and made me stop blaming myself. That night, after a taxi ride, she asked, "Do you want a nightcap?"

Her apartment was spacious and cozy. She brought out champagne, and we laughed over my story of picking up Martita's endless props as she dropped them.

"Let's forget about *Madwoman*," I said. "Tell me about your day."

"I had my hair done," she teased. "And you didn't notice."

"I told you how beautiful you looked. Everyone said so."

"Forget I mentioned my hair."

She grew serious. "I had lunch with my father's partner. He wanted my psychiatric opinion about his condition. He's sick—suspicious, fearful, deluded. One in ten people who are like that spend time in a mental hospital. He should be there now, but won't go."

"Are you saying I need help?" I asked with a smile.

"I'm not going to answer that," she replied, smiling back.

She was smart in a way different from Jacqueline—grounded in deeper realities.

"I'd like to sit on your lap," she said.

I pulled her close, kissed her, and she pulled back at last.

"I have to go to the bathroom," she said. "Why don't you get undressed?"

***

The bus crawled up Madison Avenue. Snow lingered in corners. I checked my watch, jumped out at 64th, and waited until eleven at the address. I couldn't stop thinking of Eleanor, how proud I felt with her on my arm. At the party, she shone in her silver fox coat. Everyone praised Martita, who still barked at us, though less now that magazines photographed her. Her lover Arthur had arrived from England, prancing about in her feather boa. I hoped he'd stay, but he didn't.

The night before, we'd gone to an actor's performance of South Pacific. All of Broadway was there. From the first notes, actors applauded every moment. I held Eleanor's hand as Ezio Pinza sang "Some Enchanted Evening." Later, in her bed, we both gave in to that yearning. I didn't feel the same fire as with men, but told myself it might come.

When it was over, Eleanor cried. "That would have been the most beautiful baby," she whispered. I held her.

Now I found myself climbing the staircase of the gray stone house, where Doctor Byron waited. She led me to a high-ceilinged room with waxed floors and paintings. She motioned me to a sofa.

"What do I call you?" I asked nervously.

"What would you like to call me?"

"Doctor, or Doctor Byron, or—"

"Which would you rather?"

I laughed weakly. "It's really what you want."

"Sit there," she said, and I sank into the sofa.

She was pale, with wispy brown hair and a powder-white face. She studied me silently until I filled the air with questions she would not answer. Finally, she said, "Why don't we talk about why you're here. What do you want?"

"I thought Eleanor told you," I said.

"Eleanor has nothing to do with us. Only what you say matters."

"I guess I want to be cured," I admitted.

"Of what?"

"Of being homosexual. Eleanor must have told you."

"I want to hear it from you," she said evenly.

"I'd like not to be anymore."

"You're married."

"Yes. I love my wife very much, but not like I love Eleanor."

She sat straight, pad and pencil unused. I pulled out papers. "I brought you a dream," I said.

She regarded me coolly. "Since you arrived, you've tried to please me. Now you bring me a dream. Why don't you read it?"

I did. In it, Jacqueline and I wandered a park filled with children chasing movie stars. I longed for attention, but no one noticed me. Later, I stood with Eleanor by a small river with circular boats drifting by. I begged her to join me, and though she was pale, she agreed. Jacqueline swept past us, detached as always, while Eleanor and I searched for the river beneath a shining moon.

When I finished, Doctor Byron finally took notes. "Did you and your wife have sexual relations?"

"No," I said. "Not yet."

"I'm afraid our time is up. I'll see you Thursday."

***

Jacqueline and Mary stood at the railing, searching for me. I wanted to turn and disappear, but they waved. Mary blew kisses that I half-heartedly returned.

A traffic jam at the gangplank delayed them. When they reached me, Jacqueline cut me off. "We've got plenty of time to talk later. I've got to get the car, and there's not enough room for the luggage, so you'll have to take a cab."

She directed Mary and me to the suitcases. People shoved as if in a food line. I gathered everything, found a porter, and loaded it into a taxi. Jacqueline hurried Mary toward the cars, calling, "We'll see you at the apartment."

Bags were piled in the back seat with me. I felt trapped—rain poured in when I opened the window, and I sat sweating, restless, feeling I might suffocate.

To steady myself, I thought of Doctor Byron and my months of therapy. I had never questioned the marriage until the dream. With Jacqueline returning and bringing Mary, I had no clear idea how my life was supposed to work.

From Rome, Jacqueline wrote long letters about plans for when she and Mary returned. The winter was so cold that they rarely left their flat, and her novel stalled. I wrote back about the gym and quitting smoking and drinking. I could hardly tell her I was seeing her best friend and trying to become normal through therapy.

In Paris, Jacqueline's letters changed—full of instructions and criticisms, including lists of insurance policies to arrange. She criticized my self-denial, calling my efforts to quit smoking and drinking childish. She wrote, *If we make sense about closet space, the three of us will have no trouble.*

After reading it, I found myself singing, "If you leave Paris, you'll take away the sun." It made me smile.

In therapy, Doctor Byron asked if I'd been dreaming. "Nothing except a song," I said, then recited the lyrics: If you leave Paris, you'll take away the sun, the shining lights, the dazzling nights, the fun. She asked what it meant. I said, "It's just a love song. I must be in love with someone in Paris." She asked who. "Jacqueline, of course. She's there for a month. I guess I'm saying I love her and want her to come home."

"Are you?" she asked. "Doesn't the song say if she leaves, Paris will be destroyed?"

"Yes," I said. "Then I don't want her to leave Paris? Oh my god. I don't want her to come home." The realization left me silent.

The taxi pulled up on 54th Street. I hauled the bags upstairs, unlocked the door, and sat waiting.

I thought of calling Eleanor, but feared Jacqueline and Mary would walk in. I looked around the room that Jacqueline and I had worked so hard to make beautiful, the first real home I'd had in New York. The doorbell rang, and I ran down to help with the last bags.

"I had to put the car in a garage on 55th," Jacqueline said. Mary complimented me on how well I looked and was excited to see my play. They rushed around, talking over each other.

At last, I couldn't stand it. "I'm leaving you," I blurted out.

Jacqueline stopped. "You're what?"

"I'm not going to live with you anymore."

"Did Eleanor put you up to this?"

"Of course not. It was my idea."

She unzipped a suitcase. "We'll talk about it at dinner."

I pulled off the diamond ring Jacqueline had given me. "Take this back. I don't want to be married to you."

She hurled it at me. "Get out," she screamed.

Mary pleaded, "Jacqueline, don't, please."

I left and went to the furnished room I had rented days before. As I unpacked, I remembered Jacqueline had not given me my ring back. It didn't matter.

My new furnished room was the worst place I had lived in since coming to New York. The apartment belonged to an elegant widow who wanted company without conversation. Everything was cold and sedate, with stiff furniture and heavy draperies. I tiptoed in after the theater because she was always in bed. The hush and propriety reminded me of the relatives I had fled.

For a moment, I almost regretted leaving Jacqueline, but the feeling passed when the phone rang the next morning. Jacqueline's voice was steel. "Did you see the diamond ring you gave back to me?" "No," I said. "You threw it across the room." "I can't find it." She hung up. I never heard from her again about the ring. Then came annulment papers. Her parents wanted the marriage erased, claiming I had refused to have children. It was fiction, but I signed and sent them back.

I had cared for Jacqueline. She changed after we married—cutting her hair, living in jeans. Still, I don't think I invented the woman I first knew.

Before Europe, she wrote letters full of love. If she hadn't met Mary so quickly, perhaps things would have been different. But now my life revolved around Eleanor and Doctor Byron. I needed to get out of the widow's apartment. I posted a note at the stage door for a new place.

Ralph Roberts, who carried me onstage in *Madwoman*, told me about a one-room apartment in his building in the Village. I agreed to look after a matinee. Ralph, a gentle giant, became excellent at massage and lived with his dog Bridget, a Kerry Blue Terrier.

The apartment was in a converted brownstone where 4th meets 12th, near Abingdon Square. The basement unit had barred windows, a small stove, and a tiny refrigerator. The bathroom was cramped, but it was mine. The rent was $35. I put down the deposit and moved in.

While *Madwoman* ran, I hoped for a new play, but nothing came. Agents were kind, but there was never a role better than Pierre. So I stayed, listening to Martita tell me how marvelous life was eight times a week. I even played the Subway Circuit with Eleanora Mendelssohn. She was a lovely actress, but lacked Martita's edge. I missed the voltage of Martita's performance.

By the end of the run, Martita had eased up on me. Audiences adored her. When Leora left, Roberta Haynes took over and once raked her nails down my back during the final kiss. Martita, appalled, slapped her, and the audience roared.

After the show closed and Martita returned to England, I saw her only once at lunch at Sardi's. She was exquisitely dressed, charming, not a hint of the old tyrant. She joked that she longed to be beautiful and loved, but I knew it was no joke.

However elegant, she still suggested iron beneath silk. We promised to keep in touch, but didn't. Years later, I learned Martita had died in a fire, likely from drinking and smoking in bed. The papers called it asthma. I prefer to think she exited like Miss Havisham, in a blaze that matched her force.

Sixteen

The wind whipped across the lake, sending leaves over the icy path. Eleanor and I walked close together, bundled in coats, bracing for Chicago's cold.

We ignored the cold, laughing together. "I'll never forget it," Eleanor said, and we laughed again.

During *Madwoman*, I was asked to do a TV play at the local station. TV was new to me, but I wanted the experience, even without pay. Eleanor visited and came to watch.

We rehearsed on Friday, then rushed to *Madwoman*. Saturday, two shows. Sunday, we rehearsed and performed the TV play live. The drama was about two prisoners escaping Devil's Island; after years of breaking through the wall, only one escapes. My co-star was John Carradine, who also played the Ragpicker in *Madwoman*. During the live broadcast, Carradine altered our blocking to steal the shots.

It was just like Martita, upstaging me even after a year. But I fought back, watching the live camera and getting my face into the shot. Carradine caught on and tried to pull away, but I followed. The tension actually energized the scene.

In dress rehearsal, I broke through the plaster with a rock. But during the live show, the wall wouldn't break; the plaster had been put back too heavily. I hammered desperately, but no hole appeared. Carradine, meant to be too ill to help, joined me. Suddenly, a huge hole burst open, and a stagehand's arm shoved a sledgehammer through—visible to the entire TV audience.

We finished the play. When the director yelled cut, Carradine and I collapsed in laughter. The image of prisoners being "helped" from the outside became TV lore. We left the studio laughing. Eleanor had visited me in other cities, but never for this long. We toured Chicago, dined out, and lived like a couple.

I'd been staying at the YMCA to save money, but now had a small apartment on the North Side. One evening, we ran into an actress I knew who was in town for a pre-Broadway tryout. She rushed over, ignoring Eleanor.

"Oh, just the man I want," she said. "I'm having trouble with this part, and I thought you could help."

I introduced Eleanor and said I'd be glad to help. "Could you come up to my room now?" she asked.

"Maybe for a little while," I said. Eleanor kicked me. "Tomorrow would be better," I added.

"But that may be too late," the actress protested. "I'm sorry," I replied. "It's just not possible."

In the elevator, Eleanor's anger was obvious. I reached over to stroke her head. She swung her purse at me. "Don't do that to me again," she snapped. "I'm not a dog to be patted."

"I'm sorry," I said. "She asked for help. What did I do that was so wrong?"

She didn't answer. We got off. Back in the apartment, I sat smoking while Eleanor noisily packed, still furious.

Part of me was relieved. I cared for her, but life with Eleanor left me claustrophobic. Intimacy felt like duty, not joy. I couldn't shed my true self, no matter how hard I tried. Eleanor was disappointed when I quit Doctor Byron's analysis. Besides leaving Jacqueline, two years of her "just listening" had done nothing for me. Something unspoken lingered between us; I knew it couldn't be ignored.

Eleanor walked in wearing her white silk pajamas and blue robe. "Are you still angry?" I asked.

"You hate it when I get emotional," she said. "You're afraid to express your feelings. One day, you'll learn to indulge your emotions without fear. They're real when they're there, and no one could ask for more."

She lit a cigarette. "If you question your emotions, you miss the moment. To experience anything—fear, anger, love—you must be without defenses."

I waited, then said, "You know that girl didn't mean anything to me."

"Don't you know why I was angry?" Eleanor asked. "It's my last night with you, and you were going to spend it helping some little nothing with her silly part."

"Actually, she's a very good actress," I said. "I don't care if she's Helen Hayes, you still don't get it."

She began pacing. "I wasn't going to say this. I planned to write, but maybe it's better this way. I'm going to live in Paris."

"Eleanor, isn't that a bit dramatic just because I talked to a girl?"

She took my hands. "I love you, and I thought I could go on making no demands and be happy. I never told you—one night, when you said you couldn't see me, I saw you at Five Oaks with the handsome boy I call the jack o' lantern. You looked so happy. I left before you saw me and cried in the street."

I tried to put my arm around her. "No, don't," she said. "It's all right. We never had a commitment. I cared so much it was worth it." We felt awkward, so she sat on the sofa and I perched opposite.

"You know I've always said real love is when two people are equals," she said. "That's not us."

"But I do love you," I said.

"I need more than that," Eleanor said softly.

She looked away, then said, "I want to get married. I want children."

Panic surged. I saw the life she imagined: a suburban street, children, the same kitchen every night. I suddenly felt as if I were being suffocated.

Eleanor studied my face. "I know it's not in the cards for us," she said. "But I'm going to live abroad, where I can't see you. One of my maxims is, 'You finally get what you want.' And I'm going to go in search of it." I sat beside her and held her as tightly as I could.

Eleanor went to Paris and vanished. She'd married a count who was much older than her. They had no children, and later Eleanor opened an antiques shop.

Years later, in Paris, I called Eleanor, and she met me with her husband. She looked elegant, gray at the temples. When her husband left, she took me to the train. I kissed her cheek. She burst into tears and walked beside my train, crying, until the platform ended—and so did we.

Madwoman closed, and the Subway Circuit ended. Summer was too late for stock. Television opened a door. I played Roderigo in *Othello* live with Torin Thatcher, directed by Delbert Mann.

I worked on my basement apartment: built shelves, a bed that became a sofa, a desk with a tile top to hold flowers, and I hung a screen to conceal the kitchen. Still a cave below the sidewalk, but mine.

Then I got an audition for *The Marble Faun*. I skimmed Hawthorne and drew on both my *Hamlet* self and the man who'd starved through winters. The reading went well. Anna Lee played opposite me; we fell a little in love, but she was married and commuting from the country. She nearly stayed in town to be with me, but we realized it was madness and stayed friends.

The dress rehearsal was perfect. I can still hear the Richard Strauss that opened the broadcast. For once, I wasn't scared of lines or light cues. I was Donatello in Rome, meeting the woman I loved. We finished to a curtain call, the camera panning faces. Later, I learned Wesley Addy went to the hospital after a fall on a mat jarred his arm. It was minor. We all congratulated each other and, since there was no Sardi's or morning papers, we just went home.

A few days later, my agent called. Mrs. Goldwyn had seen the show and told her husband I was going to be a movie star. He was flying in to meet me about *Hans Christian Andersen*, which was to star Danny Kaye. I shook so hard I could barely hold the phone.

I wore my best suit. Mr. Goldwyn opened his own door and spoke as if I already had the part. His wife thought I was a dancer because of the tights in the broadcast; he needed an actor, not a dancer. Nervous, I explained the tights were the director's idea, that I was an actor, not a dancer. He patted my hand and said he'd ordered the kinescope. He was sure I was as good as his wife said.

I rode the elevator down, replaying everything I'd said. Days later, the agent was gentle: Goldwyn liked me, but I'd have to play opposite Danny Kaye, and my nose was as big as Danny's. He couldn't have two large noses in one frame. Farley Granger got the part.

I hung up and thought of my grandmother. I remembered asking her if I was good-looking enough. "Your nose is too big," she said. That nose had been praised onstage, but the screen is a harsher mirror. The truth wasn't my nose—it was my panic in that room. I walked in an actor and turned into a beggar. Life is full of missed opportunities, I thought. That would make a good printed pillow for my bed.

***

Sandy Meisner accepted me into his professional class at the Neighborhood Playhouse. I worked days, but twice a week with Sandy felt like the best training in the world. He joked that when I made it, I'd fly him to my Hollywood villa and we'd swim in my pool. Years later, friends brought him to my house in Los Angeles. There was a pool, but cancer had taken his larynx and he barely remembered me.

In class, Sandy was both ruthless and generous. He could praise you as God's gift and then tear you apart. We were all terrified. I stalled before every exercise, lighting a cigarette I didn't want. Another student walked around the room until he could begin. Sandy let us dawdle, then barked one word: Relax.

All the actors were a gift. Joan Lorring, fresh from an Oscar nomination, joined because she wanted to work onstage. She called herself Dellie and made acting look easy. She once overheard women watching her movie whisper that the girl should have her nose fixed. Joan said laughingly, "I wanted to lean over and tell them I have.

Dellie became a friend and cooked Chinese food from her childhood growing up in the Orient. On Broadway in *The Autumn Garden*, she called in sick so her understudy, Gaby Rodgers, could go on. Gaby was superb. Her neckline, cut low for Dellie, threatened to give the audience more than her performance, but gravity did not win.

Gaby changed my life twice. She was seeing photographer Jerry Cooke, and when he needed an assistant, she recommended me. The mornings paid my rent while I rehearsed nights. Later, she found me an illegal walkup over Healy's Bar. The bathtub and toilet were in the bedroom; you washed your hands in the kitchen. A former tenant had painted a long letter of hate to his lover across the wall. I covered it with paint and hoped the room would remember love was possible.

I had kept my basement place in the Village long enough to make it livable. Friends sat on the floor to watch me on *Man Against Crime*. My neighbor Ralph Roberts became family. We threw a garden party to lure casting people, but forgot chairs, so we scavenged and painted them green. The paint dried to the touch, not to clothes. The next day, everyone left with stripes on their backs—a Schnookle mistake, talked about more than any job offer.

Work dribbled in. Billy Nichols, my *Hamlet* friend, got me into *Hit Parade* sketches. I never sang or spoke, only partnered Dorothy Collins or Giselle McKenzie, and the Times critic wrote a column on my pantomime but didn't use my name, unfortunately. Barbara Ames and I auditioned with Method backstories, but no one cared. She was close to Philip Loeb; when the blacklist drove him to suicide, it broke her heart. Dellie kept working and married. Ralph stayed as an actor but learned massage and ended up taking care of Marilyn Monroe. Gaby was the bright spot.

She was funny and fragile, in analysis forever. One night, she called at two a.m. She had taken a cab to Bellevue to put herself in the booby hatch. They made her wait until her fury replaced her fear; she stormed out and told me the story until we cried with laughter. Another time, she met the actress Edna Best in a home for the mentally disturbed and asked what she did all day. "I paint a little," Miss Best said. Gaby said she longed to go to the same place and paint. "Oh no, my dear, don't consider it—the brushes are not very good."

Between Jerry's photographic shoots, *Hit Parade* sketches, and Sandy's classes, I began to feel like a working actor who might become an artist. I learned to hear 'Relax' as both command and affection. Friends could carry you when the industry would not. In my new apartment above Healy's Bar, with the hateful letter sealed beneath paint, I told myself that if I kept at it, the next words on those walls would be happy ones of mine.

I ended my first year on television with *A Child Is Born*, a Christmas play in which I played Joseph. The drama centered on innkeepers opening their door to Joseph and Mary. The broadcast struck such a chord that we were asked to repeat it for the next two Christmases. Because it was live, each year we performed it again from scratch.

The winter that followed was lean, but suddenly offers came. I played the brother of the mad wife in *Jane Eyre*. Rehearsals turned into a love fest thanks to Viola Roche, a veteran British actress in her eighties, who told outrageous stories and kept us laughing. She brought her dog "Sal" to rehearsals, to which the director objected.

"Oh, don't be silly," she said, "Sal loves *Jane Eyre*." One of my favorite things she said at her advanced age was "Oh Ducky, it's no nice not to want fucking anymore."

Soon I was cast on the *Philco Playhouse*, playing a prisoner in the South and later a young Irishman opposite Una O'Connor on *Studio One*. I then played young Oscar Hammerstein in a tribute sketch. When

Sullivan introduced the real Hammerstein, he joked that I was better-looking than he had ever been, and the audience roared. Hammerstein recited "The Last Time I Saw Paris," and the audience was moved to tears.

In the fall came my most important role yet: the lead in Galsworthy's *Justice* for Kraft Television. I played a young Englishman who forged a check and was condemned to solitary confinement. Director Stanley Quinn let me find my own choices. For the scene of near-madness, he had a real cell built, sealed from the studio. Alone inside, I drew on memories of shame and ended up pounding the walls, screaming to be let out.

During rehearsal, Stanley whispered to the cameramen, "This is the masturbation scene." He understood without my telling him. The performance went flawlessly, and the cast and crew applauded when it ended. For days afterward, strangers stopped me in the street, as if I had just played on Broadway.

There were more shows: *Coriolanus* for *Studio One*, with Richard Greene; *The Idol of San Vittore* with Maria Riva, Marlene Dietrich's daughter. I met her in the hallway, praised her appearance, and she said, "Oh, I always bake bread for the cast and crew." I hadn't mentioned bread at all.

My final job that year was opposite Janet De Gore in Booth Tarkington's *The Wren*. After months of heavy drama, it was a joy to play a light romantic comedy. We sparkled together, and the audience loved it. It was a cheerful end to my first full year in television, one that began with a manger and ended with a romance.

Seventeen

Television brought recognition, but stage auditions were few and far between. Theater agents saw me as "classical." TV let me play every type; I began to believe I could do anything.

A casting director called: "Be here to audition at 3:00. You're reading for a 12-year-old boy who believes in Santa Claus." I worked for hours. I thought I could raise my voice to sound young but what could I do to seem like I believed in Santa Clause? Fortunately, the casting director called and said he'd contacted the wrong actor. I had to laugh at my being so ready to play any role.

I played Joseph of Arimathea and then Chopin opposite Sarah Churchill. The plot was improbable but charming. I mimed piano while others played. Reviews were good.

On *Man Against Crime*, I played a murderer. The director just told me when to look up or down. The camera made me convincing—film shapes as much as the actor.

I joined the summer theater in Olney, Maryland, sharing an apartment with actor, Geoffrey Barr. It was better than sweating in NYC.

The first play was a French farce starring Eva Gabor. My part was small. I discovered her gowns were padded, reminders not to believe appearances. Maurice Evans had worn an undergarment as Hamlet to give himself bigger legs and a bigger chest.

The second play, William Inge's *Come Back, Little Sheba*, starred Joan Blondell. She was unpretentious and friendly, perfect for the role.

She breakfasted with the company and told bawdy stories about her ex-husband Dick Powell and his new wife, full of bitterness and humor.

The third play changed my life: *The Happy Time*, a hit Broadway coming-of-age story. I played the rakish uncle, a womanizer with a French accent. The boy's mother was played by Mary Fickett. We spent evenings together, and one chilly night, Mary and I huddled together in the rumble seat of Geoffrey's car. Hugging became kissing, and an affair began that lasted five years.

Mary and I began planning our return to New York when Ken Banghart called. The next play starred Luise Rainer in S. N. Behrman's *Biography*. The actor opposite her was leaving. Would I take over? I was thrilled. Rainer had won back-to-back Oscars. To be onstage with her would be extraordinary.

Banghart said I had to read for her, though she'd seen my photo and thought I looked right. If it went well, I'd open in Easthampton. Mary was disappointed, but knew I couldn't turn it down.

My role was an angry young writer who scorns writing a biography of a woman only to fall in love with her. I'd heard rumors Rainer was "difficult," but gossip swirled around all stars. I remembered the director Bobby Lewis telling me he had taken Miss Rainer to dinner and afterwards to see the view on Mulholland Drive, Rainer looked at the sky and said, "Look at all those stars, and I am a star."

She arrived late for our reading, tiny but brimming with energy. Without an apology, she complained about everything, then turned to me as if I had kept *her* waiting. "Shall we begin? I have things to do."

I picked up the script while she recited from memory. It was unsettling to read while she performed, but I adjusted. After a few pages, she stopped. "It's all right. You don't have the character, but we have a week. I will help you."

"Won't the director be here?" I asked.

"I am the director," she said, daring me to object.

The week that followed was excruciating. Each rehearsal was delayed while she took calls or invented business to get attention during my scenes. Even her entrance was contrived. Some nights the audience applauded; other nights, silence lingered until she muttered, "What's the matter? Don't they ever go to the movies?"

By the time we reached Easthampton, the theater was nearly empty. Within days, the tour was canceled. The relief was enormous. Only later did I realize the actor I replaced had refused to endure her. Even if I'd been warned, I would have taken the part. The lesson was one I already knew: stars are not always wonderful people.

Life with Mary was a change and mostly happy. We spent nearly all our time together. By chance, she shared an apartment with Neva Patterson, the first woman I had slept with—something neither of us mentioned to Mary. The two were opposites. Once, a man called with obscene commands; Mary called out, "Neva, it's for you!"

Mary was deeply sexual but kept it hidden. To the world, she looked wholesome and poised. Our schedules differed, so we eventually agreed on certain nights together, mostly weekends.

Money was tight, so we cooked at home. An actor friend helped me fix up the flat, and Ken Banghart sold me elegant stage furniture from a closed show. The apartment finally looked impressive.

With Mary, I felt part of respectable society, which I never did with men. We were welcomed at parties, and casting people actually treated me differently. Yet I still wrestled with my attraction to men.

Meanwhile, television shifted as stars from Hollywood crowded in, taking roles I might have had. The phone stopped ringing. My father urged me to try selling insurance. I resisted until work dried up. After playing a diminished part in Maurice Evans's TV version of *Hamlet,* I gave in. The insurance company trained me in a polished sales pitch. My acting helped me top the class, but I hated the work. I drove all over the city, selling to families who could barely afford insurance. I felt guilty and depressed.

Time with Mary dwindled. My days were split between Jerry's photography office, insurance calls, acting classes, and gym. At Bobby Lewis's workshop, we studied Sean O'Casey, but I lost the role I wanted.

When Gaby offered me a part off-Broadway in James Merrill's *The Bait*, I jumped at it. Neither of us understood the play, and opening night sent Arthur Miller and Dylan Thomas bolting for the exit.

I was exhausted, spread too thin, and frustrated. Then came an escape: Charlton Heston was starring in *Macbeth* in a fort on Bermuda, directed by Burgess Meredith. They offered me Malcolm. I accepted immediately.

The island was paradise—bright cottages, lush gardens, cool breezes. Heston, now a star, greeted me warmly. Burgess kept rehearsals light. My role was small, but I felt lucky and, for once, carefree.

The locals clamored for tickets. Opening night lived up to *Macbeth's* reputation as a cursed play. A gale howled through the fort, we dressed by flashlight, and lines were lost to the wind. The storm blew Lady Macbeth's dummy back onstage after she had supposedly died, and a fiery finale sent smoke over the audience.

Yet the production was hailed a success, thanks to Heston's fame. On our last night, Bill Dana performed a comic abridgment of *Macbeth* with the wind obliterating most of the lines. It brought down the house. Cursed or not, Bermuda had been a triumph and, for me, a much-needed reprieve.

While I was in Bermuda, Mary called because she had been cast as Deborah Kerr's understudy in *Tea and Sympathy*. It was an auspicious start. The play was a hit, but Mary and I saw less of each other.

One day, a new actor joined the workshop—strikingly handsome, confident yet aloof. Eventually, I spoke to him: his name was Jim. He was a model transitioning to acting. I brought him into our circle, and soon he was sitting with Mary and me every session.

It was inevitable. Jim was everything I wanted to be. My attraction deepened, and even though I was still with Mary, Jim and I became lovers. It didn't last. He refused to commit, resenting my ties to Mary, while I resented his nightlife. We argued constantly.

Once Jim asked, "Notice anything different about me?" He'd had a blemish removed. No one could have seen any difference, but his vanity was too much. The imbalance between us became unbearable. After one drunken quarrel, I burned his photograph and prayed not to see him again. My prayer was answered.

Mary and I drew closer, especially after her father died. Mary grieved deeply and leaned on me. I began joining her and her mother for dinner. Her mother wasn't fond of me, but she and I made the effort.

I was cast in a new play by V.R. Lang, retelling Orpheus and Eurydice in an amusement park. It ran only a week, but I enjoyed it. I never forgot one absurd line: "Later in their love, she learned to play the glockenspiel."

Soon after, director Iza Itkin offered me Oedipus in Jean Cocteau's *The Infernal Machine*. Playing Oedipus was thrilling—brash youth at the start, a broken king at the end. For the blinding scene, I used ketchup around my eyes, but the spices burned badly. The *Times* gave us a rave, but a newspaper strike meant no one saw it, and we closed. I always regretted losing that showcase.

Meanwhile, Mary's career shifted. When Deborah Kerr fell ill, Mary went on in *Tea and Sympathy* and triumphed. She played a married woman who sleeps with a troubled student to "cure" him of homosexuality, a plot that today feels appalling but then was taken seriously. Elia Kazan attended her debut and wrote a glowing piece in *The New York Times*. It changed her career overnight.

Then came the call. Mary's voice was cool: she didn't want to see me anymore. I pressed her, and after a silence, she said, "I know all about Jim." I was stunned. I thought I had been careful. She wouldn't listen when I insisted it was over. "You broke us up," she said. "Don't try to reach me again." She hung up.

I was crushed, knowing it was my fault. I realized then that a double life is never fair. But wanting men was part of me, and I didn't know how to stop.

At that low point, Jerry Cooke offered salvation: assignments for *Life* and *Time* in Europe. He needed me as an assistant and driver. Mary wouldn't take my calls, so I leapt at the chance. Chrysler loaned us a car, and I sailed with it to Paris to meet Jerry.

It was dusk when I docked, and I spoke barely a word of French. I lurched through villages yelling "Ou est Paris?" until, at last, the Eiffel Tower appeared. Paris—an impossible dream—was suddenly mine.

***

My tiny room at the Pont Royal overlooked the Eiffel Tower. It felt like a miracle to be there.

Jerry's favorite Paris spot was a kosher deli; I hid my disappointment. Billy Nichols gave me $100 for a Paris dinner. I spent it alone at Le Grand Véfour, eating the best meal of my life.

We crossed into Italy for Jerry's Chrysler shoot at Ghia. Giorgio, the factory head, invited us to dinner—not at his home, but at a raucous restaurant with staff, endless courses, and a "nightcap."

We were driven to a parlor where women in kimonos played cards. Giorgio clapped: "My treat. Who chooses first?" Jerry was pushed upstairs. "Alan, your turn."

I chose the plainest girl out of pity. She barked, "Pagare... il tempo," scrubbed me, then lay flat staring at the ceiling. It ended quickly. Back downstairs, someone said, "Alan, like Alan Ladd." My girl replied and they translated, "If only it had been Alan Ladd." I swiped a card from her solitaire game and kept it for years.

The next morning, Giorgio assembled half the factory to see us off and urged Jerry to let me drive. I turned the key—BOOM, a smoke bomb detonated. Laughter, applause, and hugs. "If only you could have seen your face," Giorgio said. We left for Rome.

The seven-hour drive ended in blazing sun: Colosseum, Spanish Steps. My room at the d'Angleterre had a terrace. Jerry had his own plans; I was happy to be in Rome alone. The concierge suggested *Aida* at the Baths of Caracalla if he could get a ticket, then sent me to Otello for carbonara. A bellboy arrived mid-meal with an envelope: one ticket.

The opera was pure spectacle. At intermission, I noticed a small circle around one of the handsomest men I'd ever seen. I stared at the group, but no one paid any attention to me. After the show, I went to a place I'd heard of, Victor's on the Via Veneto. The man from the opera was at the bar.

He saw me and walked over. "I saw you at the opera. American?"

"New York," I said. He laughed when I told him all I'd seen of the city was the Coliseum. "Come, I'll show you Rome by night."

As we left, the bartender called out, "Addio, Principe."

He shrugged. He said his family still used their titles but he was just Alessandro, a writer living near Florence. He drove me through Rome, showing me the sights, each lit up like a stage. We drew closer without touching; I basked in his beauty and quiet pride. Two last stops: Trevi Fountain—he pressed a coin into my palm. Then the Aventine and the "most beautiful keyhole in Rome." Through the Knights of Malta door, a tunnel of greenery framed St. Peter's dome. It gave me a chill.

"It's 2:00," he said. "Your hotel won't let me stay with you. I am visiting friends, so we can't go there. It's better. I have to leave early for Florence, and you are off to Capri. Better to leave it a dream than a reality."

He was right. I gave him a silver ring. "Take this so you remember how you gave me Rome."

At the entrance to my hotel, we looked at each other for a moment. I walked toward the door, turned back. The car hadn't moved. I touched my fingers to my lips and went inside.

Jerry and I drove to Naples and took a boat to Capri. The day was bright, the water rough; we were seasick until it calmed. The real thrill was the Faraglioni. The captain shot the boat through the opening, the sun burned, spray hit my face, and I felt free.

Our first stop was La Canzone del Mare, Gracie Fields' club with a public pool. Jerry needed two striking girls by the pool; I found them. He handed me a swimsuit and posed me with the girls—my debut for *Life Magazine*. He later shot me leaping into the Blue Grotto and waterskiing in Positano. All three ran in *Life*.

Italy was a blur of hauling gear, chasing captions, and racing the light—Naples to Lake Como to Cortina d'Ampezzo. After two weeks, we pushed on to Trieste and Yugoslavia, working south from Lake Ohrid to Titograd.

When Jerry was called to Istanbul, someone had to stay with the car and the equipment. I was left in Titograd. Our hotel was grim. "How will I eat?" I asked. "No one speaks English."

"The maître d' does," Jerry said. When I asked him if he spoke English, his only word was "small" and that was all I heard for the week.

I couldn't read the papers or find a book in English, and hesitated to wander where I couldn't ask directions. Titograd had been bombed to rubble; what stood was new or under construction. I felt like an outcast.

After days in the colorless hotel, I drove into the mountains with a picnic. The kitchen gave me hard-boiled eggs, bread, and a nameless bottle. Out of town, an old car smashed into mine. A dozen people poured out, shouting. The right side was gouged. They tried to rub the scrape away. I tried sign language: your fault.

"Police," I said.

"No polis," they cried.

Everything still worked, so I waved them on. Several kissed my hand. Back at the hotel, no one understood my plea for a body shop. I gave up. That evening, a tall man approached, pantomimed a crash, and led me to the promenade. He flashed a red card: "Communist." With gestures, he promised to fix the car for $35. I cashed the travelers' checks, handed him the money, and keys; he promised to return in two or three days.

I saw him around town; he beamed each time. On the third day, still no car. I found him and insisted I was leaving. "Ready," he said, and ran off.

An hour later, he pulled up. The scrape remained, slathered with mismatched paint. A young woman arrived, unloaded food from the trunk, and left. He patted the scar proudly, shook my hand, and left. I figured he'd painted the car and spent the rest impressing his girlfriend.

I parked and decided to ask Jerry to dock my pay for a proper repair.

That night I went to settle my bill. The cashier, a woman with a pencil in her hair, counted my checks, then looked up. "Is no good, Titograd. You go back United States."

"You speak English!" I cried. "Why didn't you say anything? I needed help."

"You a baby," she said. "Go home where you belong." She turned back to her ledger.

Jerry arrived the next day and was wonderful about the car. We didn't need it, and he'd already been told to dispose of it in Rome before we flew home.

I was in Rome again, this time not just overnight. Jerry didn't mind if I stayed; he handed me money for the fare home.

"Stay a week if you want," he said. "New York's dead now."

It was midsummer, the slowest time for work. After seeing Jerry and the equipment onto the plane, I returned to the d'Angleterre Hotel. If I were careful, I could afford a week. Billy Nichols had given me a guidebook; I made a list of what to see.

By then, it was too late for museums, but the Via Veneto was the place at cocktail hour. I took a cab to the Excelsior, ordered a Negroni, and watched the crowd. Glamorous women and well-dressed young men strolled—a bazaar where flesh was the commodity.

I thought of Alessandro. Nothing had happened, which made the memory sweeter. He proved such men existed. Someday, I might find someone who completed my "half of the apple."

Then a familiar face. "Dickie!" I shouted.

Dick Camp, an actor friend from New York. We embraced.

"What are you doing here?"

"Loving Rome," I said. "You?"

"I live here. Work here. I'm late for the studio." He'd found steady work dubbing movies in Rome. "Dinner, 8:30," he said, scribbled his address, and dashed off.

A taxi passed a little pyramid to a quiet district. Dickie's apartment was spacious, warm, and full of friends, pasta, and wine.

"Stay," he told me. "You could dub tomorrow. I've got an extra room. We'll share the rent and you'll live cheaply."

With wine, the idea seemed brilliant.

The next day, he introduced me to Gisella, the head of the dubbing studio. Within an hour, I was syncing English lines to Italian lips and having a ball.

"Start tomorrow?" she asked.

"Yes," I said. That afternoon, I left the hotel, moved into Dickie's, and began one of the most pleasant chapters of my life. I acted as I dubbed, giving life instead of the usual flat sound. Gisella was delighted and kept me busy.

Days flew by from 9:00 to 5:00. Evenings, I often stayed in, reading about Rome while Dickie went out. I planned Hadrian's Villa, but work always called. When I finally made it, my agent phoned: return immediately for a film audition. I rushed back, didn't get the part, and never saw the villa.

I stopped trying to reach Mary. She was starring in *Tea and Sympathy* opposite Tony Perkins after Deborah Kerr withdrew. I sent a telegram of congratulations.

Meanwhile, I fell in love with Rome. Each morning, I stopped at a stand for juice, cappuccino, and a pastry beneath colonnaded trees. Modern shops stood in ancient walls; ruins beside apartments. The past lives in the present. And then, one morning, I woke thinking: I left home to be an actor, not a dubber. I booked passage, tossed another coin into the Trevi fountain, and sailed back to New York.

Eighteen

After unpacking, I called Billy Nichols to thank him for that extraordinary dinner in France. He invited me over. His apartment above the Morosco Theatre was, as always, an oasis in Times Square, filled with all the treasures I was used to seeing from his travels.

Over wine, I told him about my trip and made him laugh about Titograd. When I thanked him again for the dinner that made me feel rich and privileged in Paris, he stopped me.

"I'm giving you a better present," he said. "A consultation with my analyst. He'll recommend someone."

I protested that I couldn't afford it and didn't need it. Billy looked at me seriously. "Acting jobs are scarce. You still haven't decided whether you want men or women. You're charming, but you're getting older. Without help, you risk ending up a lonely, out-of-work actor."

His bluntness stunned me. I remembered a recent TV job I'd told him about, where I forgot my lines and was unable to speak. "Is this why?" I asked.

"That's just one of many things," he said.

Reluctantly, I said I would accept Billy's gift but only for a meeting. The doctor, warm and rotund, listened as I spoke of lovers, friends, and my stalled career. When tears came, he pressed a Kleenex into my hand. "You would be greatly helped by analysis," he said gently, and referred me to a younger psychologist. I hesitated, but I made an appointment.

The new doctor's office was drab, but he was calm and reassuring. I told him I was turning 29 with little money, failed relationships, and growing stiffness onstage. I spoke of my father's self-absorption, my mother's dreams, and my panic on a recent TV which should have been easy for me.

"Analysis is like a voyage," he said. "The goal is to land on the dangerous islands, not sail past them. Face the world with understanding."

I told him a dream: I had died and was diving under the sea, before golden doors with scenes from my life. I knew paradise lay beyond, but the doors never opened. He smiled. "A beautiful dream to begin." I somehow found the money to see him twice a week.

I was back in Jerry's office. I lifted weights at the YMCA, studied with Sandy Meisner, and saw the analyst faithfully. Before Christmas, I landed a small TV job and was cast as Bassanio in an off-Broadway production of *The Merchant of Venice*. Rehearsals were muddled, performances uneven, and it was no triumph.

Television was kinder. In *The Story of Mary Surratt,* I played one of Booth's followers. The new year brought two gifts: a workshop for the new Shakespeare theatre in Stratford, CT, where I ran into Mary.

Her play had closed. We hadn't spoken since our break, but when we saw each other, neither looked away. I went over to her.

"You look beautiful," I said.

"Thank you."

"Can we be friends? I'd like to see you," I said.

She admitted she wasn't with anyone. Class began, and though we sat apart, I felt her closeness. At the break, I whispered, "Meet at Five Oaks?"

"Seven o'clock," she said.

***

Opening night at the new Shakespeare Theater in Connecticut, nothing was ready. The building was unfinished, and the dressing rooms had puddles; weeks of rehearsal left us unprepared.

Backstage was chaos. Many of us had multiple roles in *Julius Caesar*, juggling costumes and makeup while avoiding Jack Palance, our Cassius, whose fights with his wife made everyone tense. Mary was in Hollywood filming her first movie. She wanted to stay, but couldn't refuse a film, just as I couldn't refuse Stratford. The audience was full of notables and movie stars. Reporters made it feel like Broadway.

As one of the Tribunes, I opened the play. The scene went smoothly, and I hurried off to become Cinna the Poet. Reports from the stage weren't good. The show was stiff and the audience silent. At intermission, the mayor of Stratford, England, stood on stage and said, "I wish you were up here with me and could look out your way and see what I see." He meant it as praise for the new building, but it sounded like a critique of the play.

Cinna's death scene was my big chance. In a pink and green costume, I was torn apart by the mob, and applause followed. Backstage, others congratulated me. I was half-dressed when someone screamed, "Shayne, you're on!" I rushed upstairs, too late. Massey, as Brutus, was already in a scene with only one soldier since I was missing. The only soldier was an extra and had no lines.

Without seeing that only one soldier was there instead of two, Massey asked if either of them had seen anything. The extra froze since he didn't have any lines. Massey turned to my empty spot, repeated the line, got silence, then sat down on his stool, which broke into pieces. Later, as Brutus' soldier in his final scene, I begged him not to die. Tears came pouring out of me as he fell on my sword. After the final curtain, Massey thanked me warmly for my emotion, never knowing I had missed my cue. Critics in the local papers said that he was drunk.

The second play, *The Tempest*, fared better. I played Sebastian opposite Fritz Weaver and fanned myself with a palm frond to pretend I hated the tropical island. Stratford life was quiet, our circle small. Among us was Leora Dana, witty and warm, and her husband Kurt Kasznar, an Austrian character actor full of jokes at other people's expense.

One afternoon, Kurt pulled up in Leora's car. "You won't believe where we're going Sunday," he said. "We're taking a yacht to Oyster Bay. To see Arthur Loew and Nick Schenck. They run Hollywood."

I thought Hollywood was now the place for me, so I begged Kurt to let me go with them, but there wasn't room for me on the yacht. Kurt finally told me to at least come to the dock to see them off. At the last second, Kurt yanked me back aboard. "Of course you're coming," he laughed.

We sailed to Loew's mansion for lunch, then to Schenck's estate. At the pool, a servant handed me a swimsuit, and I decided to impress Mr. Schenck. I dove, swam, and climbed out dripping, my idea of an Errol Flynn movie.

Schenck rose slowly. "Vell," he said, "I tink I'll clean up."

I strode over, bare-chested. "Can I help you?" I asked.

He looked me over. "You a barber?" Then he walked inside.

Kurt and Leora howled with laughter, and soon the entire cast greeted me with the same line. So much for my Hollywood break.

***

Fall in New York was beautiful, and Mary and I were happier than ever. Her Hollywood debut hadn't helped; the part was dull, and Inger Stevens stole the spotlight. Mary's performance was flawless, but Hollywood wasn't calling. She didn't mind. Her heart was in New York, where she was now a leading young actress.

I was proud of Stratford and landed the lead in a staged reading of Dos Passos' *U.S.A.* Broadway felt closer. I had a little money saved, Jerry's office work, still photographing actors, and I even won a photo contest. For once, bills weren't crushing me.

Mary had grown close to Gaby, now going with "Hound Dog" songwriter Jerry Leiber. We often doubled. Gaby's wit and beauty were dazzling; she floated through art and music circles.

That fall, my parents were on Cape Cod near Chatham, where Mary's mother had moved. We met at her cottage—charming and full of fake fisherman memorabilia.

When my parents arrived, I lit the fire, then stopped everyone before the toast.

I knelt, opened a small box, and asked, "Mary, will you marry me?" She gasped, saw the ring she'd once admired in a shop window, and whispered yes. Our mothers wept into handkerchiefs.

My mother had been waiting for this. With Mary as her daughter-in-law, she sailed on a boat called *Fame*. She flaunted Mary's Broadway success, and the phone lines in Brookline buzzed with her bragging. Announcements went out, luncheons were planned, and Mary endured them. I ducked away into a TV job on *Omnibus*.

Mary's charm pulled me closer to my parents. I'd always kept distance as protection, but now she envisioned a family circle I had fled. She laughed at my father's stories as though they were funny, but I couldn't join in.

Work dried up. Then Bobby Lewis asked me to understudy and stage-manage *Mister Johnson*. A step down, but it paid. Gaby joined the cast, Josephine Premice stole the laughs, but the play closed quickly. Summer stock was already cast, so I was back running Jerry's office and playing house with Mary.

Despite the engagement parties and gifts, we never discussed a wedding date. It felt as if we'd already been married for years.

Over the holidays, Mary went to parties without me while I worked in Bobby's next play, *The Hidden River*. Again, I understudied and stage-managed. The cast was impeccable: Robert Preston, Dennis King, Lili Darvas, and Gaby. Lili, once Max Reinhardt's star, fascinated me. She burst into tears on cue each night by slamming her foot before the line. Stagecraft at its finest.

Opening night unraveled when Dennis King lost his lines, dragging Lili down with him. Critics forgave him, but her triumph collapsed. The play closed in three weeks. Another understudy role that I never played.

By June, things brightened. I landed the lead in a summer stock tour of *Anastasia* opposite Dolores del Río. I felt ready. Moreover, I had a dream that I thought would end my analysis.

"I dreamed I went onto the roof of my building," I told my doctor. "A woman appeared with a small boy in a dark suit. He walked to the edge and fell. The boy must be me. The woman is my mother. She made me into that buttoned-up little man. But I walked away. I killed him off. I'm free. Which means I'm done with analysis."

The doctor kept writing. Finally, he said, "Remember, analysis is a voyage. Sometimes we avoid dangerous islands. This dream is one of them. Good luck with your play. I'll see you in the fall."

We rehearsed *Anastasia* in New York before touring the Poconos, Cape Cod, and the Hamptons. I was cast opposite Dolores del Río, decades older and a screen legend when I was born. To bridge the gap, I was asked me to grow a mustache and streak my hair gray.

Dolores arrived as breathtaking as ever—gracious, punctual, professional. She never varied a syllable. Competent but mechanical. Her agelessness was its own performance; she slept 16 hours a day, perhaps her secret.

One evening, she sat beside me, luminous even offstage. I asked what she had done that day. She whispered, "You don't want to know." When I insisted, she described her dinner: tiny lamb chops, green peas, a baked potato, and vanilla ice cream. Her eyes shimmered as if she had shared a hidden truth.

The tour was a reprieve from chasing jobs and the constant push-pull of money and Mary. Audiences adored Lili Darvas as the Dowager Empress as she lifted Dolores into credibility. Lili and I often ate together, and I was enthralled by her stories—her lost lover, her husband Ferenc Molnár, who refused her a divorce because he believed staying married meant he would never die.

Clarice Blackburn, brilliant as a peasant in the play, sometimes joined us. In Falmouth, we met a young Richard Harris—magnetic, witty, already remarkable. He sang with restraint, letting lyrics matter. Soon, the four of us were inseparable.

My attraction to men had been a battle since I was 15—sometimes resisted, more often not. Was marrying Mary my concession to society, or the start of a double life? Richard was inevitable. After nights at the club, he would come to my door. They were only romps, nothing lasting, but he lingered longer than most.

Back in New York, Richard and I drifted apart. But one afternoon, he stopped by as Mary arrived. I panicked and tried to usher him out another door, but timing failed. As I greeted Mary, Richard appeared at the end of the hall. With perfect poise, he said, "Good evening," and vanished. Mary asked who he was. I lied. She studied me but let it go.

Soon after, Mary entered the hospital for tests and asked me not to visit. One night, a man answered the phone. Later, I learned it was James Congdon, an actor she'd been seeing.

She asked to see me. She was pale but composed. "I've loved you," she said, "but I love someone else now. James can give me the life I want. You can't." Within a year, she married him. We never saw each other again.

Richard vanished too, until years later when we met for drinks. He was writing travel books, still sharp and charming. After a second drink, he smirked, "Did you know I was having sex with Lili Darvas at the same time I was having it with you?" I was startled, but by this time in my life, little surprised me.

When Mary left, the bottom fell out of my life. I drifted—thin, smoking too much, avoiding restaurants and friends. Bobby Lewis saved me. He was directing a new musical with Lena Horne, *Jamaica*, and offered me steady work: assistant stage manager, understudy, and a small part. It kept me busy and gave me structure.

The cast was nearly all Black—Lena, Ossie Davis, Josephine Premice, Alvin Ailey—except Ricardo Montalbán and Erik Rhodes. Harold Arlen wrote the score, Yip Harburg the book. Lena's stardom kept it alive for 18 months.

Bobby opened rehearsals by reading the play aloud, his eyes filling with tears. What saved *Jamaica* were the dancers, choreographed by Jack Cole. Alvin Ailey shone. Lena, though, faltered under Bobby's talk of "actions" and "motivations." She panicked, convinced she couldn't act. We had become friends, and she confided in me. I told her, "Forget theory. Just be Lena." She laughed, and it worked.

Opening night belonged to Lena, though Josephine Premice stopped the show with her number about leaving the atom alone. Critics were cool to the play but raved about Lena. My days fell into routine: analyst in the morning, Jerry's office by noon, gym, errands, then theater at night. I called places, ran the board, managed cues—steady, exhausting work.

The real joy was Lena. Before each show, I sat in her dressing room as her maid set her hair. She covered her freckles and chatted about her day. Her husband, Lennie Hayton, was always there with a drink, but only after the show. She called him "Daddy." Odd, but it worked. They treated me like family.

Saturdays often ended at Lena's apartment, full of music and laughter—Hazel Scott, Billy Strayhorn, Flossie Klotz, Ruth Mitchell. I belonged in that circle.

During *Jamaica*, I managed one unforgettable side project: a role on *Omnibus*, television's most prestigious show. Joseph Welch hosted an episode on trial by jury. I played a defendant pleading insanity.

I researched relentlessly. Just before the live broadcast, an ophthalmologist dilated my pupils for close-ups. When asked my favorite color, I answered flatly, "Black." The jury acquitted me by reason of insanity.

Robert Saudek, the show's creator, later told me it was "totally unfair" that I hadn't won an Emmy. *Variety* praised me. But the true prize was the work itself. For the first time in years, I felt like an actor again, wrestling with a role that mattered.

When Erik Rhodes left *Jamaica*, I asked to replace him. People thought I was crazy, but Merrick's office loved saying money. I did my best British accent, squinted into an old man's face, and got the job.

Nights, I played the governor and stage-managed: calling times, running cues, prompting lines. I only joined the curtain call if the PSM had the board. I loved the grind and the better paycheck.

Later, Lena worried Ricardo's understudy looked too young. I asked to audition. Management said I couldn't be a native fisherman. Lena insisted I audition. I knew every note and move, so I got it—another $15 a week and Tuesday understudy rehearsal.

That spring, I brought a dream to my analyst: I was the long-lost royal son, an impostor. The parents believed me because the prime minister did. The King loved bric-a-brac I had cleared away; I promised to restore it with the Queen's help. Three figurines appeared—Romeo, Juliet, and a third who came to life, kissed my hand, and said I wasn't the Prince. The Queen still believed. Then the King entered, told me to stay put, raised a shotgun—and the curtain wouldn't fall.

The doctor said my parents cared when I gave them things, even news, and noted my father's "stay put" echoed my stiffness onstage. I asked if one trauma made me this way. "No." The phone rang. Merrick's office: Ricardo was sick; I had to go on at the matinee.

I shook, babbling about never singing with the orchestra. The doctor reminded me I'd fought for the understudy, that people praised my rehearsals. "Do this for yourself, not your parents." I stopped shaking and left for the theater. I raced up four flights to my apartment, shaved in the kitchen sink, *Jamaica* cast album blaring. By the time I was dressed, the music didn't scare me; the scenes with Lena did.

At the theater, Charlie, the PSM, rehearsed one moment with the stagehands, Lena shoving me overboard. They caught me before I could hit the stage. No time for more. Lena arrived and said, "Hello, Koli. It was my character's name, and the nicest thing she could have done. You know everything," she said. "You'll be fine."

"One thing," I said. "You have to let me kiss you." She nodded. I kissed her, full passion. When she walked away, I realized she was more nervous than I was.

The announcement hit the audience: "At this afternoon's performance, the role of Koli, usually played by Ricardo Montalbán, will be played by Alan Shayne." A hideous groan punched the air out of me.

Then the overture crashed. "They don't want me. Fine. They're going to get me and like me." I belted "Savannah," faked a few Jack Cole steps, missed nothing. By curtain, they applauded hard. I had to do it again that night.

By week's end, my voice was wrecked. "Doctor Feelgood" gave me a shot; heat flooded my veins, and my voice soared. Only years later did I realize he had given me drugs. Each show, I willed myself into stardom for two hours, then I was just Alan again.

Waiting for curtain call, sweat cutting tracks through brown greasepaint, I thought of that first matinee call in the analyst's office. Analysis taught me how much of my drive belonged to my mother's dream of being an opera star. Slowly, I pushed her off the stage and started claiming it for myself.

Applause swelled. Lena's look was warm. Backstage, a few slaps on the back; the company was beginning to accept me. Ricardo's dresser wrapped me in a robe, walked me to the star's room, and patched my makeup for the evening.

My mother swept in, kissed me, and praised me. A knock: a TV actor I knew and someone with him. "This is my friend Norman Sunshine."

I was stunned by this man. He was my age, striking—dark hair, guarded eyes, strong nose. I managed formality while panic rose: what if I never saw him again?

They had dinner plans. I blurted, "Maybe a drink?"

"We have to get to dinner," he said. They left. I replayed the scene on a loop, mortified.

A week later, I reached the top of the subway stairs, and there he was, holding a portfolio. "Hello," I said.

"Oh yes," he answered. "I didn't recognize you."

"We met in my dressing room."

"I did enjoy your show. See you around." Gone again.

New York shrank to two people: Norman and me. We kept colliding—on sidewalks, at corners, never a smile, always that distant gaze. I rehearsed speeches and said nothing.

Then at the Y. he was on the bench press. Later, I found him at the lunch counter, one empty stool. I took it. He opened up: parents pressuring him to quit art and join the family business. He needed a model for a shirt ad.

"What about me?"

We went to his Jane Street apartment, panes painted white, Salvation Army furniture. He pinned the shirt tight, drew in silence, tore sheet after sheet. Finally, he adjusted a clothespin on my back, hand brushing my spine like I wasn't there.

"I can't draw you," he said. "It's not your fault. I'll write a check."

"I came to help you, not for money." I dressed to leave.

"Can I have your number?" he asked.

I scrawled it and left. He called the next morning, apologetic, deadline met. "Let me make it up to you. Dinner?"

His "artist's palette" meal was a disaster—colored foods like splattered canvases. We barely spoke. He cleared plates; I left, but I couldn't stop thinking about him. Analysis had opened me; I was 32 and done with casual sex. Mary once said I might be happier with a man; the more I thought about it, the truer it felt.

I called. "You gave me the artist's dinner, now you get the actor's."

He deadpanned, "I thought you'd died of ptomaine." We laughed, finally, easily.

I cooked a simple Hawaiian recipe, good wine, and candles. He was relaxed, witty. Desire took over; I kissed him. "Too soon," he said. I pushed; he relented. It was awkward, on the hard floor, without rhythm or joy. He thanked me politely and left.

I expected that to be the end. Then the phone rang. Norman: "I'd like to see you. Today." He arrived, more serious than ever. "I really like you. I want to see you. But we are not going to have sex—not yet. I need to know you. If I deny you, find it elsewhere."

I agreed. A strange courtship began: movies, museums, Bloomingdale's, 5th Avenue, the Met, late suppers after the show. Always, he went home alone. It drove me mad. I tried a fling and felt empty. I didn't want anyone else.

We folded each other into our lives: my eight shows a week, Jerry's office, the analyst; his fashion drawings and magazine work. I introduced him to friends. They were stunned by his mind as much as his looks. Even without sex, we were becoming inseparable.

P.J. Clarke's restaurant surrounded us, but somehow, we were alone. Months of restraint had taught us each other's feelings. I handed him a poem titled "Window Shopping" that I'd written. Part of it read:

You took in all the world.
I took in only you.
You were the world.
Not the shops, or the people, or the buses or the cars,
Not the skating rink or the Christmas tree,
Not the travel posters or the house of glass.
You -
Walking along seeing everything - happy.
Me -
Walking along seeing you - happy.

He read slowly, lifted his eyes; something had changed. "Let's get out of here," he said.

We walked close but didn't touch. Up four flights in step, no words. Inside, the silence was alive with what we'd been holding back. No negotiation, only certainty. Norman's hands found mine, then my face. When our mouths met, it wasn't hurried; it was the answer to months of patience.

The adventure was the beginning of something I'd never dared imagine: a life I could truly share with Norman.

Nineteen

The secretary's voice was impersonal, almost pompous. "I'm calling for Mr. Michael Shurtleff," she said, British accent clipped. "He would like to see you at 2:30 tomorrow at the David Merrick office. Is this convenient?"

My heart skipped. Michael Shurtleff was the top casting director on the East Coast, handling all of David Merrick's shows. I'd never managed to see him. Now he wanted to see me. It had to be about a part in one of the shows. Maybe he saw me go on for Ricardo in *Jamaica*. I agreed to the appointment, hiding my excitement.

After hanging up, I lit a cigarette and sat on the bed. Why hadn't I asked what it was about? But she was just the secretary. How would she know? *Jamaica* had just closed after a year and a half, but I'd been given another job in a Merrick show, *Irma La Douce*, as assistant stage manager. No acting understudy this time, but I knew the office tried to keep me working.

I wondered if Shurtleff was going to offer me just another stage manager job. Then I remembered that he only handled actors. Maybe he saw me in *Ernest in Love*, where I got good reviews as a snobby butler, but that was months ago. I'd heard he went to everything, especially Merrick shows.

I decided to wear a suit. If Shurtleff called me in, perhaps it was for a leading role. After 17 years of hustling for any job, maybe this was my break. I tried not to get too excited.

I arrived at the Merrick office right on time. Mr. Shurtleff was delayed at lunch, so I waited in the outer office, forcing myself to be calm. Suddenly, I heard heels clicking on the polished wood floor. A short man with scant orange hair, a paper-white face, and a tight tan suit appeared.

"Hello, Alan," he said. "I'm Michael. Sorry, I'm late."

"It's nice to meet you," I replied.

"Let's go into my office," he said, leading the way. The office was small, lined with files. His desk was covered with neat piles of paper and scripts. He hung up his jacket, waved me to a chair, and sat.

"You're a very talented actor, Alan, but you'll never be a star." I felt like I'd just been kicked in the stomach. I stared at him, speechless. "I've seen you act many times. You're always good, sometimes very good, but you'll never make it big."

"I don't understand what that has to do with this meeting," I said. "I know you're a great judge of talent, but I hope you're wrong about me."

"I'm about to tell you why I sent for you," he said. "You'll always work. You're liked, you'll get jobs understudying stars, stage managing, small character parts. You'll get older, never have enough money to do more than have a beer at Joe Allen's, where you'll spend your time with your friends criticizing actors who made it." I was livid, but I couldn't let him see it. I was ready to leave, but he didn't stop. "None of this is an insult, Alan. I think you deserve more. I want you to be my assistant."

"Doing what?" I asked.

"You'll be a casting director. Good pay, you'll see every show, have an expense account, and can even bring someone with you. It's a gateway to bigger opportunities."

"I'm an actor," I protested. "I know nothing about casting."

"But you do," he insisted. "You have talent, you see plays constantly, you know good actors. I can teach you the rest."

"You could be wrong about my not becoming a star," I said. It's just a matter of the right part. I haven't been lucky so far."

"Alan," he said gently, "I've followed your career for years. You were good in *Jamaica*, but the spark wasn't there. Stardom is a gift from the gods. If it's not in you, it never will be. You'd be a great success in casting." He stood. "Think about it. I need someone immediately, so I can't wait more than a few days." His handshake was clammy and unpleasant.

"Thank you," I replied and left as quickly as I could.

I was furious. I walked across town, too upset to even hail a cab. I began to honestly assess my career in New York, finally settling into stage management and understudying stars. The one great role I waited for would probably never come.

Back in my apartment, I tried to clear my head. Was this the life Norman and I were meant to have? Would I be at a theater every night doing some depressing job while Norman waited for me to come home? Was I forever chasing a dream that was my mother's and not mine at all?

In truth, Shurtleff offered me everything I longed for. Norman could go to plays with me. Using expense accounts, we could start having a decent dinner if Shurtleff was right about the money. We might even have a house in the country we had fantasized about. I couldn't wait to see Norman.

Norman's first response, after I explained what the meeting had been about, was "But you've described someone you don't like. How could you work with him?"

"I've thought about that. But if the money's right, we could have a better life together. Now we only see each other after I get home from the theater. If I do this, we could have dinner out, and you could come to the theater. We'd be together more. All my energy would go into one thing, and I know I could succeed."

"My worry," Norman said, "is that you'll miss acting. Won't you regret it?"

"I don't think so," I said. "I don't look back. I've grown less attached to acting, and I love you. I want a life with you, full of achievement and beauty. I'm having trouble getting that for us through acting. Why not try another way? I can always go back."

"I think you're wonderful and brave," Norman said. "I'm with you all the way."

The next morning, I called and accepted the job.

***

After Norman and I first became lovers, we struggled with how to live. We didn't want to move in together. Most gay friends we knew lived alone; couples seemed trapped or restless, rarely having relationships that lasted. We had no real models for enduring love, not even among straight couples. And there was always the social problem. With gay friends, we could relax; at straight parties, we had to pretend we were just friends.

Even staying overnight was complicated. Whose apartment? If Norman had a model to draw at dawn, he needed to be downtown. If I worked late at the theater, uptown was easier. Clothes, razors, books, one of us was always out of place. We argued over logistics as much as we did over desire. I worried we might drift apart.

Then fate intervened: Norman's building in the Village was sold. Searching for somewhere uptown, he stayed in my friend Ralph Roberts's apartment nearby. Ralph had moved to be closer to the celebrities who had discovered him as a great masseur. At the moment, Marilyn Monroe wanted him in Hollywood. The apartment was just one room, but big enough for Norman to work. I urged him to leave his old furniture behind. (He never forgave me when those Stickley pieces later became valuable.)

Living near each other changed everything. We could eat together before my curtain, then see each other afterwards. It felt almost like living together, without quite taking the step. We were romantic, if discreet, no kissing in the street, but in private, passion made up for restraint. Sex was frequent. More importantly, we were serious about our work and each other.

Our social life was quiet dinners with friends, never bars or crowds. Still, every day we chipped away at the walls that kept us hidden from each other. Was this lasting love, or just another affair? We had moments when we weren't sure.

By winter, Norman found a small apartment around the corner on 52nd and 3rd—a bed barely fit in the tiny bedroom, but he had space to draw. He was busy, under contract to Saks and illustrating for magazines like *Playboy*, even turning down an offer to move to Chicago because he wouldn't leave me. However, the industry was shifting: magazines folded, illustration gave way to photography, and the once-promising field began to shrink.

Everything changed when my ex-wife Jacqueline moved across the street. We hadn't spoken in ten years, but now she was everywhere—the drugstore, cleaners, supermarket. Eventually, we made eye contact in a checkout line and laughed, the anger of our breakup gone. We started talking again, and soon Norman was part of it. Jacqueline adored him.

One night, she introduced me to Jane Trahey, her partner. Jane wasn't beautiful—dyed hair, big nose, heavyset—but she radiated humor and energy. She ran her own ad agency and swept Jacqueline off her feet. Jane and Norman clicked immediately, their shared satire and fashion talk like a comedy act, with Jacqueline and me as the audience.

Jane teased Norman about joining her agency. At first, it was a joke; then it became serious. She saw his wit and artistic background as a perfect fit. Jacqueline added, "You'd have enough money to live together." I didn't tell her money had nothing to do with it. After nearly two years, Norman and I still kept separate apartments, valuing independence and privacy even as our love deepened.

Jane, Jacqueline, Norman, and I decided to vacation in Mexico, and one night, after dinner, Norman left us with a headache. When he didn't return, I found him shivering in bed, fever raging over 105. I phoned, but no one understood my English, and Norman wouldn't let me leave him. I stayed calm but was terrified as he called for his mother in delirium. I prayed: *God, don't let him die. I'll care for him always if you let him live.* By luck, the noise of a party next door led me to discover a doctor who examined Norman, called a local doctor, and together they brought the fever down.

"We're lucky," he said. "Any longer, and he might have suffered brain damage."

That night, everything changed. Norman became part of me; his pain was mine, and for the first time, I felt really responsible for another person. I had promised I would never leave him, and I have kept that promise for 67 years.

When we got back to New York, Norman gave up his apartment and moved in with me.

Jane Trahey persuaded Norman to join her ad agency. He'd never worked in an office, but he liked the idea of a steady paycheck after years of freelancing.

"What will I do?" Norman asked.

Jane promised, "We'll make it up as we go along. I just think you're right for this place—and for me."

The agency was a Madison Avenue boutique known for stylish visuals and sharp slogans. Jane's taste, honed at Neiman Marcus with Stanley Marcus, shaped everything. Norman became her shadow, floating from office to office, soaking it all in.

His first campaign was for Carven perfume. Jane handed him a bottle and asked him to think about it. Norman returned with a sketch of a nude woman kissing her own shoulder. His caption read *"Go ahead, be a narcissist."*

Jane blinked, then called in her art director.

"I love it," the man said.

Jane did too. Norman was thrilled; his first line. He didn't realize how tightly Jane guarded credit, and when the art director's version won an award, she let it be his. She began including Norman in everything she did.

Soon, Norman handled clients directly. The Lambert brothers, pompous jewelers obsessed with commas and semicolons, were memorable. After sending him on endless errands, one scolded him for neglect. Norman snapped, "Look, Mr. Lambert, I'm working my balls off."

The brother froze. "Mr. Sunshine, I will not have your testicles discussed in my office!" Norman left, and Jane shared his laughter.

Despite frustrations, Norman thrived. His satirical touch gave Jane's campaigns the freshness she needed. Her former partner had been the true idea generator, and without her, Jane leaned heavily on Norman. By day, he brainstormed slogans; by night, he shared them with me, both of us marveling at how easily they came to him.

His breakthrough came with Danskin. The company wanted to expand beyond dancewear, but Jane's campaign had fallen flat. Norman stayed late with a junior art director, determined to find the brand's essence.

"Everybody knows they make dance clothes," he said. "So, let's show people who are not dancing. How about *Danskins Are Not Just for Dancing?*" Paired with a photo of children flying a kite, the client loved it. The agency cheered Norman. He felt he'd arrived.

Then came a fur account. Jane had tossed a mink coat over her sofa, telling Norman the name she'd put together: "Blackglama." She had slogans circling the word "legend," but nothing was working. Norman listened, stroked the coat, and thought it was becoming for a woman to wear. He finally wrote on a piece of paper: *What becomes a legend most?* Jane didn't get it, but her art director did, and they went with it.

The next day, Jane claimed the line as her own. Norman confronted her: "I know this is your agency, but the legend line is mine." He left furious, ready to quit. That night, he told me, and at first, I wasn't sure what it meant. Was the mink becoming to a woman, or did it make her a legend? Then I realized it worked both ways. It was brilliant.

Jane smoothed things over by giving Norman a raise. Norman stayed on. Soon stars like Bacall, Streisand, and Melina Mercouri were photographed in Blackglama by Richard Avedon. The campaign became iconic, lasting decades. Though Jane and others claimed credit to their dying days, Norman knew the truth. Some people claimed they had come up with the line even though they weren't in the building on that day. Norman learned that credit in the advertising world is a fought-over commodity, but he also knew the line was his.

When Norman moved into my apartment, *Jamaica* had closed, but I was still working mornings for the photographer Jerry Cooke. Psychoanalysis and city life left me barely scraping by. My doctor never questioned my relationship with Norman. He saw only how good it was for both of us.

I kept acting, though jobs were scarce. I froze as a Roman soldier in an unheated church and mended shoes as a Confederate—better a cobbler than an actor. Both shows flopped. Then came a bright spot: *Ernest in Love,* a musical version of The *Importance of Being Earnest.* I played a butler, sang a duet with the maid, and even recorded my song in the cast album—my one moment as a recording artist.

When Neil Hartley at David Merrick's office got me work as stage manager on *Becket* with Laurence Olivier as Becket and Anthony Quinn as Henry II. I took it, though I wished I were acting. Still, being in the same theater with Olivier was enough.

Before rehearsals, I'd knock on his dressing room door. "Come in," he'd call. No Heathcliff or Hamlet, just a short, middle-aged man in an open shirt and suspenders. But once he rehearsed, the transformation was instant. Olivier could shift from rage to tears without effort, never fussing. He loathed the Stanislavsky method. His body, voice, and presence were his tools, and he played them like a master.

Anthony Quinn, his foil, blustered and sulked for attention. Olivier treated him with amused tolerance, making his own brilliance stand out even more.

In the cast was Brian, a method actor, who rehearsed barefoot in a monk's robe, as he insisted that he was "living the role." Olivier raised an eyebrow but said nothing until one day he couldn't stand Brian's barefoot posture any longer. He flicked his cigarette onto the stage. "Put this out, will you, Brian?"

Broadway lore recalls Olivier forgetting a line in a scene with Brian in *Becket*. I, as stage manager, rushed to cue him, but I heard him whisper to Brian, "What's my line?" Silence. Again, louder: "What's the line?" Brian just stared. Finally, Olivier caught my prompt from the wings and carried on. Backstage, he was furious. "Why didn't you give me the line?"

Brian replied, "I don't work that way." Any other actor would have been fired. Olivier let it go.

My fondest memory is quieter. One Saturday night after two shows, I went to say goodnight. He was tired but talkative. "I'm off to Boston," he said, "to see Joanie in *A Taste of Honey*. I can't wait to settle in a big chair with her on my lap." This was the man who had lived with the gorgeous Vivien Leigh but no longer wanted the glamour; he wanted a simple life with his adored young wife.

It made me think of Norman. Maybe a quiet life with him meant more than chasing stardom.

The first year in casting nearly did me in. Shurtleff was a drillmaster. I arrived early in the office to file actor cards for every performance I saw the night before, noting look, type, age, and quirks. At 11:00, the click of his leather heels meant more orders: replace Tessie Tura in *Gypsy*, schedule auditions, call agents, see four shows a night, and leave only after checking every actor. I dreaded when I heard his door open.

Merrick was worse. I rarely saw him except for a sudden appearance and a quiet hiss to his secretary. His all-red office suited him—he never greeted me, only stared as if I'd wandered in by mistake. The joy in the work was the auditions. I scheduled actors kindly, remembering what it felt like to be one of them. Shurtleff's eye was brutal and brilliant. I was learning fast.

One afternoon, a girl shuffled in, parked her chewing gum under the piano lid, and sang "A Sleeping Bee." It was Barbra Streisand—rags, wild hair, a face no Merrick musical would allow, but a voice I'd never heard. "What can you do with her?" Shurtleff muttered. "Merrick would never hire that look."

I hit my own wall with Merrick on *Carnival.* While Shurtleff was away, I hired a plain, small soprano with a glorious voice for Lili's understudy. When the lead was ill, she went on. At her first matinee, she was luminous. Merrick appeared beside me, watching her perform: "Find the understudy who just left. She plays tonight. Fire that girl." I made the call and told Julie Migenes she was out. She later became an opera star. Merrick had no feelings for people at all.

The grind was bearable only because of Norman. We used my expense account for dinner; he came with me to the theater. He had a clean eye for acting, and we laughed through most of the Off-Broadway also-rans.

Work improved as Shurtleff began to trust me. The turning point was *I Can Get It For You Wholesale.* We needed a raw, hungry Jew from Brooklyn for the lead. I'd photographed a chorus boy from *Irma La Douce*: Elliot Gould, long face, curly hair, cocky charm. Perfect. He auditioned beautifully and, after the usual search for a known name, got the role.

We also fought to get Streisand into the show. Merrick wouldn't cast her as the ingenue, so we slid her into Miss Marmelstein, a spinster on the switchboard. The audience roared, and history started. Elliot sweated through three opening songs in Depression suits and looked nothing like a star, but he and Barbra fell in love. Norman and I once saw them at Longchamps, hugging over coffee. No one would have guessed the roads they would travel.

A year later, Ray Stark asked me to read scenes opposite Barbra for Jerry Robbins' Fanny Brice musical. She was no longer in thrift shop clothes. She threw the script down and declared she was wrong for the part, then listed all the reasons—while proving the opposite. It was a performance in itself. The reading was fine, the meeting sealed it. Robbins left, Garson Kanin directed, and Barbra exploded in *Funny Girl.*

After the opening, Ray had me organize understudy auditions. Barbra sat with him—chic, perfect nails, no memory of me. Years later, in Malibu, she finally called, "Aren't you Alan Shayne, the casting director?" At last, recognition. "You were there at *Wholesale*," she said. "Wasn't it my idea to roll the wheeled chair during 'Miss Marmelstein'?"—her first directing, she claimed.

"I'm sorry," I said, "I wasn't in rehearsal." She looked wounded and walked away.

Through it all, Norman steadied me. I loathed the click of Shurtleff's shoes, yet I had found a craft and a partner who made each night bearable. Also, a front row seat at the moment new talent was born.

One morning, Shurtleff called me into his office. I thought I was being fired. Instead, he told me David Susskind, television's prolific producer and host of *Open End,* wanted him to cast a new series, *East Side, West Side*, starring George C. Scott.

Shurtleff proposed we go into business together. Fifty-fifty, still consulting for Merrick, with Susskind providing offices. He wanted more time to write; I would run things. Norman and I weighed it every night. I disliked Shurtleff but couldn't ignore the chance for real money and maybe a house in the country. I agreed, and a lawyer drew up the papers.

We moved into Susskind's office. Almost at once, Shurtleff announced he was off to Fire Island to "work on his play."

I panicked. "I don't know enough actors to cast a television show every week."

"Yes, you do," he shrugged. "It's only television."

I bristled. I owed my best work to TV. Still, he left, and I went at it like a man possessed: notes on every actor, seeing them in more than one performance, filling my files not just with talent but reliability. Could they learn lines, stay sober, behave under pressure?

Budgets were tight. I had to find actors who'd work for scale but could stand up to George C. Scott. He respected talent, but his temper was fierce; no one weak could survive beside him.

I cast Cicely Tyson after seeing her in *Moon on a Rainbow Shawl,* one of the first Black actors with a recurring TV role not defined by race.

By accident, I started hiring blacklisted actors. I hadn't been in the business long enough to know their names, so I suggested them freely. The network approved, and suddenly, people who had been shut out for years were working again. The blacklist seemed to end with a whimper.

I kept phoning Shurtleff on Fire Island. He always said his play wasn't ready. He finally returned to our office the day of Kennedy's funeral. The office staff was gathered around a television, fighting back tears.

I heard the familiar click of his heels. "What are you all watching?"

"The President's funeral."

"Oh, for heaven's sake," he sniffed. "What a waste of time." He clicked away. At that moment, I knew I'd never work with him again.

He announced he would take over the series I had been casting, but the producers refused. They wanted me. I told him I didn't want to work with him any longer.

"Then buy me out," he snapped. I agreed to pay him a royalty per episode, enough to keep him on Fire Island and "write." It was fair; he had landed us the job. We signed the papers. After a few months, I was on my own.

Shurtleff went on to teach actors how to audition. But for me, that day, the burden of his clicking heels was gone, and I had stumbled into my own casting business.

Twenty

I was casting movies, TV series, and even commercials while Norman worked on advertising campaigns. It was all successful, but the pressure was wearing us down. We rushed to the theater each night, ate quick suppers, and never slept enough. Tempers flared. We needed something beyond work, something for the two of us.

A weekend invite from Phil Bloom, a publicist with a Bucks County stone farmhouse, changed everything. The drive along the Delaware, with its barns and old houses, enchanted us. Soon, we were poring over real estate ads, dreaming of a country escape. On nights off, we'd sip Rob Roys and quote *Of Mice and Men,* where Lenny would beg his buddy to tell him about a house that they dreamed of having one day. We longed for a haven of our own.

We imagined a farm with a pond, a barn where Norman could paint, and gardens. We searched Connecticut, New York, and Pennsylvania, close enough for weekends. I made cards for each house we saw, jotting down details like I did with actors. House-hunting became our obsession.

We were drawn to Bucks County. One day, we found an 1840 farmhouse on 55 acres, abandoned for years. Electricity worked, but the bathroom was an outhouse tangled in vines. Rotting apples, bees, and neglect were everywhere. Still, it pulled us in. The seller wanted $16,000. We scraped together a down payment and nervously called the real estate agent from Upper Black Eddy. Our offer was accepted. We told the bank we were "business partners," afraid the truth would cost us the mortgage.

The night before closing, the owner let us stay in the house. Blankets, flashlights, and optimism. The place was a mess. In the morning, sunlight broke through as I pulled a shade that clattered to the floor. There was a huge maple aflame with autumn leaves. "Norman, wake up!" I shouted. "Look, we're going to own that tree!"

At the lawyer's office, signing took minutes. The owner looked smug, as if unloading a ruin. We left, raced back, and met the plumber and contractor. For the first time, we could create a home that was truly ours.

Renovation consumed us. Norman reclaimed barn beams for the kitchen, opened the fireplace, and transformed the house. Each Friday, we drove down, exhausted. We'd make Rob Roys, inspect the week's work, then argue about some flaw Norman spotted. By Saturday, we'd reconcile, walking in the woods, marveling at deer tracks.

We kept to ourselves. A retired farmer down the road was our only regular contact, forever predicting droughts or death. Another neighbor, old Mr. Zearfoss, never waved at us, though I always waved at her. Norman thought it pointless, but I persisted. One spring, as we laid down a garden path, Zearfoss stopped. His wife had died. Almost shyly, he offered us an old table. "Not for sale," he said. "I'm giving it to you."

The table was a monstrous Victorian piece, which we quickly hid in the cellar. But it meant more than just furniture. It was the gesture. It implied a sense of belonging in the area.

After months of work, the farmhouse was finished. Our favorite night was when we lit the fireplace, put the Beatles' first album on the record player, and wandered from room to room, giddy with pride.

After dinner, we'd climb to the hilltop, full of food and drink, and look down at our little house. It was heaven. The city was grueling, but this was a refuge. We had never been happier. Then came the pond.

Norman dreamed of a pond, and we thought the small spring could feed it. A state inspector said there wasn't enough water. A local pond digger swore there was. Norman wanted it so badly, we chose to believe the local guy.

After weeks of digging, we expected a glittering pond. Instead, all we got was a damp patch. We told ourselves it would fill with time. It never did.

The pond became our undoing. Norman clung to hope after every rain. We spent more money, another well, truckloads of clay, but nothing worked. The gaping hole haunted us. It poisoned our joy, and eventually, I insisted we sell. Norman never forgave me. For him, the house wasn't ruined. For me, it was unbearable.

Yet, for all its flaws, Bucks County was a revelation. We learned to cut wood, plant a garden, and chase off groundhogs. We watched deer, rode horses, and marveled at the stars. Each season was a discovery. It was the closest we'd felt to nature, and to each other.

Selling the farm was like mourning a death. Norman kept saying, "You were the one who wanted to sell." I reminded him that the pond would never have filled, and the Friday drives through tunnel traffic had worn us down, but nothing softened the breach.

We brought our best antiques back to the city, set them among Norman's Bucks County landscapes, and blocked Second Avenue with pots of vines. For a while, we pretended we'd carried the country home with us. But the illusion didn't last. We missed stepping out into silence instead of Healy's bar and the heavy traffic.

Work consumed us. Norman traveled for the agency and painted on weekends. I was casting for television, plays, and films. I had hired an associate, Jean Arley, but the load was still crushing.

I cast *Promises, Promises, Forty Carats*, insisting on Julie Harris, who triumphed, and Woody Allen's *Play It Again, Sam*, where Diane Keaton charmed us all. I cast her in her first film, *Lovers and Other Strangers*, alongside Anne Jackson, Bob Dishy, and Bea Arthur, whom I persuaded to return to acting after a stint as a Connecticut housewife.

I worked with directors from William Wyler (*Funny Girl*) to John Huston (*Reflections in a Golden Eye*) to Robert Mulligan (*The Pursuit of Happiness*). I even found Ali MacGraw for her first movie, a bit part with Kirk Douglas and Faye Dunaway in *Hogan's Goat,* which jump-started her career.

People thought casting was dull. My friend Billy Nichols teased, "It's just making lists of actors. Not rocket science." But it was diplomacy, persuasion, and instinct. I wasn't in charge. I had to guide producers and directors without them realizing it. My files gave me an edge. If one actor wasn't right for a role, I found another. I stayed away from parties and presents, determined not to be swayed by friendships. Actors probably thought their agents had gotten them the roles. That was fine with me.

Some agents wielded real power. Sue Mengers once swept past me in the Polo Lounge, and seconds later, I was paged to the phone.

"Is that Jack Clayton with you?" she demanded.

"Yes," I said.

"You tell him Robert Redford is the actor to play Gatsby!"

I wasn't working on the film, but I relayed the message. Jack and I laughed at her audacity, but sure enough, Redford got the part. Sue was a force of nature.

I was casting David Susskind's new television series, *N.Y.P.D.,* when he asked me to become his associate producer, focusing on his dramatic specials. It would mean giving up my casting business and working exclusively for him, but producing had always been my dream. I turned *N.Y.P.D.* over to my talented assistant, Nessa Hyams, and began casting and associate producing landmark television dramas, many adapted from Broadway plays.

The first was Arthur Miller's *Death of a Salesman,* directed by Alex Segal, with Lee J. Cobb as Willy Loman. I persuaded George Segal to play Biff, and he was heartbreaking in the climactic scene. Some months later, I produced my first original television drama, *To Confuse the Angel* by Loring Mandel. Susskind made me a full producer for the first time, and I was determined to succeed.

The lead role demanded Lee J. Cobb. When I called, he flatly refused. Alex Segal was directing again. "That man is crazy," Lee said. "He screamed his head off during *Salesman*. I've had a heart attack since then."

I pleaded, "At least read the script. Alex will promise not to raise his voice." Lee scoffed but relented. Alex phoned, promised good behavior, and Lee accepted. I was elated.

The first rehearsal: the cast gathered—Blythe Danner, Beah Richards, and Lee J. Cobb. All was well until Lee launched into a long, sonorous speech about the script.

Alex Segal shoved back his chair, slammed his script on the table, and shouted, "I'm not going to stand for your intoning! I want you to act, not sing!"

I froze; sure that Lee would storm out. Instead, he paused, then calmly continued. He delivered a magnificent performance.

There were other extraordinary experiences. Lilli Palmer and Max von Sydow starred in *The Diary of Anne Frank*. Liza Minnelli, fresh from off-Broadway, auditioned for *Anne*. She vibrated with tension, tears pouring down her face.

Susskind said, "She certainly can cry."

But I told him, "Anne Frank doesn't cry. She's never sad. She's optimistic." Liza didn't get the part.

For *A Case of Libel*, I built a stellar cast around George C. Scott: Lloyd Bridges, Angie Dickinson, and José Ferrer. One morning, George didn't show up. His agent said, "Better replace him." I reached Van Heflin, who had played the role on Broadway and was furious at being overlooked. I smoothed his ego and secured him, and the show was a success.

Later, I learned George had disappeared on a drinking spree. Yet Susskind still brought him back for Miller's *The Price*, where George grumbled at the idea of Arthur Miller coming to rehearsal to address the cast. I coaxed him into attending. He sat quietly, at least pretending to listen to Miller.

Not all playwrights were grateful. At a dinner party in Connecticut, I told Arthur Miller I'd produced three of his works for television. "They were terrible. Cut to pieces," he snapped. I was stunned. Millions who'd never seen his plays onstage had discovered them on TV, and the cuts were minimal.

Other projects brought their own joys. In London, we taped *A Hatful of Rain* with Peter Falk. One actor struggled with drugs, so I kept David Carradine hidden in a hotel as backup; he was never needed. Joanne Woodward was luminous in *All the Way Home*, utterly professional. Geraldine Page astonished me in *Look Homeward, Angel*, reviewing her scenes as if critiquing another actress, then calmly adjusting every movement or inflection.

I was thrilled to secure Celia Johnson, forever remembered from *Brief Encounter*, for *The Choice*. She was down-to-earth and told me she had filmed *Brief Encounter* just after the war, commuting for long hours each day. She was so exhausted that she barely thought about acting; she just delivered the lines and hurried home. But with her training and technique, she could "just inhabit" the role and create magic.

Producing these specials gave me a front-row seat to greatness and folly in equal measure. Stars, tantrums, brilliance under pressure, a masterclass not only in television but in human nature.

It was a Monday when David Susskind barreled in from the gym, pockets stuffed with wrinkled *Times* clippings torn out in the steam room, high on a "can't-miss" idea. He could sell anything, especially himself, and today he looked like a cat who'd swallowed a network.

"Wait till you hear," he said, glowing. "At the Emmys, I sat with Tom Moore of ABC and Truman, yes, Capote. We're doing a two-hour special, starring Lee Radziwill. Truman writes it. ABC airs it. America will watch Jackie's sister. And she's a princess to boot!"

"What's the play?" I asked.

"*The Voice of the Turtle.*"

I stared at David. "That's basically two people in an apartment. She has to carry the whole thing," I said. "Is she good enough to do that?"

"She's not great," David said, "but she has something."

"She'll be hung out to dry by the critics. You can't do that to her."

"I've already sold them on the show," David looked stricken. "What else can I do?"

"Well," I said, "do something that will be easy for her."

"Like what?" David was getting desperate.

"Like *Laura*. Do *Laura*, the Gene Tierney movie. You don't see Laura for the first third of it. She just needs to be enigmatic. Surround her with pros."

He huffed and then picked up the phone and started dialing. By morning, our war room was humming: London shoot (cheaper), British John Moxey to direct, Truman adapting the script of *Laura* in Palm Springs. David wanted "names" but "not too expensive."

I scoured files and agents and, despite refusals and egos, assembled an impressive cast: George Sanders, Robert Stack, Arlene Francis, Farley Granger, and Thelma Ritter as the maid. Even David was pleased. Then we waited for Truman Capote's script. And we waited and waited.

A week before I was to fly to London, as the Associate Producer, it arrived. I read it fast, then slowly. It was dreary. No wit. Plot holes. An ending that just stopped. I screened the original film and confirmed my dread: the studio had sent Truman an *early* draft. No time to fix it; Truman had farmed out part of the job to a young "writer" he was mentoring. David shipped me to London with four *Laura* scripts and the task of cobbling together a hybrid with director Moxey while he found a British writer to help.

Our savior, briefly, was Michael Dyne. He stayed up, rewrote, and handed me a script that wasn't good but at least was shootable. I messengered it to the Princess. Moxey, meanwhile, had been summoned to her country house. He returned star-struck by the grounds and the ritual: the tennis pro had been instructed never to make the Princess's backhand move; the Prince, an ancient Polish nobleman, tour-guided

Moxey as if he were a guest, and showed him a room where a woman was hand-painting scarves to make them look like wallpaper.

"Did the Princess have any notes on the script I had sent her?" I asked.

"She has a few changes," Moxey said. "She won't say 'I can't conceive' because 'everyone knows I have two children.' She won't spill milk on her dress. It 'won't look pretty.' And she won't *seem* to have made love to Farley because 'I won't do that with a homosexual.'"

I sent a portrait painter, Jan de Ruth, to meet with the Princess and discuss her painting, which was a feature of the show; he returned, saying she was "a frightened nouveau riche girl" and that director Moxey seemed intent on keeping her to himself. "He wants to be the next prince," Jan said. The plot thickened, hindering production.

Robert Stack arrived, delighted to walk London unrecognized. ("*The Untouchables* hasn't aired here, so I'm thrilled not to be stopped by autograph people everywhere I go!" he said.) He demanded rewrites. Shirtless, he paced and relived *Written on the Wind.* ("I practically had the Oscar until the camera caught my wife's tears.") He boasted, "I'll give the Princess her first TV kiss. After all, I gave Deanna Durbin her first screen kiss."

As I left his hotel, I remembered the Bel-Air fire story about him. Stack had screened his *Written On The Wind* movie for the firefighters while flames licked neighborhood houses.

A cable arrived from David Susskind: THELMA RITTER BROKE FOOT STOP FIND IRISH MAID STOP. Then, at midnight, Farley Granger called and woke me up: his deal, his dates, his car, his per diem —everything was wrong. I calmed him down: "We'll straighten it out tomorrow at 10:00."

The first reading, as we all sat around a table, felt like summer stock under a chandelier. Sanders looked old; Arlene rasped like an elderly baritone; Stack angled for more changes; Farley and Arlene demanded limos and quickly shared one. Lee arrived late in a tight blue dress, a daub of white cream above her lip where she'd had something removed.

On "Action," her voice was surprisingly like a shopgirl's: "gow-un" for gown, "jist" for just, and every line came with a different expression. We also discovered we were ten minutes short.

Worse, the script began dissolving. The writer Dyne, overwhelmed by all the actors' notes, quit, leaving a letter: "The script is half film technique, half television. The characters are unmotivated. It's a muddle. Never listen to actors. IT'S FATAL."

He left all four of my backup scripts with the Savoy concierge, who lost them. "They could be flying to India," the concierge said as an excuse. The hotel gave me a better room; I was left with one working script and a complaining stomach.

David Susskind cabled he had found another writer, John Hopkins, who refused to rewrite but agreed to write a scene that wouldn't alter the plot but would fill in the ten minutes we were short. He delivered a Pinter-ish duet for Arlene and Farley built of words like "Well?" "Well." "So?" "So." They played it with grand intensity. It meant nothing, but at least it didn't give the Princess more to do.

Rehearsals dragged along. On a day that Moxey saw his doctor, I ran the Princess's scenes. I rang the fake phone on the prop table. The Princess picked up the phone and said "hello" into the air before the phone had reached her mouth.

I stopped her and said, "You have to wait to say hello until the phone is up to your face."

She nodded and did it again. "Hello," she said to the air long before she was anywhere near the phone. I explained again why she had to wait until the phone was up to her ear before she said "hello." She was annoyed, and this time she bellowed "Hello" a foot from the mouthpiece.

I gave up. Moxey returned, gave her line readings, and then told her that an actress must be in love with her director. She declared him a bully and a "pathetic, mixed-up pervert," and vowed to be a bigger star than Candice Bergen.

At night, I called Norman, who listened to each catastrophe and reminded me: "It's not life and death; it's only a TV show."

Small mercies surfaced. Jan finished the portrait; the Princess loved it. I took her to lunch at the Savoy, where she dropped her armor and suddenly became charming. Lee Radziwill confided that she woke up with nightmares about *Laura*. On the other hand, George Sanders never complained about anything except his billing. He ate, drank, reminisced about Russia, and begged for a country-house invitation; Lee feared that if she invited him, he'd never leave.

David Susskind finally arrived from New York, kissed hands, beamed confidence, and declared me a worrier for saying Lee was not up to it. I pointed out she could only walk forward or backward; turns made her wobble. "I'm a great editor," he said. "Cut on the turns. Play the *Laura* theme whenever she's onscreen. It's going to be a smash." All I wanted was to go home, and David said I didn't have to stay for the actual taping.

David took over the taping in London and returned to New York euphoric. "I saved it," David told me. "Brilliantly edited." The network tape was unplayable anywhere but their facility. David decided to give a huge party at his apartment in the UN Plaza. "Then you'll see it at my place," he told me. He rented network trucks, ran cables up many flights of stairs, and filled the rooms with famous faces. "Don't bring anyone," he added, meaning I couldn't bring Norman.

It was a wake in slow motion. The show was worse than I'd feared. The script was a patchwork; the pros were stranded, played scenes with each other, and ignored Lee as much as possible. The theme gushed whenever Lee drifted through a doorway; the cuts on her turns magnified her stiffness.

People fled to "urgent" dinners. David stood in the wreckage, proclaiming triumph. The reviews were savage. Lee Radziwill never acted again, unless you count playing herself in a Rolling Stones documentary directed by Robert Frank called *Cocksucker's Ball*. It was never released.

And I, after weeks of clippings, princes, vanished scripts, and phones answered in thin air, went home to Norman, grateful that our life was not going to be edited by David Susskind.

Twenty-One

We'd sold the house in Bucks County and, after a short stretch of city weekends—the Metropolitan Museum, art galleries, films, Sunday lunches with a lot of wine—we began aching for the country again. We drove through Litchfield County, Connecticut, past white colonial houses and old dairy barns. Norman would often stop for photographs and sketches, then turn them into paintings at night.

He had a stack of Polaroids of his paintings on his desk at the Agency. One day, Gene Moore, Tiffany's legendary window designer, came to see Norman about an ad, spotted the pictures, and asked, "What are those?"

Norman shrugged, "My weekend paintings." Gene said he loved them and asked about the size. "Three by four feet," Norman answered.

Gene Moore said, "I'll put them in my spring windows."

"Your windows are tiny," Norman blurted out.

"They're not," Gene said. "We'll push the curtains back."

That April, six Bucks County landscapes glowed on 5th Avenue—barns and river views, each fronted by a single jewel. People stopped. *Vogue* and *Bazaar* clients of the Agency congratulated Norman. Everyone was impressed.

A call came from Mr. Miller from the new Adam Gallery. He wanted Norman as his opening show. "Do you have enough work?" he asked.

Norman had never declared himself a painter and still had a full-time job. But some inner voice said, "Absolutely. I'll finish a few more."

He painted after hours and on weekends until 25 canvases filled the studio. The director dropped by, enthusiastic. Norman grew suddenly serious and terrified. I'd just flown back from England and kept assuring him the work was good and getting better.

On opening night, Norman arrived fashionably late. The room was packed—friends, clients, strangers—and they never stopped coming. I found Norman looking stunned while I was so moved by his accomplishment. "I can't look at you or I'll cry," I said.

"It's nearly sold out," he looked amazed. The gallery owner said *Artnews* planned a review, comparing him to Milton Avery.

A white-haired man in a navy blazer stopped Norman. "I'm thinking of buying the snow painting on the invitation, but your bio says you're in advertising. I won't invest in you unless you're a serious artist."

For a moment, Norman froze. He looked at his paintings now on the gallery walls: flat shapes, bold color, poster clarity, hard work now, but with ArtCenter discipline. He turned to the man and said, "I am a serious artist. I hope you will buy the snow painting," and the man did.

Our life of wall-to-wall work, setbacks, and minor triumphs was going well, but something was missing. We were so consumed with our jobs, a certain distance crept in. At dinner, everything circled back to David Susskind or Jane Trahey and their latest crisis. We were growing disenchanted with both of them. We needed another house in the country, something to share, something to bring us back to ourselves.

We spent weekends chasing real estate agents across Connecticut. Finally, at the end of a half-mile driveway beside a dairy farm, we found it: a 1930s cinderblock house set on over 50 acres, with long views of the hills and, in the distance, the white steeple of the New Preston Church. It was not the early American farmhouse we'd imagined, but it was ours.

We moved in late one spring night. The movers had left our furniture in place, and outside, the air was heavy with the smell of cut grass and lilacs. We carried drinks to the terrace, looked out at the hills, and toasted our new life.

Bucks had been our beginning—mystery, innocence, discovery—when our relationship was just taking shape. Connecticut was more assured, settled, reflective of who we had become ten years later. We hoped building another home together would bring us back to our happiest days. Norman set up his studio in the attic; I turned a storage area into a study to write.

The first thing we added was a pool, designed by architect Armand Benedict. Painted black and studded with boulders, it looked like a pond we'd discovered in the woods. The living room had a massive stone fireplace, and carved into its mantle was an absurdly long sentence: *"Every man's chimney is his golden milestone—the central point from which he measures every distance through the gateways of the world around him."* We read it aloud and roared with laughter.

Nearby, in Kent, we had two friends, Bob Darden and Bill Corrigan. Bill once cast me as Chopin opposite Sarah Churchill as George Sand. They were a revelation: cultured, traveled, deeply in love, hosting lunches with Fredric March and Florence Eldridge, and sometimes Wanda and Vladimir Horowitz. They were one of the few couples we knew who showed us how full and respectable a gay life could be.

Our hilltop gave us what New York never could. Norman and I grew tanned and strong working in the gardens and woods. Nature's quiet deepened our connection. Even sex seemed more alive there. Friends visited, the choreographer Ron Field and Tom Rolla once arrived with a box of marijuana. We thought, *Why not?* That turned into a disaster. High as kites, they suggested a foursome; we declined. Norman spiraled into paranoia, and I had to put him into bed. The pot was less a present than a reminder: the gay world of the '60s spun with drugs and promiscuity. On our hill, we wanted none of it. We were content.

Then one night the phone rang. "This is Mike Nichols," said the voice. I sat bolt upright. Mike Nichols! He asked me to cast *Catch-22*. He told me his producer, John Calley, would follow up. I was beside myself. I had never met Nichols, the most brilliant, celebrated director of his generation, and now I would get to work with him.

It became one of my most joyous casting experiences. Mike's insight and gentleness made everyone feel safe. He was open to new actors. I brought in a mesmerizing young Al Pacino, fresh off *The Indian Wants the Bronx*. Mike was so taken that he offered him a choice of roles. Pacino disappeared, vanished under the pressure, he explained years later.

Other auditions brought an astonishing parade of talent: Bob Balaban, a nervous young actor with a comic edge; Anthony Perkins, darkly intense; and Orson Welles, who entered larger than life and left us sure he'd dominate any role. Nichols' generosity made these auditions a laboratory. Mike was always interested in discovery as well as casting.

The final ensemble was dazzling: Alan Arkin as Yossarian, Richard Benjamin, Art Garfunkel, Martin Balsam, Jon Voight, Buck Henry, and Bob Newhart. It was one of those rare times when every piece fell into place, and Mike Nichols was a dream-come-true director.

I look back at that time with Mike as one of the great gifts of my career. To be trusted by him, to help assemble a cast of such brilliance, was the best of what casting could be.

***

Three years after we got the house in the country, everything changed. Norman was exhausted by advertising and by Jane Trahey. Raises no longer made up for the constant arguments over credit. He began talking seriously about leaving it all behind to paint full-time.

At the same time, New York felt darker. Crime was rampant. Our friend Billy Nichols was mugged in Central Park while birdwatching, beaten so badly by teenagers that he never recovered and died soon after. Just getting to the theater at night became an ordeal: traffic, taxis, rushed dinners, always looking over your shoulder.

Weekends in Connecticut became salvation. Sundays were torture, packing up for the city. One day, I suggested, "Why don't we try living full-time in the country and commuting?" It was madness: four hours travel a day, but we did it. Through the winter, we got up before dawn and returned late at night. The experiment foreshadowed a permanent country life.

David and Joyce Susskind often said they'd love to see Connecticut. I invited them, never imagining they'd actually come. David never acknowledged Norman; why would he spend a weekend with us? But one summer, he announced they would come with the baby, nanny, and all. Norman and I panicked. We could handle two guests, but four plus luggage, playpens, and toys? With only two bedrooms, the baby and nanny had to share my study upstairs.

The limousine arrived, spilling out the Susskinds, nanny, baby, and enough baggage for a month at the Plaza. We gave David and Joyce our bedroom and retreated to the guest room. Joyce took the nanny and baby upstairs. Seconds later, shouting erupted, followed by the crash. I raced up to hear the nanny shrieking at Joyce: "I didn't leave Ireland to sleep in an attic! I wouldn't sleep in an attic in Ireland, and I won't sleep in one here!"

"It's not an attic," I insisted. "It's a charming study with a beautiful, built-in bed."

"It's an attic," she snapped.

"Then, I suppose you don't sleep, because there isn't another room."

Joyce, pale and speechless, asked me to leave them. Later, she said the nanny would stay. I never knew what was promised, but the problem was solved. Not an auspicious start to the weekend. The next day was worse.

I had been mentoring a young actor, Bob Randall, who'd written a play called *6 Rms Riv Vu*. I thought it had Broadway potential. Bob and his wife were passing through Connecticut, so I invited them to meet Susskind, hoping to pique David's interest.

It was a perfect afternoon. Norman and I sat with Bob and his wife on the terrace while David showered. Joyce greeted them warmly. Then David appeared, every inch the impresario. I introduced him. He took one look at Bob's wife, who was quite heavy, and without a word, pointed at her and said: "Fat girl!"

The air went dead. I wished the earth would swallow me whole. I knew instantly what he was thinking. He had bought the rights to a

New Yorker story called "Fat Girl" and wanted it adapted for film. Not having found a writer, he must have decided Bob, being a writer married to a "fat girl," was the perfect candidate.

But how to explain that? I mumbled something about David owning the story and being on the lookout for a screenwriter, while Bob and his wife sat frozen. They left soon after.

The three of us, Joyce, Norman, and I, turned on David the moment they were gone.

"How could you do that?" Joyce demanded.

"What?" David asked blankly.

"You called her 'fat girl,'" I said. "She's gone home to kill herself."

"Don't be ridiculous," David scoffed. "She never even noticed."

That was David all over: no feeling for people, just calculations. He was like David Merrick—brilliant, ruthless, and insulated. He made enemies easily, especially on his talk shows. Celebrities tolerated him when they needed something, but others retaliated. I once read that Tony Curtis had a portrait of David painted inside the bottom of his toilet bowl. That seemed about right.

We decided to transform our Connecticut ranch into a French farmhouse. Through our art director friend Ben Edwards, we found Iris Whitney, a decorator who became our guide. She taught us that every object should be beautiful: a lamp could be made out of a simple Chinese ginger jar; a carpet could be bold but not too garish. We couldn't afford the finest things, but Iris took us to auctions and gently trained our eyes for line, period, and quality.

She was soft-spoken and elegant, with a past that was once tabloid fodder. Thirty years earlier, movie star John Garfield had died in her apartment. He was married, but not to her, and the press crucified her as a "scarlet woman." The Iris we knew was nothing of the kind: refined, almost shy, with an apartment in Gramercy Park filled with antiques she'd picked up at bargain prices.

One day, I looked at her, quiet and gracious in her sixties, and thought of *Arsenic and Old Lace*. What about two old ladies who didn't commit murders but solved them? There hadn't been a series like that on television. Agatha Christie had Miss Marple, but she worked alone. My pair would be sisters in their sixties, living in Gramercy Park, like Iris, surrounded by antiques. One would be elegant and fey like Iris; the other, strong, practical, a maiden lady who wrote mystery novels. Together, they would be the Snoop Sisters.

I wrote an outline and, recalling what I'd learned from Susskind, knew I needed a package: a writer and a star. Hugh Wheeler, a friend who lived a short distance from us in the country, who would later write *A Little Night Music* and *Sweeney Todd*, agreed to write a script if I could sell it to one of the networks. Helen Hayes liked the idea of the no-nonsense sister, and when Mildred Natwick heard Hayes was in, she agreed to the elegant counterpart. I had my package, and I mailed the outline to myself for copyright protection. I presented it to Susskind, and he optioned it. Universal bought the project, Hugh wrote the script, and producer Leonard Stern in Hollywood took over the reins.

Months later, I saw the pilot on television and hardly recognized it. The antiques were gone, replaced by modern art. My gentle, fey ladies were made "hip." Leonard had rewritten Hugh's script, draining it of what made it unusual. Norman and I watched it and were miserable.

Meanwhile, Norman's painting was becoming more and more serious. He began a series he called his "Pinter plays," portraits of people standing together yet apart, isolated with each other. His first was of Eleanor Perry, the screenwriter, standing at our front door in silhouette against the sunset, her reflection caught in the glass. It captured her loneliness after her breakup with her director husband Frank. I had cast two movies for them: *The Swimmer* and *Last Summer*. Norman was evolving a style: the poetry of alienation.

Eleanor became a close friend. She spent weekends with us in Connecticut, savoring the quiet and loving our long walks together. On one visit, she casually mentioned she had seen Susskind at a party. They'd spoken of me, and he'd said I was a "good worker" but "not a creative person." I was livid. After years of delivering shows while he took the credit, he dismissed me with a wave. I wrote my resignation that night, agreeing only to finish two current productions.

Months later, with the second show complete, I was told to clear out by week's end. As I packed, David's daughter Pam moved in. He had asked me to train her as a casting director, and now I understood why. As I was teaching Pam, the subject of homosexuality came up. "Those people are so disgusting," she said flatly.

"What's so terrible about them?" I asked, keeping my voice neutral.

"They do disgusting things to each other."

"They do pretty much the same things heterosexuals do," I said. She didn't want to hear it.

I've often thought of a story Billy Nichols told about a dinner party. A guest launched into a tirade against homosexuals. His wife said, "Why do you hate them so? What is it that they do that's so horrible?"

He replied, "If you must know, they put a man's penis in their mouth."

To which the wife at the table calmly replied, "Well, I do that."

Her husband groaned, "Ohhh, Florence." Norman and I still say "Oh, Florence," when something absurd happens.

Susskind himself never mentioned my being gay. He ignored Norman when it suited him, as he had when he excluded him from the *Laura* screening, though in person he could be perfectly cordial to him. He preferred to employ women; in the macho atmosphere of the '60s, they posed no threat. I suspect he kept me so long because he assumed a gay man couldn't threaten his power either.

Still, silence could speak loudly. When Norman had his one-man show, a reporter from *The New York Times* asked to feature him and his apartment. The night before, Norman asked me, "What if she asks if I live here alone?" At the time, men simply didn't say they lived together.

"What do you think?" I asked.

He paused, then said, "I think if it comes up, I'll tell the truth. I'm proud of what we've built together."

The article ran with photographs of Norman painting and sitting in our living room. Midway through, it said plainly that he lived with me. That Friday, it felt like a bomb had gone off. On Monday at Susskind's office, silence thundered. No one mentioned the article. No client, colleague, not even Jane Trahey at Norman's agency. It was news that no one wanted to confront.

Susskind made his statement the way he always did, by saying nothing. For that moment, in *The New York Times*, our life together existed in print. It was, as far as we knew, the first time the paper had acknowledged a same-sex couple. The world wasn't ready, but we had quietly crossed a line.

After leaving David Susskind, I went through one of the hardest times of my life. I had never stopped working since I left home at 17. Even when acting jobs were scarce, I was hustling: I ushered, waited tables, assisted a photographer, and worked for a doctor. I didn't know what it meant to have empty, unstructured time.

Each morning, after Norman left for his long commute to New York, I went up to my small study under the eaves. If it was cold, I'd light the Franklin stove and try to think how to restart my career. I had abandoned casting when producing Susskind's specials consumed all my energy, and now I wasn't sure how to re-enter. Others had stepped in and established themselves, and I no longer had an office in the city where I could see actors. Living in Connecticut, I'd also lost touch with the new Broadway generation.

What I wanted most was to produce television, but I didn't know how to begin. My experience was technical, not entrepreneurial. Susskind had the track record to get remakes of plays financed. I didn't. I needed an idea strong enough to sell, but nothing came to mind. I would stretch out on the bunkbed, staring at the hills, willing inspiration to strike. I devoured Brontë, Austen, Dickens, Tolstoy, Dostoevsky—hoping a story might spark an adaptation. But the rights were impossible, the costs astronomical. They remained just great novels.

Once a week, I'd drive to New Milford to collect unemployment insurance. I hadn't stood in that kind of line since my early acting days. Occasionally, I'd run into actors I had once cast. I imagined them thinking, *There he is. He used to be important, but now he is collecting a check like the rest of us.* The shame gnawed at me. I was in my 40s. What if my work life were truly over?

My days settled into a rhythm: reading, scribbling ideas, long walks to shake off anxiety. In the evenings, I waited for Norman. Often, he came home after 8:00, exhausted from a full day at the office and four hours on the road. And still he made dinner, because I never learned to cook. Looking back, it was outrageous. We'd also bought an MG sports car, beautiful but absurd. Norman hunched into it for the commute, his back slowly wrecked by those endless drives.

One day, the strain caught up with him. He came home and said he couldn't do it anymore: the agency battles with Jane Trahey, the commute, the compromises. He wanted, finally, to paint full-time. He had savings, but not enough to cushion us indefinitely. Still, I knew this was the chance he deserved. I told him, "I'll support us for five years until you can get established as an artist. Somehow, I'll make it work."

Norman resigned. Jane accused him of betrayal and demanded that he clear out immediately. Even Jacqueline, one of our closest friends, turned on us. Years passed before we spoke again.

Life shifted. Norman set up his studio; I returned to my study, still searching for a project big enough to avoid reopening my casting office. Our days became quietly productive as we worked side by side. We finally ate meals together. I'd read him what I'd written, and he'd suggest changes. He'd show me the day's progress on a canvas, and we'd talk about color, shape, and feeling.

In the evenings, we walked the country roads, then came back to a drink, dinner, and a little television. No glamour, no frenzy, just the two of us luxuriating in time. We felt like the luckiest people in the world.

Twenty-Two

Eleanor Perry continued to spend weekends with us, often bringing a friend from her consciousness-raising group, a quiet film critic named Gail Rock. Gail was pleasant if withdrawn, with glasses and long straight hair that she was forever flicking behind her shoulders, and she adored Eleanor, which was reason enough to have her.

One cool fall morning, the four of us lingered over our breakfast coffee by the Franklin stove. I confessed I was desperate for something to produce. "In a month," I said, "the networks will be scrambling for a Christmas special. If I had the right idea, I could sell it now. I've read every children's book in sight. The only thing from my own life is being a little Jewish boy who wanted a Christmas tree and couldn't have one, and no one's buying that."

Gail said softly, "We weren't Jewish, and we didn't have a tree."

"Why not?"

"My father was too stingy. We went to my uncle's. They had one, so he said there was no reason to waste the money."

"That's it," I said. "That's the special."

"What is?" Gail blinked. "That's not a story."

"I'll find one. Eleanor will write it."

Eleanor smiled. "I will." She was taking every assignment to prove, after Frank left her, that she didn't need a director-husband to get work.

I kept questioning Gail. "What did your mother think about you not having a tree?"

"She'd died years before. I lived with my father and grandmother."

A stingy father wasn't enough. A grieving one might be. "Gail, go upstairs," I said. "Write about the room you grew up in. Wallpaper. Bedspread. What your father and grandmother were like. Just put it down."

"I've never written that kind of thing."

"Do it anyway." And, wonderfully, she got up and did.

While Gail scribbled, Eleanor and I roughed in a story: a Nebraska girl of ten or eleven, brainy, bossy, bespectacled, who longs for a tree. Her father forbids it, claiming "waste," but really because Christmas is an unbearable reminder of his dead wife. In the end, he brings home a tree and the paper star the mother had made, and he helps his daughter hang it on the tree.

Gail returned with notes: a distant father, a busy grandmother, a small town, a tomboy girl who once *won* a tree at school. In real life, her father had accepted the free tree. In ours, he'd erupt, and our heroine would give the tree away to a child who had none. Eleanor wrote in our kitchen, lifting phrases from life. "I don't give a fig," she overheard at the market, and it went straight into Grandma's mouth.

I took the outline to CBS. The head of specials liked the idea and the name, *The House Without a Christmas Tree,* and approved a script. (Eleanor was already halfway through.) When we delivered it, I sent it to award-winning director Paul Bogart. Paul said it was too "simple," too "sweet." I kept calling.

Finally, I said, "Paul, you work all the time for Susskind, whom you don't even like. You tell me you like me, but you won't help me get my first show on?" He sighed, heard the need in my voice, and said yes.

We had to shoot in November, and we needed snow. Toronto had served me well on other shows, so we flew up and found Uxbridge: 1950s streets, a modest house, a proper old high school. Snow never arrived, so we hired a machine and prayed.

Casting the girl, Addie, meant seeing everyone. We wanted a real child, not a pageant doll. Lisa Lucas came in: full of horses and sports, not a word about "the craft." She read cleanly, had the spark, and looked like our Addie. For the father and grandmother, my dream cast was Jason Robards and Mildred Natwick. I offered the show to both of them, expecting polite refusals. To my amazement, they both said yes.

Around then, two significant events occurred: one gift and one blow. The gift was Norman. Painting full-time now, his back often gave out, so he started making collages from children's construction paper, cut into barns, fields, and animals. When I brought home a photo of our location house in Canada and asked him to collage it as a possible logo, he produced a bright red farmhouse under a cobalt sky that made Paul stop and say, "We have to use this."

We went further. We decided Addie would grow up to be an *artist* rather than a writer, as she had been patterned after Gail originally. The special would begin with adult hands cutting papers to make a collage of a house. When it was complete, the camera would dissolve into the real house. Then, at the beginning and end of each act, we would dissolve from the live action into one of Norman's collages, matched exactly to Paul's camera frames. Norman would come to Toronto, trace Paul's selected freeze-frames from tape, and build the paper moments. It gave the piece gentle, handmade poetry and the imprint of real art.

The blow was CBS's condition. Because I'd never produced "on my own," the special had to be a CBS production. I could produce it, but they would own it. It was too late to go elsewhere, and they'd funded the script. I took the deal. It was a financial mistake; I never made any money in what turned out to be a huge success. But at least a door had been opened.

The shoot went beautifully. Lisa was totally real and winning. Jason and Millie were brilliant. Ben Edwards's spare interiors and Jane Greenwood's clothes put us quietly in the right place. Paul's edit, woven with Norman's collages, gave the show its uniqueness.

The reviews were terrific; the ratings great. The morning after the broadcast, I was called to an appointment with Fred Silverman, at that time the head of programming. He congratulated me and said, "Do another holiday with the same family."

"Which holiday?"

"You tell me."

"Thanksgiving," I blurted, buying us a year to get it done.

We ultimately made three more holiday specials. For Thanksgiving, I borrowed from our Bucks County life. The reclusive old farmer down the road, who thawed enough to give us a hideous table, became the center of the story. Barnard Hughes broke your heart.

For Easter, I raided my own early failures: a once-promising actress (Jean Simmons, luminous), and on Valentine's Day, we tried a back-door pilot. Addie, now blossoming, loses her glasses, finds a dress, and flirts with her first love. Jason, Millie, and Lisa did all the specials. The series didn't happen, but the shows are watched to this day.

Eleanor won the Emmy for *Christmas Tree* and Paul was nominated. The Television Academy recognized Norman's contribution with an Emmy for the Valentine's special. The paper worlds he built had become part of the show's soul. I received the Christopher Award, "for affirming the highest values of the human spirit."

But the true prize was quieter. It was proof that I could build something from scratch, find the story at a breakfast table, coax it into a script, assemble the right people, and make a special that felt like a memory. And to have done it with Norman's hands literally shaping the look of it, with our life inside his work, was the best prize of all.

The year after the success of *The House Without A Christmas Tree* was strangely empty. No publishers or agents called with material, and I was back in my Connecticut study, trying to find ideas with no results. Then Helen Hayes phoned. She and Mildred Natwick were in Hollywood filming *The Snoop Sisters*, which CBS had ordered for four 90-minute episodes despite the limp pilot. The ladies were miserable, hating the scripts and feeling badly treated. They insisted I come out to help them. "Otherwise," Helen said, "we won't continue."

Universal called the next day and made a quick deal to fly me to Los Angeles. Norman came with me. We thought we'd stay for a few weeks, but we ended up staying nearly 20 years. It's an old joke: you go to Hollywood for a short visit, put on a bathing suit, go out to the pool, and when you go back inside, you look in the mirror, and you're 75.

On the set of *The Snoop Sisters*, I quickly realized that no one wanted me there except Helen and Millie. As the originator of the series, they believed I could fix the show. But it was too late. The scripts were already being ground out, and the material was ordinary. All I could do was be with Helen and Millie and make them as comfortable as possible.

One night, Mike Nichols, in town finishing a film, invited Norman and me to a party at Tony Curtis's rented house. There, I ran into John Calley, now head of production at Warner Brothers. We'd become friends while working on *Catch 22*. John pulled me aside. Years earlier, when he'd first gone to Warners, he'd phoned me out of the blue and said, "The only question is whether you live in Beverly Hills or Malibu." He wanted me to take over casting at the studio. I laughed and said I was happy in New York, passing the opportunity on to my talented ex-assistant, Nessa Hyams.

Over drinks, John told me that Nessa was leaving for Columbia Pictures. Did I want the job at last? My first instinct was to refuse. I was a producer now, not a casting director. But Norman and I talked it through later at the hotel. *The Snoop Sisters* had already been cancelled. Work was scarce back east. Specials weren't enough to support us, and Norman was now painting full-time and could work as well in Hollywood. Everything I tried to get, whether a promising book or a story idea, was already taken by someone with a bigger name.

Meanwhile, New York was snarled with traffic, gas shortages made commuting maddening, and the theater world felt less welcoming. Maybe Hollywood was the solution. If Warners let me produce as well as cast, perhaps I could balance both careers.

We hired a lawyer who began to negotiate with the studio. My title would be Director of Creative Affairs and Head of Casting. The title sounded grand, but in truth, it was vague. I joked later that there were plenty of "affairs" in Hollywood, but I was never asked to direct them.

Still, the salary was generous enough for us to live comfortably, and the promise of real studio clout was irresistible.

Norman immediately set about finding us a home. We couldn't go on living at the Beverly Hills Hotel. He found a jewel of a house for rent on St. Ives Drive, above the Sunset Strip. In the '40s and '50s, the neighborhood was filled with nightclubs catering to movie royalty. By now, they'd become record stores and agents' offices, but the views were still magical. From the terrace at night, the lights of Los Angeles spread all the way to the horizon. The house itself had been decorated by its owner with tastefully matching draperies and bedspreads, and polished leaves on Ficus trees. It was stylish, temporary, glamorous. The perfect perch for our new life in Hollywood.

At Warner Brothers, my office was buried on the first floor—really, the basement. Everyone else seemed to have a view, which felt like a signal that I was there to cast, not to produce. Still, I was included in weekly meetings, and stacks of galleys and scripts kept arriving. Publishers sent new novels to every studio at once, and we were expected to read overnight and weigh in by morning. I sat on our tiny porch on weekends, reading in the sun, hoping one of them would be my way forward as a producer again.

We asked Henry, our Connecticut caretaker, to send our dachshund Snoopy to Los Angeles. Henry had been sitting with the dog each night in our empty bedroom. Weeks went by, and Snoopy never came. Henry always had a reason. At last, Norman and I flew back east to retrieve him ourselves and bought another dachshund for company. It was easier than prying him from Henry's arms.

The weekly staff meetings were held upstairs in John Calley's vast office overlooking the executive circle, where the real power brokers parked. My spot was in the lot, well down the pecking order. John's office was decorated with English country furniture and, oddly, a wooden spiral library staircase that went nowhere. The symbolism wasn't lost on me. Inside, Ted Ashley, Frank Wells, and John formed the ruling triumvirate. Reports were read in monotone, numbers ticked off, and then it was each executive's turn.

When they looked at me, all I could say was, "I have nothing to report," unless asked about casting lists. Early on, I suggested actors I knew from New York, like Richard Gere, but I was met with blank stares. What they wanted was star names like Steve McQueen. I caught on. "Robert Redford," I would suggest. "Perfect," they would all shout. I learned quickly. It didn't matter that these stars rarely materialized. The ritual of invoking their names was enough.

One afternoon, John asked me to stay after the meeting. He had grown distant, but now he came out with it: "You have to say something."

"But I don't have anything to say."

"Then make it up." He gave me examples like inventing a chance encounter with Barbra Streisand or suggesting an agent had sent me a biography. "No one will remember by next week."

I promised to try, but never mastered it. John, though, was effortless, witty, charming, a master raconteur. He was always armed with gossip from his forays around town. Only later did I learn he disliked Hollywood parties, rarely attended them, and got his stories from Sue Mengers.

One production report always came up at the meetings, *Barry Lyndon*, Stanley Kubrick's latest film. Each week was the same: delays, costs mounting. Kubrick wanted a special lens for candlelight, then scrapped days of footage, then demanded new locations.

Ted Ashley would ask, "How much will this cost?" Charlie Greenlaw, head of physical production, would calmly read out astronomical figures. Ted would turn to John. "John, what can we do?"

"I'll phone Stanley," John would say, and that was the end of it. After weeks of John always saying, "I'll phone Stanley," one executive quipped, "John, why don't you threaten Stanley with a phone call?" Everyone laughed. John smiled. He was untouchable; everyone knew it.

I developed a few ideas. I got an advance copy of *Alive*, the harrowing account of the Uruguayan rugby team whose plane crashed in the Andes. I read it straight through, and prepared a pitch. At the meeting, I described the snowstorm, the wrecked fuselage, the young athletes clinging to life, and their desperate choice to eat the bodies of the dead. I finished, moved by my own telling. Silence.

Then Dick Shepard, across the table, said dryly, "Blacks don't like snow." The project was dead. Later, another producer made *Alive*, and it became a success. The lesson was clear. If you couldn't advance your own projects, you could at least kill someone else's.

Hollywood had no rulebook, but I was learning. Beneath the polished surfaces and easy smiles, the game was ruthless. I would never be the slickest player, but I got good enough to survive.

Norman was back in Los Angeles, the city he'd once left behind, but this time everything was different. Family obligations had loosened; his father was gone, his mother was settled in a retirement home, and his siblings were absorbed in their own lives. What could have felt like a return to an unwanted past became a new beginning. Now free to move through the city as an artist, Norman experienced it with fresh eyes.

Each morning at our rented house on St. Ives Drive, Norman set up on the balcony with his pencils, pastels, and paper, staring out toward Santa Monica and the ocean. He drove through neighborhoods, noting the pink stucco, Spanish tiles, and palm trees.

Now everything was filtered through an artist's lens. His painting "Maids," showing Latina nannies gathered in a Beverly Hills park under the shadow of the pink Beverly Hills Hotel, captured both beauty and irony. It marked a turning point in his work. Los Angeles inspired a new visual vocabulary, stylized, satirical, but deeply personal.

His satirical eye expanded to Trousdale Estates, where ostentatious villas and rows of cypress struck him as absurd. He painted the houses, stacked one on top of the other, and over-decorated, mocking the place's wealth and artificiality.

The house we found for ourselves on Beverly Crest Drive was screened by trees and hedges. It was a peculiar home once belonging to Vincent Price. Part Spanish villa, part clapboard cottage, part eccentric experiment, it was bizarre but irresistible. We told ourselves we couldn't afford it, but the realtor urged us on. Vincent Price and his wife were divorcing, and for $160,000, it became ours. Norman called it "Symbionese architecture." With designer Jane Bogart's help, we remade the interiors. Outside, Norman designed a lush garden of tropical plants.

The house became a haven and a gallery for Norman's work. He hid three orchids from Vincent Price's prized collection when we moved in. Later, we confessed the theft to Vincent himself, who laughed uproariously. Dinners with Vincent and his new wife, the irreverent Coral Browne, became part of our lives. As she walked through the remodeled house, she would say about Vincent's ex-wife, "That cunt, if it weren't for her, all of this would be mine." Her wicked commentary filled every room with laughter.

From our home studio, Norman launched into painting his Los Angeles series. He painted our shelves of artifacts, framing them with rooms and pools that no one used. It was a meditation on isolation within abundance. He painted sleek women in modern interiors, cool and remote, detached from the world's troubles. His tongue-in-cheek style crystallized into something distinct, a commentary on privilege and alienation in a glossy cityscape.

Recognition followed. Through store owner Richard Dorso, producer Norman Lear and his wife visited Norman's studio and bought "The Maids," becoming Norman's first major Los Angeles collectors. Their enthusiasm was the validation he needed. That night, we celebrated and joked that soon Norman would be the one supporting us.

It was a new chapter. Norman was a full-fledged artist in Los Angeles, and I watched with pride as his work took root in the city that had once felt like his prison but was now his canvas.

Twenty-Three

Dan Melnick, producer and studio head, became another key ally for Norman in Los Angeles. At my urging, Dan took Norman's work to Margo Leavin, whose West Hollywood gallery was one of the most exciting on the West Coast. Margo had secured the rights to show prints from Gemini G.E.L., the renowned print workshop that produced editions by Jasper Johns, Ellsworth Kelly, and Roy Lichtenstein. She was also connected to Leo Castelli, the New York dealer whose artists defined postwar American art. Though her gallery leaned toward abstraction and conceptualism, far from Norman's figurative style, Dan convinced her to look at his work. To Norman's surprise, she offered him a show that October. It was his first in Los Angeles, only his second anywhere.

Norman worked with enormous energy and optimism in the months before the opening. The day the show was installed, Margo phoned to say it looked terrific. By afternoon, several paintings had already sold. That night, Norman arrived late, as he had learned to do in New York, to find the gallery packed. We hadn't been in Los Angeles long, and his name was only just beginning to circulate, yet the room buzzed with energy.

Dick Dorso rushed him over to meet Billy Wilder, whose legendary private collection was the talk of the town. Dan Melnick introduced him to Tina Sinatra, who had just purchased his shelf painting, her favorite piece in the show. Everywhere Norman turned, he saw red dots marking sold works. He had been to countless art openings, but never anything with this intensity. When he found me in the crowd, I had tears in my eyes.

The evening rolled into a party at Ma Maison, one of the city's most exclusive restaurants, where the celebration continued. Norman could hardly absorb it all. The show was a complete sellout. He felt, finally, that his leap from the security of advertising into painting was vindicated. That night, he told me, was his chance to repay my faith in him. Tomorrow's reviews would be the proof, but already he had crossed a threshold.

Friday mornings had always been exciting for us in New York, the day the theatre reviews appeared. Now, in Los Angeles, it was the same for Norman with the art reviews in the *Times*. He woke early, anxious, and went downstairs for the paper. Within minutes, he was back in the garden, pale and devastated.

Henry Wilson, the leading critic, had written a brutal review of his show. In a few sharp sentences, Wilson dismissed nearly the entire exhibition as derivative, "second-rate Hockney." Only one canvas, the women discussing art, was deemed promising. What Norman had deliberately done, the flatness and poster-like quality he had cultivated since art school, was criticized. He felt as if the paper had published his obituary.

When I found him outside, the *Times* limp in his hand, I knew. He thrust the review at me, his voice raw with hurt. I read quickly, trying to find something to cling to. "But he praises the painting of the women," I said.

Norman was inconsolable. "Don't you see? He's saying I'm finished before I've even begun."

I tried to reassure him. "It's one review. Everyone else loves the work. Reviews get thrown out with the garbage by nightfall."

But Norman could not let it go. He reminded me of the promise I made when he left advertising. I would carry us for five years until he established himself. "It's been almost five years," he said bitterly. "What if I never succeed?"

I told him that five years was nothing in an artist's life, that he painted because he *had* to, not for critics. The people who had bought his work and filled his openings had put their faith in him. "You can't give up," I said. "I won't let you."

Still, he remained silent, wounded. After our morning swim and a half-hearted breakfast, I kissed him goodbye and left for the studio. Later, I learned that as soon as the door closed behind me, Norman stormed into his studio, seized a brush, and painted over two nearly fin-ished canvases in heavy white strokes. "At least," the maid overheard him say, "no one can criticize these."

It was only a few days after Norman's art review had appeared in the *Los Angeles Times* when the call came. I was sitting in my bleak under-ground office, the phone a welcome distraction from the dull routine of the studio.

"Hi," I said, relieved. "I'm glad you called. It's boring here—"

"I'm in jail," Norman whispered. "I need the money to get out." Then silence.

I was shocked, but I managed, "I'll be there as quickly as possible. How much do you need?" He told me. He gave me the address. We hung up.

I had only a few dollars. The banks were closed. He said the money had to be in cash. Swallowing my pride, I panhandled my way through the casting department, begging the women for loans. God knows what they thought, but finally, I gathered the $250 he needed. I drove to the jail, paid the bail, and found Norman waiting, pale and silent. We drove home without a word. I never asked him what had happened. At that moment, none of it mattered; only that I was there for him.

It wasn't until years later that Norman told me the full story. He said he had been restless, aimless after the show. The review had destroyed him. Days passed with no phone calls, no visitors, no word from his dealer or friends. He blamed me for dragging him back to the city he had once fled, and we barely spoke. I tried to reassure him that reviews didn't matter, but he only snapped at me not to lecture him.

One morning, sunk in despair, he decided to drive back into the Hollywood of his youth, searching for some spark, some vision that might reignite him. He wandered through old haunts, his childhood streets, the house where his family had imploded, the park where he once played. Nothing matched his memories. The city was a parody of itself, its glamour peeled away, its beauty paved over. Finally, he stopped at a public restroom near Griffith Park.

He was alone at the urinal when suddenly a man appeared at his right, too close, rubbing himself. Then another on his left, doing the same. Norman felt his heart beat. *Danger. Get out.* He stepped back, fumbling with his zipper. At once, strong hands clamped down on his arms. A second pair of hands snapped cold metal around his wrists.

"You're under arrest. Lewd and obscene behavior."

The words made no sense. Norman's voice caught in his throat. He wanted to shout his innocence, but terror smothered him. The two men were vice cops. They shoved him into the back of their car. "Please," he begged, "what did I do?" They didn't answer.

At the station, they stripped him of everything—wallet, keys, coins. His name and address were inked into a ledger. His fingers were pressed onto cards that would brand him forever. Then they threw him into a hot, airless cell with six other men who stared at him with hostility. He sat against the wall, sweat running down his back, his chest tight, unable to breathe.

Later, an officer read the charges aloud: loitering, obscene conduct, indecent behavior. Lies, every single one. It was the policemen's word against his, and he had no defense. He was told he would face a hearing, that jail time was possible, and that he would carry a criminal record. He said it was like being buried alive. Bail was set at $250. He made his call. That was when I came.

As soon as the papers were signed and the cash was handed over, they released him. He walked beside me like a man underwater, his eyes down, his face locked tight. In the car, he turned to the window, away from me, as if the city itself had betrayed him. We drove in silence. At home, he barely spoke.

I wanted to ask what had happened, but I didn't dare. Part of me was afraid of what I might learn. A gulf grew between us. We became formal with each other, as though politeness could bridge what neither of us could face aloud.

Later, Norman found help. An old fraternity brother, now a prominent lawyer and gay activist, took his case. With influence and persistence, he persuaded the judge to erase the charges. The poisonous words "lewd and indecent" were replaced with "trespassing." The record was scrubbed clean, but the scar remained. Norman could never forgive the vice cops who had humiliated him.

We never spoke of it again. Years later, when I asked him to tell me everything, I thought of my own brush with the police as a boy, when I might have been arrested and ruined for something I hadn't done. I knew then, as I know now, that Norman hadn't done anything either. He had been hunted, cornered, and branded because of who he was.

Twenty-Four

I decided the best way to love him was not to probe or force him to re-live it, but to let it rest. He was the man I loved, and that was all that mattered.

Despite the harsh review in the *Los Angeles Times* and the trouble with the police, Norman was soon back at work. His greatest strength was resilience. Almost immediately after saying he was done painting, he surprised even himself by grabbing a brush, squeezing out paint, and starting again.

One morning, he saw downtown Los Angeles shimmering in the pale light and made it his new subject. He painted the city repeatedly, each scene framed by the window at a different height. The series was exhibited at the Bernard Jacobson Gallery, and this time, *The Times* praised his work, calling it a combination of abstraction, minimalism, and realism. Norman was pleased but announced he would never let a review sway him again, good or bad.

At the same time, I was casting Paul Newman's *The Drowning Pool* at Warner Brothers, and the work was going well. Still, film meetings made me so nervous that I started smoking again after 20 years without a cigarette. The endless talk of profits and losses left little room for conversation about writing or actors, except the stars. Movies were treated as packages, not art. Norman worried about my smoking, and I would sneak outside for a cigarette. Eventually, I quit again, but the relapse showed how much pressure I was under. Looking back, I wonder if I took it all too seriously; often, no one cared about others' input.

Irwin Allen, king of disaster epics, moved onto the lot with *The Towering Inferno*. He summoned me and led me to a wall covered in fabric with four slots labeled with character names and four knobs. He spun the knobs, and star names—Newman, Redford, Dunaway—rolled into place like a pinball machine. "What do you think?" he asked, though he never waited for an answer. He only wanted admiration. Afterwards, he served Kentucky Fried Chicken on Spode china, with Cokes in Baccarat goblets. As I left, he assured me I had helped him enormously.

My two-year contract was ending. Norman and I were living well, traveling, and making friends. But I had little to show except casting *The Drowning Pool* and *The Last Warrior*. The exception was *All the President's Men*, the one project that demanded everything I had.

To prepare, I went to Washington, D.C., to meet the real people behind Watergate. When I met Ben Bradlee, editor of *The Washington Post*, I immediately thought of Jason Robards—his voice, manner, and humor were a match. At the studio, I said so. "Oh, he's washed up," one executive scoffed. "Can't you do better?" Fortunately, director Alan Pakula agreed with me. Jason played Bradlee and won an Academy Award.

Robert Redford was a joy: pleasant, professional, magnetic. On the set, a replica of the *Post* newsroom, your eye went to him, no matter how crowded the room. It was as if a spotlight was always on him. Years later, Norman and I went to Sundance hoping Redford would consider a remake of *Saratoga Trunk*. He agreed to watch the old film if I screened it there. He arrived with his children and their friends, who fidgeted through the film. Redford slipped out halfway, but was charming, showing us his house. He never mentioned the project again. Such was Hollywood: projects died quietly, and you moved on.

Working with Dustin Hoffman was different. I first saw him years earlier in Ronald Ribman's *Harry, Noon and Night*, where he played a German transvestite brilliantly. I called my friend, the agent Jane Oliver, the next day: "Sign this boy, he'll be a star." She did, and within a year, he was in *The Graduate*.

Now, Dustin was a major star. He insisted on improvising with every actor before I could cast them and would only see them a day or two before shooting. I often sat outside his dressing room with nervous actors for hours. He never rejected any of them, but the process was agony. For someone who once struggled himself, he seemed to have little regard for others.

In the end, *All the President's Men* was the finest cast I ever assembled. I drew on the best actors I knew, not for looks but for their essence—taciturnity, aggression, belligerence, whatever the real people had. Director Alan Pakula's taste matched mine. Years later, I read a critic who said the casting deserved an Academy Award. In my day, casting directors were listed at the end of the film, along with the caterer or the hairdresser's assistant. Today, they receive top billing and awards. They deserve it.

Shortly before my contract ended at Warner Brothers, I was told it would not be renewed. They were happy for me to stay, but without a contract. They felt I was already paid enough and didn't want to keep raising my salary. I didn't blame them. I had been hired to cast and develop film projects, but I hadn't delivered one. Agents with books or scripts never brought them to me. I was too far down the pecking order. If I chased a property, it was already out. Nothing reached my desk until it was rejected everywhere else. I realized I was only seen as Head of Casting; my years producing TV specials were forgotten.

At that time, Mike Nichols came to Warners to direct *Bogart Slept Here*, Neil Simon's comedy about a New York actor in Hollywood. I was to cast the film, and working with Mike again felt like being back in New York. We assembled a smart, funny cast, with Robert De Niro in the lead.

While I was busy with the film, Ethel Winant, head of casting at CBS, called. I'd known her since my acting days. "Are you happy at Warners?" she asked.

"It's all right," I said.

"Why don't you take my job?" she said. "You'd love it. You don't have to do casting every day. The studios bring you actors for pilots and movies of the week, and all you have to do is approve or disapprove. And you're in command."

I hesitated. In Hollywood, television was considered a stepsister to movies, but the idea tempted me. I was tired of spending as much time finding actors for bit parts as I was chasing stars, and I no longer fooled myself into thinking I was a true film executive. Ethel was powerful and respected; all the studios courted her approval. I felt buried by comparison.

"What do I do?" I asked.

"Go see Perry Lafferty," she said. Perry was vice president of West Coast Programming at CBS.

I met with him, and on Ethel's word, he insisted I leave Warners as soon as my contract ended. He promised a different world: no isolation in the Valley, but an office in the city next to the Farmers Market, where the energy of Los Angeles surged around you. It sounded like freedom.

Norman and I spent long hours talking through it. In the end, we agreed I would go to CBS. Executives there didn't have contracts, which suited me. I could always leave if I didn't like it. They allowed me to finish the Nichols picture and produce another *House Without a Christmas Tree* special. I said goodbye to Warners and moved on.

Soon after I settled into my new office, Frank Wells, President of Warner Brothers, called. "Can you come right over?"

I drove to the studio, wondering if they wanted me back. When I walked into Frank's office, John Calley and Ted Ashley were waiting.

"We need your help," Ted said. "Mike's picture isn't working. He thinks it's the material. We think another cast may solve it."

John added, "Start with the lead, De Niro's part. Bring actors to show Mike."

"But De Niro is the star," I said.

"He's wonderful," John replied, "but he may not be right. We've seen the dailies, and it just isn't working. Who can we get?"

I went to my new CBS office by day and returned to Warners at night, parading actors in front of Mike. He met every young talent in town, worked with them, and listened. But nothing clicked. The material sagged. At last, we ran out of actors, and the picture stalled. Later, with rewrites and Herb Ross directing, it was reborn as *The Goodbye Girl*. Richard Dreyfuss and Marsha Mason starred, and Dreyfuss won the Oscar.

Meanwhile, I learned more about my new life at CBS. My office overlooked Beverly Boulevard, not a parking lot in the Valley. I could wander the Farmers Market at lunch or meet with producers and agents. Instead of one or two films, I was consulted on dozens of shows. It was a healthy change.

One day, Perry Lafferty brought me a problem. "We've got Linda Lavin under contract, but it's up at the end of the week. If we don't use her, we'll lose her. Do we have anything?"

I remembered a pilot script from Warners—*Alice*, based on Martin Scorsese's *Alice Doesn't Live Here Anymore*. CBS had rejected it, but I liked it.

"What about *Alice*?" I asked.

"Oh no," Perry said. "We passed. It isn't funny."

"Put Linda Lavin in it," I said. "She'll make it funny. Did you ever see her in *Last of the Red Hot Lovers*? She was fantastic."

He remained doubtful, but after some pressing, he agreed if I promised a great cast. Vic Tayback returned as the diner's owner. For Vera, I brought in Beth Howland, unforgettable in *Company* singing "I'm Not Getting Married Today." For Flo, Diane Ladd refused, so I gambled on Polly Holiday, an actress Dustin Hoffman had recommended. She wasn't the obvious choice, but she was brilliant and won the part. The boy from the film refused, too, but after exhausting every boy in Los Angeles, we found Phillip McKeon. *Alice* was launched.

At CBS, I was treated warmly and no longer had the crushing pressure of film meetings. But I was still casting as much as ever. Ethel had promised me a world where casting people paraded actors past me for approval, but if someone wasn't right, I had to find the replacement. Back I went to files and auditions.

Socially, things changed. My new position meant Norman and I always had good tables at Ma Maison or Trader Vic's. We gave large parties, mixing actors, directors, producers, artists, and even a few movie stars. Our home, with Norman's paintings and the sweeping view, was perfect for entertaining. It was obvious we were a couple. No one questioned it, but I was aware I was the only executive openly living with a man. That gave me new confidence.

Still, I wasn't satisfied. There was no challenge. After a few months, Warner Brothers called again. They wanted me back, this time as Vice President of Production. No more day-to-day casting; I would hire someone else for that. They offered more money, a bigger contract, and a better car, the car being a badge of rank in Hollywood. I returned to Warners as if I had never left.

As soon as I was back, I was casting again. This time, it was the lead in a *Wonder Woman* pilot. For years, Warners had tried other pilots, but the network always turned them down. I saw every beautiful girl in Hollywood. Agents sent them in, I watched reels, and we even advertised nationwide. Hundreds of pictures poured in from hopeful young actresses. After months, I narrowed the choices to a few, but none felt quite right.

Talking with a manager who knew many glamorous women, I said I was having the worst luck. "Have you seen Lynda Carter?" he asked.

"Yes," I replied. "She's beautiful. However, I watched two television shows she appeared in. She's stiff, she acts like what she is, a beauty queen."

"I think you should see her again," he said. "She has something."

So, I called her agent and made another appointment. This time I spent more time with her. She was ingenuous, warm, and more appealing than I realized. I persuaded producer Douglas Cramer to include her in the screen tests. When we ran the network tests, no one was excited. Lynda looked magnificent in costume, but executives said she was too heavy. We promised she could lose a few pounds. They weren't thrilled by her acting either, and finally, the network said, "Postpone until next season and find someone else."

I'd had enough. "Look," I said, "I'll never find anyone who looks as sexy and beautiful as Lynda. And if I do, she won't act any better. Lynda doesn't realize how gorgeous she is or how fantastic her body is. But she has a sweetness. Her goodness will shine through and make the show work."

At last, they gave in. *Wonder Woman* ran for years. By the time it went on the air, everyone, Lynda included, had forgotten I'd found her and fought for her. With encouragement from her manager and her soon-to-be husband, she began to believe she was a star. Sudden fame is hard for actors. Some grow better with it; others start to believe their publicity and behave like royalty until the public turns to someone else.

Several months later, after a film meeting, I was asked to stay behind. Ted Ashley and Frank Wells informed me that the head of the television division was returning to England, and they had decided to exit the television business altogether. They were losing too much money, and they weren't producing any hits. They needed someone to take over in the interim while they phased out the operation. Would I consider doing it temporarily?

"You're the only one of the executives with television experience. We would be very grateful."

I was shocked. I only wanted to work on movies, but I asked my friend John Cally what he thought.

"Do it," he said without hesitation.

I agreed when they told me it would only be for several weeks.

Twenty-Five

Norman had thrown himself into his work. He found a studio in an old sweatshop in Little Tokyo, and each morning after breakfast, he'd head to the freeway. Hours vanished at his easel. Sometimes music played, mixing with city sounds, but mostly it was quiet. No longer confined at home, his downtown studio became a new world, sparking a creative breakthrough.

One afternoon, I called him, letting the phone ring until he finally put down his brush. "I have incredible news," I said. "Guess what?"

"You sold a movie?" he asked.

"Better than that. You've been nominated for an Emmy Award for the collages you did in *Addie and the King of Hearts*. There's a new category, Graphics and Title Design. I didn't tell you, but I submitted your work."

"I can't believe it! I'm thrilled!" Norman shouted, his voice echoing in the cavernous studio.

Addie had been the last of the specials we'd done together, featuring his art. Now, against all odds, he was being honored for it. What made the nomination even more surreal was that he was up against *Wonder Woman*, produced by Douglas Cramer.

Doug had commissioned slick, animated pop art sequences in the style of Roy Lichtenstein. Norman's collages were handmade, childlike in their simplicity: construction paper cutouts, bold and colorful. Technically, they seemed no match for Cramer's comic-book fireworks. But Norman's work, to me, had more heart.

We had agreed not to appear together at industry events. As one of the few openly gay executives, I was cautious. Homophobia was always near, and I knew it could be used against me. Norman was furious when I told him I wouldn't go to the ceremony. "We did this together," he said. "This award is for both of us."

A trusted friend told him, "Better for Alan if you're seen with a woman. Makes everyone more comfortable." Reluctantly, Norman agreed. He asked his dealer, Margo Leavin, to accompany him to the Craft Emmy Awards luncheon, where the behind-the-scenes awards were given.

The luncheon was at the Beverly Wilshire Hotel. Margo and Norman were photographed as they entered and were seated near the stage. Norman, sure that he wouldn't win, let his nerves settle into just enjoying the wine. Mike Connors of *Mannix* emceed and looked Norman right in the eye, saying, "You are the creative people who make us look good."

The ceremony dragged on. Norman checked his watch, worried about missing his flight to Palm Springs, where Doug Cramer was hosting us. Finally, Connors announced the Graphics and Title Design category: "And the winner is...Norman Sunshine for *Addie and the King of Hearts*."

Norman froze. Only when Margo hugged him did he move. Applause swelled as he reached the stage. Connors shook his hand, and a woman handed him his statue. Norman babbled a thank-you speech he barely remembered. Rattled from wine, he returned to his table, Emmy in hand. The triumph felt hollow. He thought, "Why wasn't Alan here? Who are we still hiding from?"

After the ceremony, Norman rushed to the airport, only to learn that his flight had been canceled. Furious, he called Doug. "Give me Alan," he barked.

I grabbed the phone. "I'm so happy you called."

"I'm so angry with you," he shot back. "You should have been there."

"What happened?" I asked, steadying myself.

"I won! That's what happened. I won! But you weren't there."

"It's just as well," I said. "I would have cried."

"I know," he admitted, and then, at last, we both laughed.

Spying a Hertz counter, Norman hung up, rented a car, and barreled down the freeway, making the two-hour trip in ninety reckless minutes. He screeched up to Doug's house, honked, and thrust the Emmy at Doug and me. "And neither of you was there to see it!"

We hugged him, congratulated him, and poured wine. Norman and I clinked glasses, but the truth hung between us: we hadn't shared that moment. How many men and women had accepted awards, unable to thank the person they loved? Norman said he had acknowledged me in his speech, but only as the "producer," not his partner. I told him I would never let anything like this happen again.

***

When I first took over Warner's television division, I felt like Ronald Colman in *The Prisoner of Zenda*—suddenly impersonating the King without knowing the rules. I was lost. Luckily, Barry Meyer (legal and financial affairs) and Richard Kobritz (technical production) steadied me. The creative side was a disaster, but together we formed a team, staying late, plotting how to keep the division alive. Even if Warner was phasing out television, I was determined to make it work.

Ironically, the only shows on the slate were ones I'd already touched: the *Alice* pilot with Linda Lavin and the cast I'd assembled at CBS, and a handful of *Wonder Woman* specials with Lynda Carter. By coincidence, I was inheriting my own work. Not knowing too much helped; I could trust instinct over habit.

Alice, however, was in trouble. I'd told CBS how funny it could be, but the pilot wasn't funny at all. CBS ordered just four episodes—a half-hearted gesture, almost an obituary. The tone was depressing: The character of Alice seemed like a singer trapped as a waitress, the diner felt dreary, and the cast had no spark. There was no joy or rhythm. The writing was flat, the production uninspired.

Most people shrugged: "Why bother? *Alice* will be canceled." But my theater background told me otherwise. If a show had potential, you fought for it. I started asking around, keeping lists of good producers and writers. Everyone said it was hopeless. Still, I pushed.

I reached out to John Rich, who'd directed *Barney Miller* and other sitcoms. At first, he wasn't interested. I begged. Finally, he agreed. John was commanding and blunt. The cast didn't like him—trainers rarely win affection while causing pain—but he transformed the show.

He saw immediately that *Alice* wasn't about a waitress pining for a singing career. "This is a comedy," he said. "Forget the singing. The show is about the family: Alice, Flo, Vera, and Mel. They fight, love each other, and fight again."

He also insisted that each episode be performed as if it were opening night on Broadway. Though taped, he demanded the energy and precision of live theater. Suddenly, the show crackled. The audience laughed. *Alice* had found its heartbeat.

It went on to run for nine years. Producers came and went until Madelyn Davis and Bob Carroll, of *I Love Lucy* fame, took over for the last seven. Three different actresses played Flo. Somehow, it endured.

There were constant flare-ups. The cast didn't always get along. We held "consciousness-raising meetings," where actors vented their beefs while the producers and I sat like psychiatrists, intervening only when things got too heated. Tempers flared, egos clashed, but after everyone spoke, they returned to work until the next time.

Six months in, *Alice* was working, *Wonder Woman* was strong, and we had a miniseries with Elizabeth Montgomery. Suddenly, everything changed. Warner decided not to shut down television. Ted and Frank, buoyed by the turnaround, asked who I'd recommend as the new president. I helped make lists of top executives, but one by one, the candidates said no. They were already successful elsewhere and saw no reason to join a studio that had nearly abandoned television.

Norman and I had become close with Ted, the head of Warner, and his future wife, Joyce Easton. Ted had just completed est, a program of group awareness training meant to help you unlock your potential. He found it miraculous and insisted that Norman and I do it too.

We agreed, and it was unlike anything we had ever experienced. For two weekends, from early morning until late at night, we sat on hard folding chairs in a hotel conference room with hundreds of people, doing exercises meant to tear down our defenses. Est was infamous for forbidding bathroom breaks except during brief pauses, so we survived by not drinking water. But the discipline worked. The noise of the world fell away, and all that remained was yourself: who you were, whether you were happy or not, and what you wanted.

We both usually swam twenty laps each morning. On the second Sunday of est, after three grueling days, something extraordinary happened: we kept swimming, lap after lap, until we reached 100. That week, Norman returned to his studio and began painting larger canvases with more energy. I, too, had a revelation.

A cornerstone of est was "sharing." People stood and declared, "I want to share with you," before speaking their truths. As I sat there, I realized: *I had made Warner Television a success. Why hand it over? It should be mine. I deserved it.*

The next day, emboldened, I asked Ted's secretary for a meeting with him. "Ted," I said when I stood before him, "I want to share something with you. We've searched for someone to take over the television division and found no one. I rescued it from oblivion. I've proven I can do the job better than anyone else. I should be president."

He looked startled. "I'll talk it over with the others," was all he said. I left without another word, but as I walked back to my office, I wondered, *Does it always have to be like this? Do you have to ask for everything? Can't it ever just come to you?*

Weeks passed. I heard nothing. Then Joyce Easton quietly told me the real reason for the delay: they were debating the problem of my being gay. Would it be a detriment? How had I not seen this coming?

"Of course," I said to Norman. "I should have known. They'll never give me the job. Remember when I suggested Doug Cramer? Perfect credentials. They turned him down flat because he was gay. No anger, no insult, just a statement of fact, as if *gay* and *president* could never belong in the same sentence."

"That's outrageous," Norman said. "There are plenty of gay men in important positions. Everyone knows who they are, and they still do their jobs."

"But they don't live openly with another man," I reminded him. "They show up with women and keep their gay parties secret. Directors, producers, fine. But executives *represent* the studio. They want someone who can sit in a football box, play softball, and drink beer with the network presidents. They don't think I can move in those circles."

"That's ridiculous," Norman shot back. "If your shows are good, the networks will buy them. Period."

"Why don't you call them and tell them that?" I said bitterly. "They're probably in a meeting weighing the upside and the downside, and the downside is winning. Joyce is pleading for me, but it won't matter. I should never have asked." I tried to convince Norman and myself that it didn't matter. "It's not important," I said. But it was. I feared they would deny me the credit I had earned.

Then, one afternoon, my secretary buzzed me. "Ted Ashley on the line." My stomach tightened. All he said was, "Congratulations. You are the new President of Warner Brothers Television."

Tears welled up in my eyes at Ted's news, but luckily, he couldn't see them. I thanked him, hung up, and sat quietly, stunned. Even though I felt I deserved the job, I was overwhelmed with gratitude. Reality had met my wildest dreams. I called Norman, who was astonished and thrilled. We couldn't wait to talk it over that evening.

There wasn't much time to savor it. The next day, I was flown to New York to meet Steve Ross, head of Warner Communications. I'd seen him briefly before, but never spent time together. He was charming and warm, but I soon realized that the real purpose of the meeting was to discuss my contract.

If I had known we'd be negotiating, I never would have gone without a lawyer, but I was trapped. I nodded, smiled, and agreed. I didn't mind; all I cared about was the opportunity. Only years later did I realize how much more secure a stronger contract could have made me.

Steve explained I'd earn a large bonus for every television series that made it to a fifth year. He named an astronomical figure, and from that moment, I barely heard another word. I left his office flying high, dazzled by visions of affluence. What I didn't understand was how slim those chances were. Reaching five years and syndication was almost impossible; anything less wasn't covered. In the end, I managed to have six shows—*Alice, Scarecrow and Mrs. King, Growing Pains, Head of the Class, Night Court*, and *The Dukes of Hazzard*—reach that milestone during my ten years as President.

Back in California, I plunged into work. There were press releases, congratulatory calls, and ritual gifts. I was given a Mercedes convertible in the color of my choice and could now park in front of the executive building, a privilege reserved for presidents.

Many executives spent their first year redoing their offices, indulging in fantasies regardless of budget. My friend Dan Melnick installed a tin ceiling copied from a New York bar; another created a South Sea retreat. I wanted something simpler, Californian. Jane Bogart replaced the carpet with Mexican tile and plastered the walls for an adobe effect. Norman designed a fireplace that looked like a Mexican bake oven. We joked that all I needed was a woman making tortillas for the network executives.

I hung Norman's paintings on the walls, including a snow scene called *The First Day of Spring*. We started collecting art, adding prints of Ellsworth Kelly and other minimalists. I chose straw furniture, and my desk was a thick tree trunk with a glass top. A Ficus tree loomed over me. It was bright, airy, and relaxed—an office that felt alive, that felt mine.

It quickly became a gathering place. In the evenings, after the phones stopped and most of the lot had emptied, staff would drift in. We'd sit by the fire with wine, unburden ourselves, and hatch ideas. That was when the real work happened. Other executives hurried home to families or secret liaisons, but I thrived on keeping late hours.

It was often 8:00 when I rushed home, where Norman and I shared our stories. He recounted his day in the studio, and I shared mine at the lot. When we stayed in, Norman cooked, I cleaned up, and we curled up to watch TV until midnight, then slept, ready for another day.

We enjoyed going out with friends, but often groaned when the calendar pulled us away. Our greatest joy was simply an evening alone together—and it still is.

Twenty-Six

The first years in television were hectic. We developed pilots, fought for network approval, cast them, and if they made it on a network schedule, fought to keep them on air. Competition was fierce. The odds of getting a show on TV were slim, and survival even slimmer.

Fortunately, I'd earned respect as a studio head. Network brass took my calls and even listened when I pleaded for a show in trouble. That open door let me hustle for series, movies of the week, and miniseries that could elevate Warner Bros. Television's reputation.

I still sat in on film meetings, no longer feeling tense. My authority was unquestioned, and I quietly watched for projects slipping through the cracks. That's how I grabbed *The Thorn Birds*, which Warner Films had abandoned as too expensive. I loved the novel and knew Richard Chamberlain was perfect for the lead. I conspired with his agent, signed him before selling the project to ABC, then handed it off to David Wolper and Stan Margulies. It became a massive hit and a beautiful work.

I'd always thought *The Corn Is Green* was miscast with Bette Davis as the schoolteacher. She was too young, and the romance with the miner felt wrong. I'd seen Ethel Barrymore in the role without romance, just mentorship. At a dinner party with George Cukor, I suggested Katharine Hepburn for a new version and asked if he'd direct. The next day, he called: he and Kate would love to do it.

That began Norman's and my friendship with both of them. Kate insisted I call her "Kate." She lived simply: plain English furniture, overdone lamb, peanut butter cookies. George Cukor, by contrast, filled his home with art and gourmet food. Visiting Kate in Wales, where the picture was filmed, was unforgettable. She brightened her tiny house with colored wool draped across the mantle and stuffed wildflowers into a vase as they grew, no arranging. Simplicity was her perfection.

She never hesitated to speak her mind. When she learned I'd worked with David Susskind, she unleashed her disdain, recalling his TV version of *The Glass Menagerie*. She called him cheap and unreliable. At the end of taping, she told him, "You live near me, and every day you drive by my house, you'll know that I know you're a mutt."

I could see her delivering the line with relish. David, I suspect, would have laughed it off. He brushed away criticism as if it belonged to someone else. I hadn't seen David since leaving his company until years later, when I was president of Warner Bros. Television. My secretary buzzed me: "David Susskind is on the line." I hesitated, then picked up. His voice was as hearty as ever. "Can you have breakfast with me tomorrow at the Polo Lounge?"

Why not, I thought.

The next morning at the Beverly Hills Hotel, the maître d' said David had taken my usual table. He looked older but still had Brillo-thick gray hair. He hugged me like we saw each other every day. Then he got to the point: "I want you to come back. Be my partner. We'll own everything equally."

I was floored. I had one of the best jobs in television, and he was asking me to give it up for his now-failing company. I should have felt triumphant. He'd fired me, now he was begging me to return. Instead, I just felt sorry for him. He'd given so much to television, but his time was over.

"David," I said gently, "I'm very happy at Warners."

He nodded, turning my no into his familiar maybe. "Well, just keep it in mind."

We ate, reminisced, and he launched into a long harangue about how stupid everyone in Hollywood was. When it was time to leave, I slid into my Mercedes with the top down and waved as I drove away. David stood alone in front of the hotel, looking old, small, and out of place.

Norman and I had been together for over 20 years, both in our 50s. I rarely saw him during the day, though we spoke on the phone constantly. My private studio line lit up only for his calls, always giving me a lift. We met after work unless I had a business dinner. If anything, my position made our relationship stronger. I felt no qualms about going places openly with Norman. People assumed we were a couple, but it was never said. We didn't flaunt anything. We simply behaved as two men who loved being together. I loved him more than ever and couldn't imagine life without him.

Our sex life, though less frenzied than in our 30s, was still deeply satisfying. We argued, but never for long. It was hard to stay angry amid all we had built: our home, our work, our admiration for one another.

The studio was chaos. From the moment I arrived, the phone rang with fresh disasters: a director in hysterics, an actor refusing to shoot. Patrick McGoohan was the worst, hurling scripts at me and screaming. He drank heavily and ended his series *Rafferty* before it had a chance. My job was like a fireman's, racing from blaze to blaze, trying to douse each one before it spread. If the star was the problem, nothing could be done. The network would never replace them. If the producer caused trouble, they were gone.

Alice was in constant trouble. The cast chemistry was volatile. To relieve pressure and create another series, I spun off Polly Holliday into her own show, *Flo*. It was a mistake. The public didn't buy it. Later, when Eileen Brennan of *Private Benjamin* was struck by a car, I begged Polly to step in. She did, but audiences wanted Eileen. The show died too soon.

Outwardly, I kept calm, but inside I was ground down. Years later, I would suffer a severe arrhythmic attack, knowing it came from those years of strain. Every day, I was in meetings, on the phone, or rushing to sets. Every evening, I watched dailies and rough cuts of shows. My life was divided into sitcoms, dramas, made-for-TV movies, and miniseries.

The worst days were network "selling" weeks in New York. Each year, executives flew east to sit in hotels, waiting for calls that would decide the fate of their shows and jobs. Rumors flew and schedules shifted hourly. Once, I heard nothing at all. CBS was considering two Warner pilots, but I was told we had sold nothing. On 5th Avenue, agent Bill Haber stopped me and said, "You've got nothing."

I was devastated. The division depended on us selling something. I muttered that I might as well go home. Bill looked at me as if I were insane. "You've got to get them to buy your shows."

"How?" I asked.

"Tomorrow at 8:30, they're finalizing the schedule at CBS. The head of it all, Bob Daly, will be there. Stand outside and tell him he has to buy them."

I dismissed it at first, but that night I couldn't sleep. I thought of my acting days, working myself into an emotional state for a scene. Maybe that's what I'd do with Daly. The next morning, I met Barry Meyer outside CBS. When Daly appeared, I launched myself at him, half mad with desperation.

"You've got to buy my shows!" I shouted, tears spilling down my face. "We'll be out of business. We'll change anything you don't like. They'll be successful. You've just got to buy them."

Daly looked stunned, then put a hand on my shoulder. "It'll be all right," he said. "We'll buy your two pilots for back-ups."

He promised they'd go on as replacements when new shows failed. It wasn't glory, but it was survival. We lived to fight another season.

Scruples came next, Judith Krantz's novel of sex and glamour. I took her to lunch at Ma Maison, and she laughed, it was straight from her book: studio head in the garden, the power table. We bought the rights, made the miniseries, and it was a smash. It heralded an era of glossy, sexy sagas, with Warner Television at the center.

Through it all, Norman was my anchor. He painted in his studio, I fought in boardrooms and on sets, and at night we came home to each other. Sometimes the battles seemed endless. Sometimes the triumphs left me in tears. What I learned was that television was never steady; it was always a tightrope between collapse and miracle. And perhaps that was why, despite everything, I loved it.

Twenty-Seven

The 1980s brought new affluence and an art-collecting mania. Auction prices soared, and young, ambitious artists were everywhere. Except for Warhol, they were unlike Norman's generation: Schnabel, Salle, Basquiat, and Fischl all painted in a loose, figurative style that felt bold after minimalism. Their work filled top galleries, but they lived and worked in New York.

Norman and I joined the frenzy, visiting galleries in New York and LA and assembling a small but impressive collection: Schnabel, Kelly, Stella, Rothenberg, Shapiro, Dine, and more. The LA County Museum asked Norman to lead a group fostering interest and donations from the entertainment world. He even led a Q&A with Jim Dine, who became a friend and supporter. Later, we donated a major Dine piece to the museum.

As we bought works from young artists, some just out of art school and already commanding high prices, Norman wondered, Where am I as an artist? Despite success and admirers, he felt far from the center of the scene and increasingly frustrated. The word "failure" haunted him.

Norman turned his frustration on me. He lashed out; I sometimes lashed back. He began to resent the lifestyle I provided, believing our friends were there for my status, and his identity was being overshadowed. His career struggles made it worse.

Norman felt he needed to stop or even quit. He wanted time alone, maybe in New York, to figure things out. It became a test of our permanence.

One evening at Spago, Norman and I sat at our favorite table, watching the blur of cars along the Sunset Strip below. We enjoyed Wolfgang's signature pizza, sipped chardonnay, and reminisced. Producers and actors occasionally stopped by. I sensed Norman felt overshadowed by my career, but he didn't resent my world. For awards and fundraisers, I often went alone to network gatherings and played the Hollywood game.

Barbara Lazaroff, Wolfgang's wife and designer, made her usual grand entrance to the restaurant that night. She stopped at our table and said, "Wolf and I were just named one of the city's most romantic couples by the *L.A. Times*. The two of you should have been on the list. It seems unfair."

We were touched. After she left, Norman said, "Wow, I guess we're out."

"It's not that people don't know," I replied. "Nobody ever mentions it."

Norman finally said, "If I'm ever going to have a real career as an artist, I need to go to New York for a while."

I stopped eating. "What's wrong?" I asked. "I thought we were happy. What's happening?"

"No, it's not about us not being happy," Norman said. "I'm just frustrated about my career. Irving Blum and Brooke Hayward visited my studio last week. They said if I wanted a real career as an artist, I had to be in New York. Get a loft, go to galleries and openings, and become a presence. Irving and Brooke offered to help."

"But you're doing all right here, aren't you?" I asked.

"You know it's not happening, not the way I hoped."

"Norman," I said, "we both know you started late, but I believe in your talent. You're having shows, your work is in collections and museums. What more can you expect? And what about us?"

"You're not hearing me," Norman said, annoyed. "I feel angry all the time. It's not about us, but I'm always pushing down my frustration about the work."

"You didn't go to Yale; you're self-taught," I said. "You're catching up, and I think you're amazing. I always said I would support you and never regretted it. I love you and want you to be happy. Why beat yourself up?"

"Don't you see what I want is good for both of us?" Norman said. "If one of us is miserable, it can't work. Why not try New York? We could rent a loft, I'd fly back and forth, and you could visit. We'd have another base. Other people are bicoastal. Why not us?"

I looked at Norman as kindly as I could. "If you really want this, we'll look into it."

Then Norman added, bitterly, "The problem is always the art world, isn't it?"

One month later, Norman was in Chelsea, New York, standing alone in a cavernous room carved from an old commercial loft. The reality was stark: a double bed, two folding chairs, and a stack of canvases with scattered tubes of paint. Four bare windows faced a brick wall ten feet away, letting in little light. For years, he had imagined New York as a place of energy and possibility, but instead, he found himself gasping for breath. On the phone, he told me he felt trapped. He had wanted a glamorous studio, but this was the best he could find. Part of him already longed for the sunlit hills of Coldwater Canyon.

We had discovered the space only weeks before, after flying in together to look at rentals. That trip had two purposes: finding Norman a base in Manhattan and seeing Lena Horne's triumphant one-woman show, the sensation of the season. We hadn't seen Lena since the *Jamaica* days, and word had reached us that she had changed—more political, deeply engaged in the Civil Rights Movement, hardened by Lennie's death, and embittered by years of prejudice that had kept her from the Hollywood stardom she deserved.

On stage, she was incandescent, more beautiful than ever, her voice steeped in fire and sorrow. Between numbers, she spoke of her life. The pain of losing *Show Boat's* Julie still lived in her words, her fury at the racism of hotels and restaurants still raw. The venom shocked us. It felt as if the wounds had been cut open that very day, not thirty years earlier. She was justified, of course. The world had failed her. But seeing her anger so naked, after knowing her once as radiant and playful, left me unsettled.

After the ovation, I slipped a note to the stage door man asking if we might see her. "You don't need a note," the doorman barked. "She sees everybody." We followed the narrow hallway to a crowded anteroom. Dozens of admirers, many elderly African American women, waited patiently. A man stood guard, sharp-eyed and unfriendly. When I introduced myself, he said flatly, "I know you. I was one of the singers in *Jamaica*. I'm Lena's manager." Gone was the urbane gentleman who had once overseen her affairs; this man was tough and almost combative. He told us to wait.

Eventually, Lena emerged in a plain dressing gown, stripped of stage glamour, her beauty now fragile with fatigue. She bypassed us, greeting each woman with warmth. Only when she circled back did she stop in front of Norman and me. Her eyes narrowed. "Mr. Mogul," she said to me, her voice thick with sarcasm. "How come you never got me a job, Mr. Mogul?"

The words hit me like a slap. For a moment, I was speechless, then I stammered out how magnificent she had been. "Well, if you think that," she said sharply, "get me work." She turned away. Norman and I slipped out quickly, my cheeks hot with shame.

Norman tried to soothe me. "She comes from the heyday of the movie studios," he said. "She probably thinks that with your title, you're like Jack Warner, able to hand out movies with a flick of the wrist."

But it didn't help. She had been my friend, and now she made me feel as if I had betrayed her. The next day, I sent her flowers, but there was never a reply.

Back in Chelsea, Norman settled into the routine of his new life. He rose late, walked the noisy streets for coffee, then returned to the silence of the loft. At first, the emptiness gnawed at him, but gradually he began to use it. Without the comfort of our home or the distraction of friends, he pushed himself harder. His canvases grew larger and bolder, and the struggle that had driven him from Los Angeles began to find its way into the work. Still, at night, he often phoned me, restless and lonely. I would listen, reassure him, and then hang up to face my own loneliness.

When I visited, I saw both sides: the thrill of Manhattan's energy and the harsh solitude of his studio. We walked through galleries together, sometimes encouraged, sometimes daunted. Each parting was a small test of our permanence. The loft gave Norman room to search for his voice, but it also showed us how hard it was to live apart after so many years together.

After I returned to Los Angeles, Norman spent days visiting galleries, starting in SoHo. What had been a derelict neighborhood of warehouses was now a hub drawing collectors from uptown and abroad. He went to Mary Boone, Leo Castelli, and other new spaces, staring at canvases smeared with reckless paint, near-pornographic nudes, and oversized ironic words. None of it spoke to him. He had hoped to feel excited, provoked, or even influenced. Instead, he felt disconnected, left out of a conversation he didn't understand.

Thinking he might feel more at home among established artists on 57th Street, he went uptown. But those galleries were only interested in stars. He came away no less alienated. The nights were easier. He dined with old friends from his past. Irving Blum and Brooke Hayward, who had promised to help, proved good only for long lunches and a few laughs. No one would open doors for him. He would have to do it himself.

But when he sat down to paint, he felt out of step with the city. New York had changed so much in 20 years that it no longer felt like where he belonged. One afternoon, he walked back to Greenwich Village, to the grimy doorway of his old basement apartment. He thought about his younger self, the ambition that had carried him through so many careers, and then about the life we had built together. Then came the darker question: *What am I doing at my age trying to start over?*

He told me seeing old friends was always warm but brief. They went back to their lives, while he returned to the solitude of the loft. Meeting new people was nearly impossible. The art world was a closed circle of dealers, curators, collectors, and favored artists, and he had no entry. He watched it up close at the Sonnabend Gallery: an older woman stood while the receptionist ignored her. When he finally spoke, she explained she had transparencies and wanted to see the director. The answer: they weren't looking at new artists; shows were booked two years ahead. She left, shoulders bent by another rejection. Norman saw himself in her defeat and felt a wave of humiliation. He was too old to stand in line with his portfolio, too proud to beg. And yet, here he was, subjecting himself to just that.

He called me every night. I thought I could fly east every other week, but Warners consumed me. A month passed before I was able to manage a visit. Norman pretended to enjoy New York, but I knew better. Our conversations, once effortless, had grown stilted. Living apart was opening a gulf between us. When we came together, the closeness felt more like an obligation than joy.

I asked to see his work. At first, he resisted, saying he wasn't ready, but when I pressed, he relented. He showed me a striking portrait of Brooke Hayward: she clutched her arms as if cold, surrounded by chic possessions—leather sofa, bronze and ceramic animals, a pastoral painting. All of it appeared through a subway door scrawled with graffiti. The contrast was surreal: the safe world within versus the dangerous world without. It was ambitious, unlike anything he had painted before.

I studied it carefully. "It's wonderful," I said at last. But we knew each other too well. He knew I didn't mean it.

The distance between us grew with every visit. Our nightly calls couldn't replace the constant mutual support that had always bound us. I was used to Norman waiting at the end of each day, ready to listen to my battles and help me make sense of them. Now he seemed torn between wanting to return and refusing to admit New York had been a mistake.

On my next trip, I sensed it even more sharply. Norman looked restless, as though he could hardly wait for me to leave. In more than 20 years together, we had been satisfied, passionate, joyful. But now I felt something shift. It wasn't betrayal—neither of us had broken rules, though monogamy had always been unspoken. It was worse. It was estrangement. I began to wonder if his move to New York had less to do with the art world and more to do with being away from me.

On the flight back to Los Angeles, I kept replaying the weeks apart. Had we lost what had always defined us? Was our home, the life we'd built, slipping away?

Twenty-Eight

While Norman was in New York, I was bereft. At the studio, I was busier than ever. I got Tony Randall to do *Love, Sidney*. We'd known each other since *Antony and Cleopatra* in 1947. Tony first brought me the idea as a movie of the week, which we produced. When it succeeded, it spun off into a series, the first sitcom with a gay lead character. Tony was fearless, embracing his feminine side and love of the arts. Many assumed he was gay, but in all our years, I never saw any sign of it. What mattered was his openness; perhaps that drew him to *Love, Sidney*. He needed attention, clashed with people, and could be cutting, but he was worth it. The show ran two seasons. The gay theme, even softened, may have cut its run short.

Alongside *Love, Sidney*, I had *Flo*, *Private Benjamin*, *Scruples*, and *Bare Essence* to shepherd. The days rushed by, and I stayed late, reluctant to return to an empty house. I played with the dogs, then waited to call Norman in New York. He rarely got home before 11:00, so I waited until 8:00 my time. I stretched our conversations, then faced the blankness of the night without him.

I hadn't discouraged Norman from going. He had to try. I shared his pain at not being embraced by the art world and would have done anything to help, but I couldn't give him success. I spoke quietly to dealers; they praised his work but dismissed it. It wasn't what they were showing. The world wanted young, edgy names. Norman was neither. I hated them for it. I also feared New York wouldn't help. But I couldn't face a future of him saying, "If only I'd gone to New York."

We began to bicker. The smallest thing started an argument. He felt blocked and overlooked, and I felt unconsidered. My days were relentless, and I needed him as much as he needed me. But Norman no longer seemed to think about what I wanted. I kept hearing Anne Jackson's line in *Lovers and Other Strangers,* which I had cast: "What about me?"

One evening, after another fight, I snapped. I drove with nowhere to go. My life was home, and home was Norman. I wandered Santa Monica, walked along the ocean, then drove back. Nothing had changed, but I knew something had to.

In Norman's absence, I leaned on friends. Paige Rense, editor of *Architectural Digest,* became my companion. Our friendship deepened. She joined me for dinners and premieres; I joined her for design weekends. People assumed we were a couple, and for a time, I was grateful for the illusion.

I also confided in Barry Lowen, a collector and executive who later died of AIDS. With Barry, I admitted my darkest fear: that Norman's move wasn't only about art, but about leaving me. The suspicion grew with every month he stayed in New York, with no sign of wanting to return.

At Doug Cramer's beach house, a young man flirted with me. He was beautiful, and though I suspected he wanted my money more than me, I was flattered. I resisted, but the temptation shook me. Loneliness gnawed at me. I decided I had to see Norman before it undid me.

The New York loft was bleak. Norman had barely started another portrait of Brooke Hayward. His talent was obvious, but the painting felt thin after three months. He hadn't broken into the art world, and his circle was mostly old friends who couldn't help. What worried me most was how little he was painting. I said nothing critical. I encouraged him, though inside I felt disappointed and scared.

That night, we made love, but for the first time in years, there was no passion. Norman said everything was fine, but I knew it wasn't. We slept apart, and in the silence. I felt a foreboding I couldn't shake.

Back in Los Angeles, I couldn't stop thinking: Norman was having an affair. After a week, I couldn't stand it. I called Norman, but he wasn't home. I tried several more times, growing agitated. Why wasn't he painting? Where was he? When I finally reached him, I blurted, "Have you been with someone?"

There was a pause. Then, softly: "Yes. But it was nothing."

I put down the phone and sat, drained. My life felt over. I interrogated myself: How could he do this? Was this his real reason for New York—to get away from me? I thought of the years I supported him. What had I done to deserve this?

Then I thought of Norman, alone in that miserable studio. I knew what it was to be alone. I remembered Knoxville.

Almost 20 years earlier, I went to Tennessee with David Susskind's production of *All the Way Home*. I had cast the film and found Michael Kearney, the 7-year-old lead. Director Alex Segal had me come as a dialogue coach. The work was monotonous. Funeral scenes dragged on for days. Michael was restless and wanted to play, not act.

Jean Simmons was a saving grace—beautiful, sharp, unpretentious. I taught her how to make a bed for a scene; she had never made one before. We talked and laughed, but I sensed her sadness. Evenings, I saw the rushes, ate alone, and waited for Norman's calls. I was very lonely.

One Sunday night, after a day with Jean and her daughter, I wandered into a bar. I ordered a scotch. The bartender chatted, then told two men that I was with the movie company. They came over, eager to meet Jean Simmons. One, handsome and attentive, kept asking questions. For a moment, I thought he might be flirting, but I brushed it off and went back to the hotel to bed.

Later, there was a knock at my door. Expecting a revised film schedule, I opened it. It was the handsome man: "Thought I'd come by for a nightcap," he said, pushing past me. He lay on my bed, shirt off, asking for a back rub. Suddenly, the room turned menacing. Then his friend arrived, and the mood darkened. "This faggot was trying to have sex with me," the first one said. "We've got to beat him up."

I denied it, but they laughed, drank, and toyed with a knife. They threatened to throw me out the window. In desperation, I offered them money. They took my checks, grabbed my razor, and left, warning, "Don't try picking up anybody else in Knoxville."

I lay awake all night, shaken. Had I led him on? Had my loneliness shown? The truth was, I had been tempted. What if it had gone another way? I never told Norman. But the scar of that night stayed with me, a reminder of how dangerous loneliness could be, and how close I'd come to disaster.

Now, years later, Norman had succumbed to the same temptation. Alone in New York, feeling rejected, he gave in. How could I condemn him when I knew that ache so well? I called him again. When he answered, I said, "Please come home. This isn't doing either of us any good. I need you." I could hear him breathing. "Please," I repeated, "I don't care what's happened. Let's forget it. Just come back."

After a pause, he said, "I want to. I'll come right away."

I remembered the episode with Norman and the police years earlier, and how I'd resolved never to press him for answers again. But this time, I chose differently. I told him everything about Knoxville—how I wandered into danger, possibly led them on, and took the blame. In doing so, I invited him to share his own truth.

He paused, then began a story that hurt and healed us both. "I suppose it was inevitable," Norman said. "I was sitting on a bench in Washington Square, feeling displaced. I barely noticed a young man at the other end, lost in a musical score. I tried to read *The New Yorker*, but my mind drifted back to you, your world so defined and relentless, mine so formless. I envied you even as I pitied myself."

"The young man kept tapping his thighs, humming. Then he looked at me, took off his glasses and cap, and we started talking. His name was

Steven, a Columbia music student in his early 20s, about the age I was when I lived nearby. He was wholesome, earnest, with pale blue eyes and an openness that felt like my hand reaching across the years."

Norman continued, "He practiced piano four hours a day. I confessed I could barely paint and felt out of place in New York. He asked if I'd like to hear his music and invited me to dinner. I protested, said I was too old, that I lived happily with someone in LA. He teased me—if I could complain of being too old, he could complain of being too young. He promised nothing more than music and food, said he just liked me. Against my better judgment, I agreed."

I continued listening. "The next evening, I took the subway uptown with two bottles of wine. The area around Columbia looked rough, and I almost turned back. But there he was, neat, tall, smiling. He hugged me as if I were already a friend. The apartment was modest—a large room, upright piano, thrift-shop furniture. He cooked chicken stew with noodles. The food didn't matter. It was nice to be seen by someone so young and eager."

"After dinner, he played for me—earnest, diligent, not gifted, his effort touched me. When he suggested we go to the loft, I said it was time to leave. But his trusting blue eyes stopped me. I followed him upstairs. There was a foam-rubber bed under an Indian coverlet. He knelt, pulled me toward him. I regretted it even as I gave in. It was brief, almost perfunctory—not about sex, but contact, being wanted, even for a moment. That's all it was. I never saw him again."

Norman's voice faded. Silence hung between us. His confession was raw, but honest. Like my Knoxville story, it wasn't about betrayal so much as loneliness and the hunger to feel less alone.

For the first time in weeks, we felt closer, bound by truth instead of secrecy.

When Norman returned to LA, he found solace at our Palm Springs house. The desert's stark beauty inspired a series of charcoal drawings of Joshua Tree's rock formations. He absorbed their quiet, abstract forms and, back in his studio, turned them into haunting drawings that later inspired woodcuts and plaster reliefs—works four major museums eventually acquired.

Meanwhile, I kept busy at the studio. November in LA brought the Santa Ana winds, rattling pines, and covering our pool with needles. Across the street, Rock Hudson's gardeners raked obsessively. The city warned of fire danger, but we felt safe. Life seemed good: I was secure at Warner Brothers, Norman was working joyfully, and our weekends in Palm Springs were filled with friends like Lee Remick and Tony Randall, Nancy Walker, and David Craig.

One weekend, Norman drove to Palm Springs a day before me to visit Joshua Tree. When I arrived Friday night, I found him on a chaise with the dogs, bathed in the light of the San Jacinto Mountains. We shared a glass of chardonnay and turned on the news.

The big story was houses burning in Coldwater Canyon. Norman and I looked at each other, afraid our house was involved. We tried calling home, but the line was busy. Then the phone rang. Our security service reported that a neighbor's faulty wire exploded, and the Santa Anas carried a fireball into our trees. Our house was gone.

We clung to each other, shaken but grateful to be alive, and sped back up Highway 10. By the time we arrived, smoke was still rising. Fire trucks flooded the street with light. Our gate was hacked open, and water was everywhere. The fire chief led us inside: blackened rooms, Norman's paintings destroyed, his closet gone, his work erased in ash. My bedroom survived, but the kitchen was a melted mess, its appliances warped into grotesque shapes that might have been modern sculpture if they weren't the ruins of our life.

Friends appeared—Barry Meyer and our contractor, Gary Pastor—just to be with us. Their presence steadied us. But the smell of smoke, ruined canvases, and the holes burned through Norman's portraits were unbearable.

By midnight, with no power or phones, we sat by the pool in shock, drinking warm chardonnay from the melted fridge and nibbling crackers. We slept in my smoke-soaked bed, fully clothed, barely closing our eyes.

Dawn revealed the destruction. Then came the vultures: insurance adjusters, shoving forms at us. We laughed at the absurdity until Tina Sinatra appeared, bringing a basket of food and wine, a perfect act of kindness. She'd seen the fire from her rooftop and came to help. We never forgot it.

The final surprise was Rock Hudson. We'd met him socially, but he was always a glamorous enigma, throwing parties across the street. That morning, his houseman summoned me. Rock called from New York.

"I heard about the fire," his voice said. "You can't stay in that ruin. My house is yours for as long as you need it. Two months, three, it doesn't matter. I'll be in New York. That's final."

And just like that, it was done. Through that generosity, Rock Hudson became a friend—and, in time, a tragic figure whose humanity we came to know.

Living in his house was like inhabiting another Hollywood. The place was grand but not ostentatious: gardens, Mexican doors, stucco walls, cool tile floors. Norman had a studio in an outbuilding that wasn't damaged. I drove to Warner Brothers each morning. At night, instead of returning to ruins, we both entered Rock's sanctuary. It was comforting and strange, like living in borrowed clothes.

Visitors came often—people curious about Rock's home, neighbors, friends. We played host, pouring his wine, serving on his plates, always aware of this generosity. Rock occasionally called from New York, checking in, asking after Norman's work and my studio battles. Behind the glamour, he was a deeply kind person.

Slowly, we pieced life back together. Adjusters fought, contractors planned, and the rebuilding began. But in that strange interlude, sheltered in Rock's house, Norman and I found more than survival: a renewed closeness. The fire had burned through our possessions, but reminded us what we still had—each other, and resilience no flames could destroy.

***

I'm sure some in Hollywood thought I'd been fired. No one left a studio presidency unless they were being offered a bigger job or were ill. You didn't just walk away from power and money. But I'd had enough.

A line from *Haywire*, a miniseries I produced, haunted me. Lee Remick, as Margaret Sullavan, sits in a sanitarium and says, "I've lost my zest." That's how I felt. I dreaded the office; every phone call was another crisis. I didn't want to die at my desk haggling over an actor's demands. I'd been president for ten years. It was time for something else.

At 60, I was too young to retire. My Warner Brothers contract still had years, but I could convert it into a producer's deal. Producing would free me from all the sitcoms and let me focus on stories that mattered. Years earlier, Fred Silverman asked for "innovative" ideas at NBC. I proposed a series of classics starring Hollywood names, with paperbacks released in tandem. Fred stared and said, "This place is going up in fucking flames, and you're talking about great books?" But now, maybe I could pursue what I cared about.

There were other reasons. I wanted to read books, not just scripts, to listen to music at night instead of endless TV, and spend more evenings with Norman. My job meant constant separations—industry dinners, awards, and events where I was expected to be accompanied by a woman on my arm. It left Norman isolated. Producing might give us the freedom to be more visible as a couple and to finally participate in community work together.

And death was everywhere. In recent years, I'd watched friends, brilliant men, die of AIDS. I remembered a lunch at Tony Richardson's house: a pool filled with beautiful young men. Within a decade, almost all of them were gone, including Tony. The losses changed my perspective. I realized how quickly time passed, how little remained.

Norman and I still lived well—traveling, dining with friends, hosting parties. Margaret, George Cukor's cook, now made our meals. But something had shifted. Driving over Coldwater Canyon each morning,

I no longer thought about stories. I thought about the money I was making. The thrill was gone.

George Cukor used to answer the phone with, "How's life?" I always said, "Great!" Now I couldn't. That was the clearest sign. It was time to step down.

The two years left on my contract gave me a chance to see how well I could do as a producer. I would try to get shows on, and if I couldn't, I had enough money to retire. I knew I'd be competing with 30-year-olds. My decision to leave shook Norman, but he understood I wanted a more creative life. He always supported me. We both knew what I was leaving. I was used to 40 calls a day. The day after it was announced I was stepping down as president, I got one.

Warner threw a goodbye party for me at Chasen's, also welcoming my replacement. Most of the attention went to the new president with power; actors and agents swarmed around him. Stars from my shows were there, but the shows were no longer mine. It felt like a memorial service, but I covered up by joking and saying goodbye. I wasn't leaving the lot, but everyone knew I wouldn't see most of them again.

In the following weeks, I got letters and calls congratulating me on production. Quinn Martin wrote that I had "single-handedly brought back Warner TV from the dead." I was called the "Dean of Hollywood studio TV Production Chiefs," which made me feel old. Bob Daly, the current Warner chairman, offered to speak about my years, but knowing I'd tear up, I refused. People's kind words moved me. They called me a "class act" and "gentleman," terms already rare in Hollywood. The best part was that Norman could be there with me, and I didn't care what anyone thought.

I quickly settled into my new office, a huge room with vaulted ceilings. I used John Calley's English furniture and hung Norman's landscapes. It was handsome, but I needed to do something in it. I didn't want to just take the money. I plunged into work and faced the same problem as the president: where to find good material?

I managed to get some things going. Norman Stephens, head of TV films, suggested *The Bourne Identity*. Richard Chamberlain was interested if he liked the script, so ABC ordered one. I struggled to find a writer, but Carol Sobieski, who had adapted The Women's Room for us, was willing to try. She was brilliant and wrote an exciting script despite being ill. Her death was a tragic loss.

While the script was being written, I tried other projects. I'd long been fascinated by Thomas Jefferson and Sally Hemings. Gore Vidal agreed to write a miniseries for CBS if he could include Sally. Brandon Tartikoff at NBC greenlit a Nantucket miniseries. I pitched ideas everywhere, but I was no longer greeted with the same enthusiasm. Many projects stalled at the script stage. I was at the mercy of the writers. I never liked to pressure them, but maybe that was a mistake. Many ideas went by the wayside.

I kept waiting for Gore Vidal's script, but he kept promising "a month," then "two months," then "the end of the summer."

Finally, his agent Bill Haber said, "Forget it. He's never going to write it."

"But why?" I asked. "He seemed so excited."

"He's just not going to write it," he said.

I never heard from Gore again. It reminded me of George C. Scott's agent telling me to replace him on *A Case of Libel* and never explaining why. I got a fine writer, John McGreevy, to do it. We worked on it for a year, but CBS kept stalling, asking for rewrites. Eventually, all three networks and PBS rejected it. Years later, DNA testing confirmed the Sally Hemings story. I think no one had the courage to do it before then.

Producing was a different kind of battlefield. No longer shielded by the title of president, I was just another producer, one of many pitching scripts. The phone, once busy, went silent.

When we started shooting *The Bourne Identity*, Roger Young, the director, told me he wanted me on set from dawn until the last shot of the day. Other producers came and went, or didn't show up at all, but Roger wanted me there to handle any problem. I agreed. If that was what he needed, I would be there.

So, there I was, sitting in a Zurich parking lot at 2:00 in the morning, snow falling on my cap with earflaps, clutching my coat tighter while the cast retreated into their heated Winnebagos. Jaclyn Smith had just shot a harrowing rape scene, reluctantly agreeing—after much persuasion—that her attacker should tear part of her clothes so the audience would believe the violence. She hated nudity of any kind, but in the end, the scene worked. The actors returned to warmth. I sat alone on a stool in the snow. That was when the thought first struck me: maybe this wasn't worth it. I wasn't creating, I was enabling.

Yet there were moments I'll never forget. Richard Chamberlain, half-nude on a makeshift operating table, waited for Denholm Elliott to stumble in as a drunken doctor. I saw Richard staring at the ceiling, utterly intent. Was he preparing for the scene? Some Stanislavski ritual? No. He was arranging his chest hair into a perfect line down to his navel, watching himself in a mirrored surface above. So much for *An Actor Prepares.*

Richard was devoted to his partner, Martin, a charming man. But whenever Martin was nearby, Richard lost focus. The director asked me to intervene. I gently asked Martin to handle "associate producer" errands, such as meeting actors and assisting with logistics. To ease the sting, Norman and I invited him to a cooking class at Moulin de Mougins.

For four days, Norman and Martin sat in a sunlit kitchen, drinking wine, eating extraordinary food, and pretending to learn recipes while the chef did all the work. Richard and I joined them for the "graduation." It was the happiest time we shared during the shoot.

When *The Bourne Identity* aired, it was a triumph, nominated for an Emmy as Best Miniseries—a rarity for action thrillers. On Emmy night, Norman came with me. No longer an executive, I didn't care who saw us together. We didn't win; the cameras didn't even linger on our row.

But I had promised myself that if I had won, I would have thanked Norman publicly, for all the years when I couldn't.

Richard turned down my hopes for a sequel. A pity. He had been perfect as Bourne. Years later, Matt Damon picked up the role and made it a billion-dollar franchise. I sometimes thought back to the quiet Zurich parking lot, snow falling, and wondered if I hadn't been right—maybe enabling was enough.

Twenty-Nine

The Man in the Brown Suit was the last film I made, and it was miserable. The Christie estate, after giving me *Poirots* and *Marples* at Warner Brothers, withheld the best titles. If *Brown Suit* succeeded, maybe they'd relent. That was the calculation.

I courted Rosalind Hicks, Agatha's daughter, in her damp Dorset home and later endured her son Mathew's drafty Welsh house. Henry Moore sculptures outside didn't help. It seemed romantic in theory, but it was English country living at its coldest.

The book was weak; no writer wanted it. The one who did delivered a script with an absurd ending. We patched together something usable, hired an English director who hated both me and the script, and filmed in Spain, doubling for Africa.

The cast was strong: Stephanie Zimbalist, Rue McClanahan, and my friend Tony Randall. But the director's disdain poisoned everything. One morning, I found the band in blackface. "We don't do that in America," I snapped. He sulked, I ordered it redone and our relationship never recovered. He excluded me from the wrap party.

The film was overlong and incoherent, rescued only in editing and drowned in music. That ended my Christie connection.

It was ironic. We made eight Christie films at Warner, including Helen Hayes' *Marples*, which still aired and sold on DVD. But *Brown Suit* exhausted me. Production was no longer enjoyable, and the industry was undergoing a shift. I'd fought the battles, won some, lost many. Perhaps it was time to lay down my arms.

I thought *Murder with Mirrors* would be straightforward. Another Christie, another Helen Hayes as Miss Marple, plus a juicy supporting role. At a meeting, someone said, "What about Bette Davis? The two queens of entertainment in one picture."

It sounded irresistible. I should have known better. Robby Lantz, Bette Davis' agent, assured me she was fine after her stroke. We sent the script, and she wanted a meeting. The director and I went to her modest apartment. I expected grandeur; there were only a few cheap pieces of furniture and posters. Bette entered in a silver suit, hair waved, face half-paralyzed. It was shocking.

She said she liked the script but demanded her character not be ill. "My fans won't want to see me sick."

"Miss Davis," I replied, "the story is about a woman being poisoned. If she isn't ill, there's no plot."

"Then I won't do it."

I thought we were free. Then she disappeared with her secretary. Minutes later, she returned: "I'll play sick."

The network insisted we proceed. On set in England, Bette's behavior was erratic. She demanded to see every costume, complained about hotels, and dragged trunks of clothes for interviews no one wanted. She refused to be civil to her co-star, Helen Hayes.

On the first day of shooting, Helen, ever gracious, approached her: "Bette, I'm so glad we're working together."

"Let's not waste our breath saying hello every day," Bette snapped. "We're here to work." They never spoke again.

When the dailies arrived, Norman and I watched in horror. Bette looked like a cadaver; the camera accentuated her paralysis. She could barely stand, her words slurred. I called Robby Lantz: "We have to replace her. She's ruining the picture."

"Darling," he purred, "you can't replace Bette Davis. The world would hate you."

The network agreed to soldier on. The director cut around her, Helen carried the film, and we finished. When Bette returned to LA, I sent her flowers. Her note came back furious about her scene being cut and her lines given away. She added a smiley face, as if mocking us all.

It was a painful lesson in producing. You chase big names but end up managing decline and ego. The "two queens" gave us headlines, but the film sagged under their feud.

That night, as Norman and I sat in our garden with a glass of chardonnay, I told him I was finished chasing Christies. He smiled, knowing I meant more than that.

By the time *Murder with Mirrors* aired, I knew producing was less about creativity and more about crisis management. Every project was a battlefield—wrangling egos, budgets, and networks afraid to take chances.

There had been triumphs—*The Bourne Identity* most of all, with Richard Chamberlain's performance—but the costs grew heavier. Sitting in the snow in Zurich at 2:00 a.m., persuading Jaclyn Smith to allow realism in a rape scene, or pleading with a director to scrub blackface off an orchestra—these weren't creative victories, just reminders that the job was damage control.

Norman and I sold our Palm Springs retreat and bought a house in Malibu. He set up his studio in the garage while I tried to finish the Christie film in Spain. Then Norman called, excited: Frances Lear had summoned him to New York to help rescue her new magazine—*Lear's*, aimed at women over 40.

Frances, now divorced from Norman Lear, was dramatic. She sent Norman a first-class ticket, a suite at the Regency, and the premiere issue. He found it respectable but flat, more of a catalog than a magazine. At her apartment, surrounded by Rothkos and de Koonings, he spoke his mind. Frances listened, then sprang into action—calling her art director at midnight. Minutes later, the woman had quit, and Frances handed Norman the phone: "You have to take over."

And he did. For six months, he threw himself into *Lear's*, creating six issues while juggling Frances's manic brilliance and volatility. She once arrived at our house in full flight, whirling and chanting, "I am the center of the world because France is the center of the world and my name is Frances."

After she left, Norman sighed. He told his analyst, "I want Alan and me to be happy. And I miss my painting."

The analyst said, "Then quit before she cuts your balls off." Norman did, leaving Frances screaming in her penthouse, and came home to me and his canvases.

But Norman's New York sojourn brought one good thing: a friendship with Sonny Sloane, who had a house in Roxbury, Connecticut. Sonny saw how lonely Norman was and invited him for weekends. The rolling hills and stone walls of Litchfield County worked their spell. Norman began to wonder if we might want a second home back in the country.

At one of Sonny's parties, Norman ran into Carolyn Klemm, the whirlwind Connecticut realtor who had sold our old house to Richard Holbrooke and Diane Sawyer. "Since you're up here," she said, "let me show you some houses."

That was all it took. Norman tried to brush her off. "We already have Beverly Hills and Malibu."

Carolyn just smiled. "Just for fun."

The next day, she drove him all over: colonials, farmhouses, barns. Norman was tempted but not sold—until Carolyn showed him a weather-beaten barn. It was raw but filled with promise. When I flew east to see it, something clicked. Walking the plank floors and looking up at the timbered ceiling, we felt that old spark.

We rediscovered Connecticut that weekend—the crisp air, quiet lanes, and sense of rootedness Hollywood never gave us. Against every vow never to complicate our lives, we bought the barn and renovated it into one of our most wonderful homes.

The irony wasn't lost on us: Frances Lear's chaos had inadvertently led us back to serenity. Producing had run its course. The industry gave me everything and drained me dry. But in our Connecticut barn, with Norman back at his easel and our dogs at our feet, I realized we had found the one production worth holding onto.

The barn was more than a house; it was a reclamation. After years of crisis-driven producing, endless notes, difficult directors and actors, and the bitter lesson that management had replaced imagination, Norman and I walked through the raw spaces of an old barn in Litchfield County. We looked at each other and knew, without words, that this was where our next chapter would unfold.

We gutted and rebuilt it, leaving great beams exposed and letting natural light spill into open rooms. Norman made one side his studio, with space to stretch his canvases and experiment in ways Los Angeles never allowed. The other side became a gathering place, where fire crackled, and friends filled long tables with laughter and wine.

After years of Hollywood artifice, what struck me most was Connecticut's authenticity. People cared about ideas, books, gardens, and each other. The parties were glamorous but quieter, more lived-in. You might sit next to Arthur Miller at dinner or hear that Stephen Sondheim was at the farmer's market. Fame wasn't the currency—community was.

Norman thrived. The Connecticut light brought new clarity to his work. He produced large canvases that explored form and shadow, later exhibited in museums nationwide. I watched him come alive, fully present in his work in a way that wasn't possible during the years of *Lear's* chaos or my network calls.

For me, the barn marked a new balance. I could still fly to Los Angeles and keep a hand in the industry, but every return to Litchfield County was a return to sanity—time to read, walk, and be with Norman without a phone screaming about ratings or budgets.

We had built and rebuilt many homes: Coldwater Canyon, Palm Springs, Malibu. Each was tied to ambition and the business that consumed me. The barn was different. It wasn't about Hollywood or contracts. It was about us.

Visitors sensed that difference. Actors, directors, and producers from the city would sit at our table and talk about books, politics, or meaning—not deals. It reminded me of what I once believed television could be: a medium for ideas and truth, not just ratings.

When my contract with Warner Brothers ended, I knew it was time. Producing was more about crisis management than imagination, and I no longer wanted to live in the trenches of other people's anxieties. I announced my retirement, not in bitterness but in relief. For the first time in decades, I was free to build a life on my own terms.

I began volunteering, recording for the blind, and co-hosting a small radio show, but my real desire was to spend my days reading and writing. I remembered visiting Ralph Waldo Emerson's house in high school, standing in his study and promising myself I'd have such a place one day.

In our Connecticut barn, at the top of a silo, I finally built it. A carpenter curved bookshelves into the round walls, and I filled them with volumes I'd collected but never read. Around me were tokens from a lifetime: an etching Roger gave me when I turned 16, a Sironi painting from Rome, Norman's drawing of me done in Napa, a dodo bird from Mauritius, and a watercolor from Helen Frankenthaler. On one shelf, Proust's *In Search of Lost Time*, which I began to read. I suppose many retirees turn to Proust, or at least intend to.

Here, in this aerie, I found peace. Sometimes a bird pecked at my window as if to say, "Come out." But after a lifetime of chasing deadlines, I wasn't quite ready to leave.

Norman's art entered a new phase. After years of painting, he began a series of bronzes culminating in *The Golden Apple of the Hesperides*—a 16-foot sculpture commissioned by Michael and Zena Wiener. Suspended between two abstract shapes, the shining apple symbolized the artist's struggle for perfection. When it was installed in their sculpture garden, Norman and I stood together, looking up at the bronze, knowing it would endure long after us. That's the miracle of art: it outlives the battles and compromises.

For me, inspiration came from an unexpected place: a TV home-maker urging viewers to throw out old Christmas ornaments. I couldn't let go of the thought—what would happen to those ornaments full of memory? I wrote a story where they journey back to the Christmas tree to prove their worth. It was called *The Minstrel Tree*.

Norman was skeptical about illustrating it—he was focused on painting and sculpture—but eventually he relented. His drawings gave life to my characters. We printed 5,000 copies, stored most in the garage, and had a signing where we sold nearly 200 in one evening. After that, the books just sat, waiting.

Then fate intervened. Over dinner, we met Ellen Levine, editor of *Good Housekeeping*. I gave her a copy. Months later, after September 11th, she called to say she wanted to publish *The Minstrel Tree* in the Christmas issue. For the first time in 25 years, *Good Housekeeping* would feature a children's story, and ours was chosen because its message of togetherness felt right for the moment.

There were quibbles, even an editor who thought the story was about "coming out of the closet," which made us laugh. But we let it go, knowing the exposure mattered more. The magazine included ordering information, and in one month, we sold 4,500 copies.

For me, the study, the apple, and *The Minstrel Tree* became the symbols of this final act: a life balanced between solitude and partnership, art that endures, and stories that offer hope. I had been an actor, executive, producer. Now I was simply a man in his study, surrounded by books and memories, with Norman in the studio next door. And that was enough.

One afternoon I got a call from a man I barely knew, a friend of my ex-wife Jacqueline's. His voice was flat: Jacqueline was dying. "Did she ask you to tell me?" I asked.

"Absolutely not," he replied. "She'd be furious if she knew."

It had been ten years since Jacqueline and I had spoken at a Christmas tea. Since then, we'd only exchanged curt greetings, even though she lived nearby. In Hollywood, during my Warner years, we briefly reconnected—she was producing specials like *Sybil*—and sometimes found our way back to friendship. But she had grown more rigid, living alone, dining nightly at the Palm, her beauty hardened. The world called her "Jackie," but she always insisted I call her Jacqueline.

I thought about all the years, the love, and the wasted time. In our youth, we promised to spend our golden years together on a porch, rocking chairs creaking as we reminisced. Instead, we were estranged. And she was dying.

That evening, I went to our sculpture garden, the cloister Norman designed behind the barn. Four bronzes stood among the boxwood, apples glinting in the fading light. I thought of Jacqueline: brushing her hair before bed, laughing with Jane Trahey, broken-hearted when Jane left her. I remembered her tenderness, her stubbornness, her fire. I wanted to reach out but feared a call would upset her. Instead, I sent flowers with a simple card: "Love, Alan."

After she was gone, our friend Rose told me Jacqueline had mentioned the flowers.

"They made her happy," Rose said. It was enough.

Months later, at a Thanksgiving party, a woman named Jan told me, "She said you were the only man she ever loved. She said you were handsome, smart, funny—and then she cried. I'd never seen Jackie cry before."

I was stunned. Her *New York Times* obituary ended with the line that our marriage ended in divorce. Still hiding, even in death. Yet in her tears, in those words passed on to me, was the truth we had never been able to live openly: she had loved me, and I had loved her.

Two closures, so different yet connected. Producing was behind me. Jacqueline was gone. But I was not left empty-handed.

What followed was not an ending, but a beginning.

Thirty

I was the one who suggested we get married. It wasn't romantic, but a flash of anger. Missouri had just passed a new law banning same-sex marriage—a redundancy, since marriage was already defined there as between a man and a woman. But they wanted to say it again, louder, crueler. For reasons I still don't quite understand, I—never an activist—snapped and wrote a letter to *The New York Times*.

We'd never thought much about marriage. A piece of paper wouldn't make our love stronger. But as we got older, we saw what the law denied us. Heterosexual couples could pass tax-free estates to a spouse. For us, half a century together meant nothing to the government; half our estate could be claimed, and one of us might not keep the home we built. Worse, in some states, I couldn't be admitted to Norman's hospital room or make a medical decision for him.

So yes, marriage mattered. Not for proof of devotion, but for recognition, fairness, and dignity. I poured those thoughts into my letter. *The Times* declined to publish it, saying too much time had passed since Missouri's decision. But the words stayed with me.

A few weeks later, over dinner, we saw friends' wedding album—two men married in Nantucket, their ceremony joyful. That night I turned to Norman and said, "I think we should get married. Lou and Mike did it. Why not us?"

There was no proposal, just a calm certainty. A federal judge we knew warned that Massachusetts might repeal same-sex marriage, but if we acted quickly, our union would be recognized. It was a window of opportunity.

I wrote to a justice of the peace on Nantucket, Catherine Flanagan Stover, explaining we'd been together over 40 years and wanted a simple ceremony. Her reply was immediate and welcoming.

Everything happened quickly: a private plane to avoid the drive, a booking at the Wauwinet Inn, last-minute rings from Tiffany's, two gold bands in blue boxes. Armani jackets, white shirts, white pants—formal enough, but still us.

Then the delays: fog grounded our plane, rain made us quarrel, and we got lost driving in Nantucket, Norman snapped that we should call it off. For a moment, I agreed. But back at the hotel, a bouquet of flowers from Lou and Mike was waiting. We laughed through our irritation. We remembered what it was all about.

The next evening, Catherine led us down a deserted beach in her black robe, the wind lifting her red hair. A photographer and his daughter followed. As we stopped, the clouds parted and the sun spread golden light around us.

Catherine asked us to take each other's hands and look into each other's eyes. I burst into tears. Norman led me to the water's edge until I could breathe again. When we returned, Catherine read a simple poem about walking life's path together, sometimes leading, sometimes following, never afraid.

Then Norman read what he'd written the night before:

"You are the miracle of my life. You are the rock of our relationship. You are all love, all concern, all wisdom and all generosity... From the beginning, so many years ago, we simply became married. Now, after so much time, love, and shared experience, there is no doubt that we deserve the term marriage."

I tried to read a Shakespeare sonnet, but managed only two lines before tears overcame me. Catherine steadied me. We exchanged rings, said our "I do's," and she pronounced us "spouse and spouse."

We kissed, instinctively, without prompting. In that moment, on that beach, after years of being careful in public, we were simply ourselves. Not hiding. Not excusing. Married. I felt we were floating on air. After years of being who we were in the privacy of our homes, we were out in the world, under the sky, no longer pretending.

***

I knew it was coming, but didn't mark the day. Over breakfast, I looked at Norman and asked, "Do you know what today is?"

He shook his head.

"It's 50 years today that we've been together."

He smiled, unruffled as always. "How wonderful."

That was it. No speeches, no cake. We've never been much for anniversaries, but 50 years deserved something. I got tickets to *South Pacific* at Lincoln Center and, almost miraculously, a reservation at Per Se. We celebrated our half-century with Rodgers and Hammerstein and one of the best meals of our lives.

The next day, driving back to Connecticut, I looked at Norman—still handsome, hair streaked with gray, eyes as deep as ever—and thought how quickly those years had gone. I wondered why we lasted when so many couples, especially gay couples, had not. Fidelity was part of it. As a young man, I chased beauty and affirmation but found it hollow without connection. Casual sex didn't build the trust deep love needed. With Norman, I found something enduring. By being faithful, we built a reservoir of love to draw on in hard times.

There were fights, silences, days we lived parallel lives. But always, the connection returned—a glance, a word, his smile, and the distance would collapse. That's the secret of endurance: not ever disconnecting, but always coming back.

Most days now are filled with quiet happiness: mornings together, Norman's optimism, the comfort of our home, knowing we have enough. We never made a fortune, but we owe no one and live well. Whatever remains will go to charity. That feels right.

Not long ago, we went to a party. No place cards, so I sat next to Norman. The hostess teased, "Don't you ever get enough of him?"

Without a pause, I answered, "Never."

And I meant it. After 50 years, after tears on a Nantucket beach, after everything, I never have.

***

It's late afternoon. We've finished our painting and writing for the day, and it's time for our walk to the mailbox. The driveway is a half-mile long, plus another half-mile on the dirt road to the mailbox—a good two miles round trip. We rarely miss a day.

The hills, fields, and woods around our home have burst into yellows, reds, and oranges. Autumn, tinged with melancholy, is our favorite time. The sky is cobalt blue against the golden world. We walk side by side in silence, taking it all in before beginning our usual banter—one of countless conversations over the years.

As we walk, I pick up fallen twigs and toss them into the woods, my attempt at tidying up after nature. Norman, meanwhile, wants to improve on nature, always planning new bushes and trees. Pale ocher ferns flutter at the base of the trees, and leaves sprinkle down onto the pond and path.

We've seen so many autumns, but each one still surprises us. "How did we get so lucky?" Norman asks, looking at the field and our house. I don't answer; I don't have to.

"Look where we cut down that dead ash," Norman says. "It looks bare. We should plant some white birches." The view is perfect, but Norman always wants to make it better.

We pass the fenced sheep meadow. The sheep were taken away yesterday, their job done until next year.

"I'll miss the sheep," I say.

Norman laughs. "Those blank expressions, I find them impossible to connect with, but I know you enjoy them."

"We both look forward to their arrival in the spring. They make me feel like I'm in Ireland or Wales," I say. Passing the empty shed, I add,

"When I see them grazing, I think of *Sheep May Safely Graze* and feel at peace."

As we continue, the path rises, and Norman is a little out of breath. "I need to rest," he says.

"Take it slower," I say. "We're not racing. Let's stop for a moment."

He smiles. "And take the moment as a gift?" It's something I always say.

"How did you know I was going to say that?" I ask.

"I know your every thought," he answers.

A gust of wind comes. "Look how fast the leaves are falling," I say. "They'll be bare in a couple of days. We've watched the leaves fall together for more than 50 autumns."

Norman stands quietly, letting my words sink in. I reach out and hold his arm. "What an amazing trip we've had," he says, "and are still having."

I put my hand over Norman's. "Does it depress you, getting older?"

"No, but it doesn't thrill me," he says. "It just makes me think about how precious time is." We stop to inspect the tiny waterfall that appears after the rain. "What do you think our best time was?"

"That's tough. There've been so many good times," I reply. "What do you think?"

"I'd have to say right now." Norman looks at me, then at the trees and the stone walls lining our road. "And I can't imagine anyone I'd trade lives with."

We reach our destination, the green mailbox at the road. Norman sifts through the mail—bills, a magazine, a couple of catalogues. Walking back, he thumbs through a seed catalogue and realizes I've gotten ahead. Out of habit, I pick up a crushed beer can to toss in the trash at home and catch up to him.

"Just think if we were starting our life together now," I say. "Today, two men who love each other can marry, adopt children, even get their wedding picture in *The New York Times*. It would have been so different for us. We'd never have had to pretend."

"And no double life!" Norman says. "We could have been out there with nothing to hide. I think our life would have been even better. And it's been pretty damn good." We descend the hill, both lost in thought. Norman stops and turns to me. "Could you imagine doing it all over again?"

"I could start with the very first day," I say, "and replay every moment, like a favorite movie I never get tired of."

Looking back, I sometimes marvel at how full my life has been. There were the years in the theater, the heady days in Hollywood, the stumbles and the standing ovations, the brushes with stars, and the madness of show business. All of it gleamed, and all of it felt—then as now—slightly unreal, like a ravishing stage set long since struck.

The real story was never in the soundstages or screening rooms. It was here: on quiet country lanes, in the studios where Norman paints and I write, at kitchen tables cluttered with drafts and coffee cups, in the long conversations that stitched together many years of mornings and evenings. Those were the rooms where life happened.

People ask what it's like to be 100, what I've learned. I can only tell you what I discovered when Norman and I were finally able to marry in 2004, 46 years into our partnership: the day after the vows, nothing essential had changed. No miracle clarified the universe. We didn't love each other more or less. We woke to the same errands, the same balky air conditioner, the same flu shots and cleaning appointments—and the same unshakable companionship that had carried us that far. At 100, it's the same truth, just easier to see. The day after the candles, you're still living your life. Perhaps with a few more doctors.

If I'm pressed for lessons, I borrow from the famed director Mike Nichols, who introduced our book *Double Life* with Freud's spare wisdom: "Work and love, love and work, that's all there is." I'd add one more, but let me begin where he began, with work.

I've been working as long as I can remember. I sold cookies and magic cloths as a boy and bought myself the English bicycle my family couldn't afford. At 14, I worked in my grandmother's shop. At 16, I was acting in summer stock, then pushing racks at Filene's Department Store, then announcing at WMEX. I joined the road company of *Junior Miss* and was promptly fired. I went to New York to be a "serious actor" and walked on in a play. I was a busboy at the Stage Door Canteen, and to pay rent, an usher and a waiter. Eventually, I acted on Broadway, then on early television. I was a photographer's assistant, an understudy to the stars, a stage manager, a casting director, an associate producer, and at last a producer and creator of *The Snoop Sisters* for Helen Hayes and Mildred Natwick.

That led to casting at Warner Bros., followed by a position as head of casting at CBS, then back to Warner Bros. as a film executive, and finally, my long, improbable decade as President of Warners Television. I took that charge with a salesman's grit and an artist's stubbornness. I was committed, every day, to doing the best job possible: protecting writers when their voices were fragile, fighting for actors when the right face didn't fit into a neat box, giving directors the freedom to take risks, and insisting that the work reach the audience at its best. I took real, daily pride in the shows we made, in the people we launched, in the rooms where argument sharpened into insight and insight became a series that lasted. My title never mattered half as much as the responsibility did. You hold the door for talent, and you keep it open. That was the work. When the studio lights dimmed, the pride remained.

Since leaving the executive suite, I've written five books—another kind of producing, quieter but no less exacting. You learn that drafts, like dailies, don't flatter. You cut, you rethink, you begin again. And then one day it speaks.

Now for love. I had a bit of a wild time in my 20s and fell in love a few times. Everything changed when I met Norman. We've now been together 67 years. It was not always easy. For a long time, we lived carefully, as if cupping a match against the wind. We supported each other's work, traveled widely, made and remade homes, and moved—slowly, gratefully—from the fierce heat of youth to the greatest companionship two people can share. We survived near-death experiences—Norman in Mexico, me in the Great Barrier Reef—and every ordinary challenge in between. If anyone remembers us after we're gone, I hope it's not only for films or paintings, but for the way we tried to live: openly when we could, quietly when we couldn't, always with love.

Success, when it came, came in flashes: a fine performance, a greenlit pilot, a show that ran. Failure came on time, too. Both fade. What lasts, what truly lasts, is the life we built in the shadows and in the sun. It is the truest production I know.

There is, for me, a third cornerstone. I'm not a religious man, but I hold to a steady sense of the unseen, a force that guides. I have known moments that felt like intervention, mercies beyond reason. I can't explain how the door opens just when the room grows airless, or why the right hand appears when you are far from shore, but I have felt it, more than once. Call it grace. Call it luck. I call it the mystery that threads work and love together, keeping the flame alive.

So, if I may gently revise Dr. Freud, after a century of days: love and work and the mystery that carries them. They are the cornerstones. They have been mine.

The credits roll on their own. The set is struck. In the quiet that follows, I see the eager faces and the shiny studios, the kitchen tables, the morning light on Norman's brushes, the evenings when the day's small triumphs were enough. I see the office doors I opened for others, the actors who found their success, the writers who heard their voices out loud for the first time. At the beginning of all of that, I see a young man selling cookies and a much older one still marveling at his tender ambition.

If you ask what endures, I'll answer simply: the work, done with care; the love, kept alive; and the mystery, welcomed and honored. That is the whole of it.

And it only took 100 years for me to learn that.

www.ingramcontent.com/pod-product-compliance
Lightning Source LLC
Chambersburg PA
CBHW060632080726
47818CB00003B/115